"At a time when our country and world ~~face~~
gridlock, Dr. McLaughlin does a wonder~~ful~~
coming together rather than cutting each ~~other~~
book to everyone as she articulates with ~~great~~ ~~cla~~ ~~beautiful steps we can~~
take to embrace our differences and unite as one."

Josh Nadzam
Executive Director
On the Move Art Studio, Lexington, Kentucky

"Reading this book has been an empowering experience in the face of social/
political realities that threaten personal, community and even universal core
values of civility, respect and compassion toward each other. Talking Together makes a strong case for civil dialogue as a way forward by presenting not
only conceptual components of this important and timely topic, but practical
applications and rich stories that translate concepts into lived experiences
that support points of working together in pursuit of civil dialogue. It flows
in an easily readable manner while offering civil solutions to urgent and often
long-standing problems and civil futures. The interviews with change agents
add another layer of illumination. I have learned so much about civil dialogue
through so many lenses — cognitive, emotional, spiritual, social and cultural.
As powerful as a group setting is for learning how to talk together, I think that
reading Talking Together is also entirely effective as an individual pursuit of
knowledge about self and those in the closest personal spheres of living. It has
hit me where I live and where I aspire to live. Many lessons have stuck to me
like Velcro, long after laying the book down."

Jan Romond, PhD
in Positive Psychology; Author

Talking Together: Getting Beyond Polarization Through Civil Dialogue

©2017 LifeForce Press

ISBN 978-0-9994424-1-8

First edition.

To Allen - dear friend & beloved colleague - with wonderful

Talking Together

GETTING BEYOND POLARIZATION
THROUGH CIVIL DIALOGUE

memories and gratitude for that unforgettable introduction!

By Kay Collier McLaughlin

With dearest love always - Kay

Foreword by
Michael D. Fitzpatrick
Founder, Millenia Music

Kay Collier M'Laughlin

Interviews from Change Agents

Kremina Todorova and Kurt Gohde, Founders of "Unlearn Fear and Hate"

Rabbi David Wirtschafter, Rabbi of Temple Adath Israel; Leader, Activist, Organizer

Josh Nadzam, Executive Director of On the Move Art Studio

Hiroko Driver Lippman, International Suzuki Association and
Teacher of the Suzuki Talent Education Method of Violin

Everett McCorvey, Director of the Haitian Children's Choir, the University of Kentucky
Opera Program and the National Chorale of New York City

Stacy Sauls, Episcopal Bishop and Founder of Love Must Act

Donald Lasserre, Executive Director of The Ali Center

Jim Brown, NFL Legend and Founder of Amer-I-Can

TABLE OF CONTENTS

TABLE OF CONTENTS

DEDICATION

To those whose presence in my life
wove the tapestry which led to this book:

To Dr. Pearl B. Rutledge
Anam Cara, and companion on the way to a world of authenticity
and possibility we are fortunate to glimpse
in our work of growing people and communities

To Dr. Marvin J. Rabin
Who gave us all the experience of the relentlessness of work for harmony
and the joy of its accomplishment

To Dr. Shinichi Suzuki
Who continues to show us that there is hope beyond conflict and the
possibility of peace and prosperity in the listening and the blending
of playing the music of life together across our diversities

And to The Rt. Rev. Stacy F. Sauls
For leading with truth and integrity and expecting it from the rest of us

ACKNOWLEDGMENTS

- To those who gave me the song, especially Tom Siwicki, Dr. Marvin J. Rabin, Joseph Beach, Dr. Kenneth Wright, Dr. William Worrell, Dr. William Starr, Margery Aber, John Kendall, Virginia Schneider, and those who have been part of the song....Paul and Lorraine Landefeld, Cathy McGlasson,, Kazue "Kim" Baber, Rodney Farrar, Brice Farrar, Terry Durbin, Donna Wiehe, Don Trivette, the students of Lexington Talent Education Association and Suzuki Talent Education of the Bluegrass and hundreds of colleagues in the world of Suzuki Talent Education, and 1A classes and demonstration groups, and to Robert W. Burton, Robert Quade, Walden Moore, Bruce Neswick, Jeffrey Smith, Vaughan Mauren, Erich Balling, Kathleen Balling, Owen Sammons, Jim Fitzpatrick, and all of the choristers whose voices sing on in my heart

- To Michael Fitzpatrick, who takes the song far and wide, and has provided a symphony of words to tie these ideas together in perfect harmony

- To Leslie Guttman, editor and mentor, who recognized the song and insisted it be sung

- To the men who showed me what it meant to be a team: to compete with integrity on the field and in the game of life, especially the players and coaches from Paris High School, the Cleveland Browns, the University of Kentucky, the Kentucky Pro Football Hall of Fame, and the Blanton Collier Sportsmanship Group

- To Neil Chetnik, Marcia Thornton Jones and The Carnegie Center Author's Academy for inspiration, opportunity and support

- To the Very Rev. Dr. Robert W. Insko, the Rev. William Yon, the Rev. Dr. Joel P. Henning, Dr. Pearl B. Rutledge and colleagues in the worlds of Human Relations and Emotional Intelligence

- To the Rt. Rev. Stacy F. Sauls for carrying the vision forward through our work together

- To Representative Mike Doyle, Democrat, of Pennsylvania's 14th Congressional District, and to Representative Joe Barton, Republican, of the 6th Congressional District of Texas, managers of the 2017 Congressional baseball teams, who epitomize Talking Together, offering a much-needed example to our country.

- To the several writers whose heart for harmony and permission to incorporate their words as affirmation and support of my thoughts has in the long days of research and writing often lifted my spirits and kept me going

- To members of the Leadership Team of the Episcopal Diocese of Lexington who pioneered

- To Benjamin "Bungee" Bynum, Mary Louise Dean, Carolyn Witt Jones, Ann Whitfield "Whitty" Herman, the Rev. Laurie Brock, the Rev. Carol Ruthven, David Sawyer, Charlotte "CC" Johnson and all those who pioneered the "next step" with me,

- To Cindy Adams Centers for cover and page design that never fails to capture and illuminate my vision with creative professionalism and beauty beyond my imagination; and for years of joyful partnering in the creative process.

- To Ben Woodward for e-book expertise, Kim Larimer for web page, and Callie Lindsey for social media counsel

- To preliminary readers Jan Romond, the Rev. Peter Helman, Nancy Waterfield Walton, Stephanie Wagner Whetstone, Mikell Gorman Calkin, Benjamin Bynum, and Carrie Reuning Hummel

- To Holli Rickman Powell, copy editor extraordinaire

- To Jim and Monique Brown, Donald Lasserre, Hiroko Driver Lippman, Dr. Everett McCorvey, Josh Nadzam, the Rt. Rev. Stacy F. Sauls, Kremena Todorova and Kurt Gohde, and Rabbi David Wirtschafter, whose extraordinary work as change agents is an inspiration

- To my family – my husband Raymond, daughters Diane and Laura, and son-in-law Brad for constant support

- And to the most amazing gift of my life, my grandchildren, Virginia, Drew and MaryChun, who make saving the world imperative!

- To all whose generosity enabled the initial publication of this book at a time of crisis in our country.

- Eight individuals who have pioneered in their own ways of making our world a better place have been interviewed for this book. Six of these individuals have pioneered in their area; two have the formidable task of carrying the legacy of a pioneer forward for future generations. Each has answered the same questions, giving those who are looking for guidance to pursue their own way of working for a better world some markers to consider. The interviews are set apart by screened pages, interspersed between the chapters; a "collective wisdom" section follows the Coda, bringing a synthesis of their remarks together. I am grateful to these men and women for being the change we all want to see in the world, and providing inspiration and model for us all.

Every effort has been made to secure permissions and attribute quotes appropriately. Should there be any omissions, corrections will be immediately corrected digitally and in future editions.

Kay Collier McLaughlin, PhD
Lake Carnico
August 2017

Talking Together:
A Promise to the Future of the Planet

"Only the song through the land hallows and heals." —Rilke

Foreword
Michael D. Fitzpatrick

Michael Fitzpatrick is the recipient of the Prince Charles Award for Outstanding Musicianship conferred by HRH the Prince of Wales. The producer of The Beatles, Sir George Martin, stated, "He is beyond a marvelous talent and I could not agree with him more: Music is the only thing that can change the world."

When we're kids, we have heroes. Growing up during the late 1960s in Yellow Springs, Ohio, a small town of five thousand people, Muhammad Ali, Jim Brown, and Kareem Abdul-Jabbar were my heroes. The Beatles were my heroes. Martin Luther King was my hero. When, many years later, I met Ambassador to the United Nations Andrew Young, who was pivotal in the Civil Rights Movement, I shared: "As a kid watching Dr. King on TV, I knew he was my friend."

But then we moved to Lexington, Kentucky, a "big city" of over one hundred thousand, a town ringed by horse farms and dominated by the energy of the Kentucky Wildcats basketball team and its new Rupp Arena. Flourishing amidst this was the Lexington Talent Education Association, pioneering the innovative music-learning methods of Dr. Shinichi Suzuki, who recognized youngsters' innate ability to learn languages due to their constant exposure to it being spoken in the household. Dr.

Suzuki translated that constant exposure to a "musical language" in the household and invented a whole new method of learning music. Kay Collier was one of the American teachers in the forefront of bringing Dr. Suzuki's ideas to the United States and to anchoring the "Suzuki method" in Lexington.

Once settled in Lexington, I began learning to play the cello and had the great fortune of taking cello lessons with Rodney Farrar, whose approach to teaching and playing the cello seemed nearly identical with the way my soccer coach, Amir Karimi, an Iranian engineer and master soccer player, taught soccer: all based on reflexes, repetition, strategic thinking, intuition, and fearlessness in the game and on the stage. Once a month, the cello group would gather with the violin group of students led by Kay Collier and the teachers of Lexington Talent Education Association for fantastic concerts in auditoriums and churches and any place else in town where a concert could be put on. We all loved Kay because she always had such super-positive energy and treated us like adults, and we liked the fact that we got to call her Kay. Her presence was exhilarating because she had a sparkle and a joy that surrounded her, and she made the music-making seem like the most important thing in the world. Kay became my hero.

Sure enough, after a couple of years, our very own Central Kentucky Youth Symphony Orchestra was invited to do a concert tour of the Soviet Union and, under the dynamic leadership of Lexington Philharmonic conductor Dr. George Zack, became the first Youth Orchestra from the West to perform behind the Iron Curtain. It changed our lives, impressed upon us the power of music as the truly universal language, and led to my decision to become a musician for the rest of my life.

I lost touch with Kay when I left Lexington in 1982 and headed out into the world to make a go of it as a concert cellist. Over the past thirty-five years, many things happened and music connected me to exceptional individuals and took me to extraordinary places, among them His Holiness The Dalai Lama and Muhammad Ali, and recording with Tibetan and Trappist monks inside of Mammoth Cave, the largest cave-system in the world with over four hundred miles of tunnels and caverns. So when Kay and I reconnected serendipitously via social media recently, it brought me full circle back to how the journey all began. It's an honor and a joy to share a few core insights from the journey.

The Dalai Lama has said many times that the "twenty-first century must be a century of dialogue and compassion." His friend, the late Thomas Merton, had said years earlier, "It's obvious that we have to plan the future" - and went on to conclude: "the whole purpose of life is to live by Love." How can it be possible to create a future built on dialogue, compassion and love, given the myriad challenges the world currently faces? First, as all the great traditions teach, it must begin within, or to paraphrase Tom Petty, there's gotta be a change of heart.

But how does this change of heart occur? It must occur because it feels something, and this is most readily achieved by two key elements: silence and music. In the silent space, one is alone with one's thoughts and one's energies. The longer one sits in the silence, the more one's awareness deepens. Once the mind becomes calm, the heart can open to the fullness of all that is going on in one's own life - the joys and sorrows - and open to the joys and sorrows of the world. One can then make a commitment, from this silent place, to offer something, anything, of goodness, back into the world's space.

A music that originates and emanates from this depth of silence has a greater capacity to transmit feelings of compassion and love than a music that starts sounding amidst the "noise and chaos" of the world. Think of the singing of the National Anthem, and how that reverence and respect conveyed by the crowd, that "moment of silence," always affects the power of the performance. From the silence, from the feeling, from the sounding of love, profound dialogue can then occur. This quality of dialogue is essential to chart the world's future course.

There is an opportunity now in the world for people of all faiths and traditions to bring forth their gifts of goodness, anchored in compassion and love. This is an ongoing work, one that, as Congressman John Lewis said regarding the Civil Rights work in the sixties, is designed to carry forward for generations to come. Our capacities as a human species to "transform the jangling discords into a beautiful symphony" have never been more needed, nor more inevitable.

It is this inevitability of goodness that Kay has imparted to all who know her, and which she now makes available to readers far and wide.

PROLOGUE
Call It Possibility: Beyond Dystopia and Utopia

"There came a moment in the middle of the song when we suddenly felt every heartbeat in the room, and after that we never forgot we were a part of something much bigger."
—Brian Andreas, contemporary poet, Story People 2017

"I listen to prepare my answer."

"I listen to understand where the speaker is coming from, and to better inform myself on the subject."

Participants in the informational session for the upcoming Talking Together: Getting Beyond Polarization Through Civil Dialogue seminar were reading a document entitled "The Difference in Dialogue and Debate" when Councilwoman Sally Shields slipped in the room after a long day of back-to-back meetings. She would be speaking about the process of becoming a Compassionate City, one of the local efforts to move beyond fear and hate asked to share information at this session. She listened intently as the group completed the first reading and then read together "A Covenant for Creating a Culture of Courtesy." Tiredness and her intent to leave after her own presentation forgotten, she told the organizers at the end of the meeting, "I was hooked after I heard those first two documents. I couldn't leave. I needed to understand the process. If we had been running the meetings I'd been in all day using those documents to guide us, the meetings would have been very different, and much more effective!"

Sally's statement encapsulates much of what this book is about. It is no secret that the state of conversation in our culture has sunk to an all-time low, holding interactions between individuals and organizations hostage. Cynics may scoff, and idealists despair at the idea that it is possible in today's world to talk together with anything approaching civility. We are, after all, a large and messy conglomeration of people of differing ancestries, geographies, personal and professional stories, habits, and psychological makeups who call ourselves Americans. Part of our DNA seems to be the independent mind, the challenge of prevailing thought and accepted norms for the betterment of a "common good," the definition of which is as varied and messy as those who would define it. It was a smaller country and a less diverse band of pilgrims who braved a new world and the great experiment of democracy. Perhaps the dream of the difficult freedoms established by our forefathers and the simple desires named by change agent Josh Nadzam, who says, "At the end of the day, we all want opportunities, a safe place to reside for our families, fairness, respect," could be the shared core of what makes America and Americans. I invite them – cynics, idealists, and all who are tired of the vitriol of our world – to come, talk together. It is the possibility between dystopia and utopia.

I know the lived reality of harmony. I have experienced it as my French Horn and I joined all of the varied instruments of an orchestra, our different textures weaving together to produce a sound richer than any one instrument's singular beauty. I have known it in the sweep of hundreds of violins playing music together although their players share no common spoken language, and in the awe-filled moments when voices soar majestically and whisper softly. Meanwhile I have cheered harmony as an underdog National Football League team set star power aside and pulls together to win a world championship. I experienced harmony as the Democratic and Republican managers of their respective baseball teams shared the podium at a joint press conference following the shooting of Congressman Steve Scalise and Capitol police, and the prayer circle before the congressional baseball game. And I experience it each time a diverse group of human beings find their way through their differing stories, ideas, and perceptions to love each other unconditionally. I recognize it when values and purpose of a board or governing body override opinions, giving negotiation, compromise, and decision-making a chance.

We have been running, headlong, into unparalleled change for several decades, not stopping to notice that along the way, such harmony, and the civility, common courtesy, and respect that makes harmony possible, were being discarded. Kentucky born and Kentucky bred, I grew up with and later challenged the southern ethos that peppered my world with the ubiquitous phrases "Yes, ma'am", "No, sir", and "Bless their heart", part of a behavioral code of politeness that ruled both personal and professional lives. Rebellion followed my recognition that the prevailing code precluded honest communication, barely masking biases and fears that simmered, unnamed and undealt with, just below the surface of politeness.

My work as a consultant across the United States and beyond has brought me full circle, as previously unthinkable, unacceptable behaviors have smashed the code and upended conventional relational norms in ways that have not only brought the simmering to full boil, but prevent any sort of real conversation in our country. I have come to appreciate the "Kentucky code" as one regional manifestation of basic norms of civility that have allowed people to function in the midst of strong differences.

My belief that what many consider impossible – seeing and hearing each other through a process known as civil dialogue – is possible has twin roots in the summer of 1968. Dr. Marvin J. Rabin, my high school youth orchestra director, invited my four- and six-year-old daughters to be in a demonstration group at the University of Wisconsin. The children would be introduced to the first steps of playing the violin from the founder of a method which was new to America at the time, Japanese pedagogue Shini-chi Suzuki, who was making his first teaching tour in the United States. For five days, this class of youngsters had group and individual instruction in front of several hundred music educators who were there to learn what this new method was all about. Ten boys and girls, toddlers through first grade, followed the slender seventy-year-old man in his perfectly tailored black suit. He led them through multiple exercises, from learning disci-plined stances on cardboard foot charts to vigorous "games" that trained the children's shoulders, arms, and heads to be in correct position to play this complicated instrument. Shinichi Suzuki was a slight dynamo of perpetual motion, leaning over to be at eye level with each child, flashing a contagious smile and, when searching for a word in this, his new language, offering the apology, "So sorry. My English made in Japan!" The children laughed, learned, and at break time fought to be one of the tumbling tod-dlers spilling out of his lap.

Teachers and parents were learning, as well. A philosophy lay under the methodology. After World War 1, Shinichi Suzuki, a Japanese violinist, grieving that the children of his war-torn country would grow up know-ing nothing except the devastating aftermath of conflict, decided to give them the only gift he had to give – the gift of music, so that they might know something of beauty and joy. He began to teach children, creating a skill-to-skill building block pedagogy that he called "The Mother Tongue Method." It was his deeply held belief that music was a common language that could save the world.

Today, children the world over are taught by the Suzuki method, and can play the Suzuki repertoire and beyond together, without sharing a common spoken language. The great Pablo Casals, upon hearing a Japanese Suzuki tour group play, wept, and as he embraced the tiny musicians, com-mented, "Perhaps it is music that will save the world." That was Dr. Suzuki's intention.

One week after meeting Dr. Suzuki, I attended my first Human Rela-tions Laboratory Training. Diverse men and women met together in small groups over five days, learning the skills and experiencing the dynamics of coming to know each other and communicate effectively with each other through both shared perspectives and inevitable differences. For me, the community that emerged at the week's end carried the kind of deep harmony that I knew from playing music in ensemble. These two back-to-back events gave me powerful visceral memories which would continue to be reinforced over the years by experiences of people coming together to "make music", whether the music of violins and voices, or the harmony of deep human connections.

Years later, author and psychiatrist Scott Peck would express his experience of the possibility of human harmony after participating in his first small group work at National Training Laboratories in Bethel, Maine. In his book *A Different Drum*, he wrote, "Four times I have been a member of a group of very different people who loved one another in a sustained fashion. It might never happen again. But I did have a sense that it could be a replicable phenomenon. And ever since knowing that a group of very different people loving each other was potentially repeatable, I have never been able to feel totally helpless about the human condition again."[1]

It was not long after our first experience with Dr. Suzuki that I was cooking dinner when my very distraught children rushed into the kitchen. I sat down on the floor and gathered them to me. Diane, now seven, was trying to console her four-year-old sister, Laura, who was crying. "A very bad movie came on TV," Diane explained, her face wearing an expression that clearly wanted verification from Mom that it was a bad show. "They said that America fought Japan, that our soldiers killed Japanese people." Both girls looked at me hopefully, waiting for a grown-up to assure them that this terrible thing had not happened. We had just returned from the violin workshop where they had forged a bond with this teacher from Japan. It was hard to have to tell them that not only was the TV story true, but that it was a story of the reality of ways we humans have dealt with our differences throughout history.

This scene with my innocent children being wakened to the brutal reality of conflict was a deep-down punctuation to all of the experiences which made a clear call on my life. I knew there were better ways. It was not simply a cognitive knowing, but a soul-deep knowing of lived experience. I knew there were good people working toward these better ways. Many of them had been part of my own experiences; many more were part of a far-flung network across the world I might never know in person, but the knowledge of whom strengthened my own resolve.

Two other experiences were core in leading to the work I do today. One of the first teachers in my life was my father, Blanton Collier. As a child, learning environmentally, I absorbed his teaching in natural ways. If I had analyzed it, I might have assumed that everyone lived with such a teacher. Life was an ongoing lesson: Rudiments of mathematics. Gin rummy. Basketball. Calisthenics in our pajamas. How to row a boat. And perhaps most powerful for me, how to swim when you are totally terrified of water. My father was a coach. First, a high school coach, then an assistant football coach, in the Navy and with the fledgling Cleveland Browns, and then head football coach at the University of Kentucky. Finally, the head coach of the World Champion (pre-Super Bowl) Cleveland Browns. Following his death at age seventy-six, I wrote a book about his teaching philosophy. My research included interviews with as many former players and students of all levels as I could find. It was through them that I learned that whatever he was teaching, at whatever level, was characterized by a consistent, relational approach that built both individuals and teams, and was as applicable in academic classrooms, corporate offices, religious organizations, and non-profits as on the football field.

- Know the student, and what makes them tick.
- Begin where the student is, not where you think he is or where you'd like him to be.
- Deal with the basics, the fundamentals. Know them so well that they are a part of you.
- Break the basics down into skills that are necessary to get the job done and teach the skills. Repeat them over and over again, until they are internalized and become a part of the student, on automatic.
- Believe in and stand on what you are teaching and the student's ability to accept and learn it. Never give up on a student. If one approach does not get through to the student, try another. It is the teacher's job to find the way to teach every student.
- Accept the responsibility for teaching – for getting the necessary information across in an understandable way. That will not necessarily be the same for all students. If the student fails, it is the teacher's fault.
- Instill confidence, both in you as the teacher, and in the student himself.

- Analyze results and performances and learn from them as teacher and student. No detail is too small to learn from.
- Reinforce achievement through praise. Never criticize publicly. Talk over mistakes one-on-one.
- Continue to learn yourself, and do not limit your learning to a given field.
- Love what you're doing.

Brian Sipe, one of the quarterbacks my father tutored after retirement, spoke of how my father taught him to perfect the fundamentals until they were automatic, while simultaneously talking about "intangibles." "He who wanted to define everything about football and break it down into its smallest details also had this great ability to work with something that is virtually impossible to define – intuition, and a feel for the game," Brian said.

In the often brutal, physical world of professional football, he was an educator plagued with inoperable nerve deafness, a sensitive, unassuming man who at 5'10" tall was often dwarfed by his gargantuan players. If you'd met him on the street, you'd have guessed him to be a college professor, a dean perhaps. But never would you have picked him to be on some wind-swept sideline, leading his troops against the likes of Vince Lombardi and George Halas. He did not yell, curse, or demean his players; he simply taught in a patient, reasoned way. He was fiercely competitive during a game, and collegial when not on the field. Of both players and daughters he demanded the same two things: recognize and own your mistakes, and give one hundred percent of your ability. He modeled forgiveness and loyalty because that is simply who he was. Perhaps Jim Brown, the greatest running back of them all, characterized him best when he said of his coach, "I was prepared for his genius. I was not prepared for his humanity."

If the first major influence of my life came to me at birth, the fourth arrived at the other end of the continuum. I was coming upon retirement age when I was asked by the sixth Bishop of the Episcopal Diocese of Lexington to develop an office of Leadership Development and Transition Ministries for the region surrounding Lexington, Kentucky, that would build healthy human interaction throughout the system. The idea was that this would free the organization to pursue its mission and to live out the Episcopal baptismal covenant to "respect the dignity of every human being." Over a decade, leaders were trained to facilitate the work, local entities experienced new and positive ways of living and working together, and the concepts began to be known in wider communities. It was clear that the desire to have healthy relationships was not, and is not, limited to one organization and locale! While consulting with groups across the country had long been a part of my career, post-Diocesan work has brought opportunities to spread these concepts as an independent consultant and discover ever more examples of how "this stuff" works.

Recent conversations which began with casual questions about "exactly what is it that you are doing?" have brought queries as to my willingness to work with businesses, office staffs, corporate and academic boards, as it "sounds like these are skills that are applicable in so many settings." My questioners could not be more on target. Wherever human beings endeavor to live and work together, there is great need to learn the skills of what I call civil dialogue, or Talking Together.

All around us, violence, in attitude, speech and action, are the norm. I call this trouble – the kind of trouble that can end the world you and I know and live in, that can lead to extinction of life on our planet. It is a lack of civility, a lack of reasonable and acceptable behavior.

The Institute for Civility in Government says:

> Civility is claiming and caring for one's own identity, needs, and beliefs without degrading someone else's in the process. Civility is about more than politeness, although that is a necessary first step. It is about agreeing without disrespect, seeking common ground as a starting point for dialogue about differences, listening past one's preconceptions and teaching others to do the same. Civility is the hard work of staying present even with those with whom we have deep-rooted and fierce disagreements. It is political in the sense that it is a necessary prerequisite for civil action. But it is political, too, in the sense that it is about negotiating interpersonal power such that everyone's voice is heard, and nobody is ignored. Civility begins with us."[2]

It is the last line of this daunting definition of civility that makes what otherwise might seem impossible possible. That moves the issue from nebulous to named. For, if it begins with me and with you, that is a place to start. I cannot change anyone else. I can choose to change me. This book is one such starting place for thinking about the kind of changes in my behavior that will lead to civility, and learning the skills I need to practice to encourage civility wherever I go in my own life. If civility, kindness, respect

---

2 Definition of Civility from the Institute for Civility, Houston, Texas. Cassandra Danke and Tomas Spath, Co-founders. Used with permission.

is the destination, this is one guidebook for the journey. Philosophically, it is a journey that holds aspects of pilgrimage, because it is one of moral and/or spiritual significance. It is a book for thought leaders and change agents, whether or not you have ever thought of yourself that way, and whether the institution that is the base of operations and your circle of influence is a Fortune 500 company, a school system, a faith-based operation, or some other variety of what contemporary poet Brian Andreas means when he says, "I never thought of it as working for world peace; just trying to get along in a really big, strange family."

The core values of what it means to be human are in jeopardy. We have forgotten what it is to be kind, respectful, and civil. It is making life extremely uncomfortable at best, and dangerous at worst. It is easy to name the trouble with fear-based tags and stereotypes that raise emotional temperatures and bring on verbal hand grenades. Terrorism. Nuclear power. Isms of all sorts. Would-be tyrants. Isolationism. Greed.

But the trouble is not exterior, it's interior. It's lived out in the ways we think of each other, speak about each other. As Rabbi Ed Friedman, whose seminal work Generation to Generation highlighted the importance of learning from patterns in our history, says in his book A Failure of Nerve, "the most immediate threat to the regeneration and perhaps the survival of American civilization is this...we are polluting our own species."[3]

This trouble is so widespread that it can feel overwhelming. And when any problem reaches the stage of overwhelming, too big for anyone to know how it happened to begin with, much less too big to begin to imagine a solution and try to fix it, it's easy to run for cover and try to avoid the fallout.

In the next chapters, we will not only look at some specific examples of the behaviors that divide us, we will also have a glimpse of specific examples of behaviors that enable respectful, rational interactions. Changing behavior requires:

- Naming destructive behaviors and the impact of each
- Owning how I have been sucked into as well as having observed the very behaviors I name
- Committing to changing my own behavior
- Practicing the changes as consistently as possible in my own sphere of influence
- Making the change a way of life

---

3 Friedman, Edwin H. Failure of Nerve: Leadership in the Age of the Quick Fix. Seabird Books, New York. 2007. Used with permission received September 2017.

As a consultant, I have used the steps in this book in numerous systems – educational, religious, family, not-for-profit, corporate – with a high degree of success in freeing the organization to focus on their goals rather than on squeaky wheels and loud voices who perpetuate cacophony instead of making the music possible in their system. These practices are taught in workshops I lead across the United States, as well as in my home state of Kentucky. The stories are true, and the individuals in the stories are real people. Their names and identifying details have been changed for the sake of privacy, and in cases where the same story has played out again and again, details have been clustered into one representative story.

We can change our own parts of the world, and by so doing, begin to change our larger world. There are crucial issues to discuss, bridges that need to be built. We cannot tackle any one of them together until we learn how to be together in respectful ways. To want to hear the "other" as well as to be heard by them. To be open to the possibility that each of us has as much to learn as we do to teach. To be willing to see with new eyes.

Whatever song has moved your heart, be in touch with it now.

John Philip Newell, in his book *A New Harmony*, calls us all to join in that harmony as he writes:

"We live in the midst of a unique moment. It is a decisive moment, in which we are being offered a new-ancient way of seeing with which to transform the fragmentation of our lives and world back into relationship. But if we miss this moment, choosing instead to continue our patterns of wronging the earth and one another, there will be a degradation of life on this planet like none we have ever known. We must explore the brokenness of our harmony, whether as individuals or families, or as a nation or species. Knowing and naming the extent and depth of our disharmony is essential to finding the way forward. What will we choose? Which path will we follow?"[4]

It is past time for talking about how we got to this place and what could happen if we don't do something to get out of it. It's time to step forward in our own circles of influence and begin to practice the ways of living kindly, respectfully, and civilly. To begin truly talking together.

A song has echoed in my heart since as a seventh grader, our small-town band and chorus performed it at high school graduation in the Southside Gymnasium in Paris, Kentucky. "Our call is for freedom, our song is a song of peace…." I cannot speak to the quality of that long-ago

---

4 Newell, John Philip. A New Harmony: The Spirit, the Earth, and the Human Soul. Josses-Bass, a Wiley Imprint, San Francisco, CA. 2011. Used with permission.

performance. I can tell you that we sang with our hearts as well as our voices. We were singing a senior class into a new chapter of their lives, beyond our small school and town. We were singing about a world of promise, and standing shoulder to shoulder in that ordinary gym, a world that seemed possible. There was something about making music, matching our pitches, feeling the vibration of the instruments next to me that raised the possibility of harmony beyond that moment. There was an implicit linking of musical harmony to world harmony.

When someone says, "have you always wanted to change the world?" I feel the Southside Gym, turned performance venue for the night. I hear the strains of Brahms First Symphony, to which the words were set. And the words leap from deep within to my consciousness:

Our call is for freedom, our song is a song of peace
With peoples united, our troubles and cares will cease
When troubles grow longer, courage grows stronger
bringing the throng release
For every day must show us the way
to find freedom, and peace.

Let us begin.

Kay Collier McLaughlin
Lake Carnico, Kentucky
August 2017

At the conclusion of each chapter, there are questions that are intended for groups of people to use, sitting in quiet reflective time to allow answers to emerge, and sharing their answers in a community. This is how we begin to Talk Together, and to form new habits in order to move beyond polarization through civil dialogue. Thank you! I hope you will share your experiences of Talking Together with us at kcollierm@gmail.com.

Moving Forward to Action: *Questions for reflection and sharing*

1. What is the song that you hear calling you? Perhaps it is a song you listen to again and again, or which keeps playing in your brain. It might be a well-known song, or it might not be well known at all. It could be pop, rock, bluegrass, country, oldies, classical, religious,

new age, etc. Perhaps it's not a song at all, but a poem or a line that jumped out at you from a book. What are the words and what do they mean to you?

2. Is there a message of the song that you are singing repeatedly that seems to go beyond you? Are you singing it with someone else? To someone else?

3. Who are the mentors that have sung a song that you have heard? What messages were they sharing with you?

4. If you have a personal mission statement, how does this song fit with it? If you do not have a personal mission statement, begin to write one now. You may want to share evolving versions of it with your group, or the person with whom you are doing these exercises as you read. Be aware that it may change as you change in the process of this book and/or seminar.

CHAPTER ONE

Discordance

Discordant: Harsh and jarring sound due to lack of harmony; producing an unpleasant sound.

Ammon Weinstein is an Israeli violin maker in Tel Aviv who has spent the last two decades finding and restoring violins that were played by Jewish musicians in concentration camps during the Holocaust. He dedicates his work to the four hundred relatives he never knew, the grandparents, aunts and uncles of his parents. By painstakingly repairing these instruments so that they can be played again in concert, Weinstein not only gives voice to the voiceless, but reminds the world that music helped sustain life and hope during the Holocaust, where every avenue was explored to crush the human soul.

There is only one he has not repaired. It was sent to him by an American violin maker who had discovered inside it a drawing of a swastika and the words, "Heil Hitler." He believes that the work was done by an apprentice, not a master violin maker. "There is widely accepted knowledge that most 20th century German violin makers were not supporters of the Nazi party," said Weinstein. "We will never repair the violin. It will remain as a badge of shame for the Germans. Let them see how far they went in their hatred of the Jews and the culture." His story adds a level of deep authenticity to the movie Playing For Time, where the Women's Orchestra of Auschwitz can be seen performing as prisoners are marched to the gas chambers, the ultimate discordance between life and anti-life; between good and evil.

We are confronted by this discordance today, and the huge questions it raises about not only the kind of society we are, what kind of society we want to be and whether or not it is possible to bring some common visionary intentionality to the kind of society we truly want to create.

This discordance has been building just off the radar screen of critical issues in the country. It exploded exponentially across America following the November 2016 Presidential election. Crescendos of reactivity have greeted many of the decisions of the new administration, seeming to reach a high following the shooting at lawmakers and their staffs at a Republican baseball practice. But more was to come: demonstrations and death in Charlottesville, the great statue debate, and as this book goes to press, the continuing devastation of Hurricane Harvey and conflicting opinions over the "Dreamers." More than the aftermath of a hard-fought campaign and the conflicting emotions of elation of those who "won" and sadness of those who "lost" continues to be laid bare. There is no harmony to be heard in the protests, the fear and anger that continue to pervade the news, voices crying out to be heard.

When you and I react to the vitriol—when, in continuing shock, we cry, "they said WHAT?"—the fabric of the country we thought we knew and of which we sang appears frayed and fraying to a point of desperation. When we encounter the angry shouts into an unhearing universe that passes for conversation today, we are facing the reality that is a part of our lives today, every day.

In this chapter, we are going to see in that hard reality both examples of how ordinary people like you and me can be impacted by the reality and how ordinary people like you and me can bring about extraordinary change.

In Chapter Three, we will look at taking back power, and recognize that this is not a problem beyond solving. In order to solve the problem, however, we have to name it, and recognize it, no matter how difficult that might be, rather than deny its existence or accept it as normative.

I'll begin with a story from my own experience. I turned on my car radio and was blasted by an angry voice shouting over others who were trying to speak. "You're a liar!," the man yelled again and again. The angry voice belonged to Ken Ham, Chief Executive Officer of the organization Answers in Genesis. He was talking about The Ark Encounter, a northern Kentucky theme park featuring a Noah's Ark, built to Biblical proportions.

Ham was being interviewed by WEKU's John Hingsbergen on "Eastern Standard", a Kentucky public radio program. The other guests on the program were from the state tourism department and an organization dedicated to the separation of church and state. The person Ham was accusing of lying was a woman who had called in to share some data on tax incentives for which she was attempting to provide the source. The host was doing his best to maintain a dialogue. Ham kept interrupting, his booming voice so accusatory that it hit my ear with a physical force. I was so disconcerted that I pulled over into a gas station parking lot to listen. Despite the host's efforts to include the other two members of the panel in the discussion, Ham barreled on, interrupting anyone who was speaking.

I grew more frustrated and angry with the crosstalk and vitriol. Grabbing my cell, I punched in the station number. It was the end of the program, and I doubted my call would be answered, much less aired. However, with moments to go before the end, I was put through. "I find the tone of this conversation to be divisive, rude and completely unacceptable for public radio," I said. "It is impossible to hear any content, to learn anything when there is shouting, interrupting, talking over each other and name calling. It would be helpful to me as a listener if there were some guidelines for on-air conversations that become unacceptable that would contribute to a positive model for listeners rather than modeling more polarization." There was the obligatory 'thank you' from the station to a caller and the show was over.[5]

I sat in my car, watching people pumping gas, stopping for milk and bread, and going about their daily business. I thought about what I had just heard and my own compelling need to respond. The behavior of the one man, a featured guest on this radio show, crossed every boundary that could be set for acceptable human interaction, despite the astute professional behavior of the host and the two other panelists. Unfortunately, such behavior is the rule today, rather than the exception.

As a trainer in leadership and organizational development over the past four decades, it has always been important for all training sessions to begin with establishing norms and standards of behavior that will enable any group or organization to function. In recent years, there has been increasing variation in what is considered "acceptable."

A Widespread Problem

Polarizing behavior and talk is happening everywhere – in person, as well as on radio, TV, and social media (which seems to have started because of the ease of anonymity). It is oversimplification to blame the Internet alone. Perhaps the roots of today's wild west of incivility began in the 1980s, with the explosion of cable television and the twenty-four-hour news cycle. Pressure grew to capture audiences and ratings. Pundits became more and more provocative, even outrageous. Then came the web, social media, and today we have a world that hasn't been fact-checked,

---

5 "Eastern Standard," WEKU Public Radio, June 2016. Used with telephone permission from John Hingsbergen, August 18, 2017.

where faux "news" sites with oblique names pop up hourly with radically contradictory "breaking news" that is often disproved shortly after it is released –but not before it has informed the consciousness of millions of folks attached to their digital devices. Reality television added another shocking model in the way of "entertainment", and the "Survivor mentality" made its way into the "in" vocabulary in the culture, as speaking to—and about—each other in whatever derogatory words and tones of voice to throw competitors off the island and be the survivor became a sign of being "cool" and "with it."

Incivility leaked its way slowly into both our public and private domains, like poison gas snaking stealthily under doors and through window cracks until suddenly it is making its way into everyday encounters. An irate customer storms out of a drugstore having screamed at the pharmacist after discovering that her prescription had not been called in by the doctor's office. "You could have let me know and I wouldn't have driven over here and stood in line to find this out." The pharmacist refrains from asking how he was supposed to know the prescription should have been called in. Score one for not getting sucked into the vitriol!

A son and his mother have been trying to avoid a political discussion, well aware that they are aligned with different parties and supporting different candidates for the state senate race. But in exasperation one day, the son bellows, "I cannot believe you would be that stupid! What is wrong with you?"

Two candidates for local office are speaking at an open forum in their county. A man in the audience jumps up from his seat, ignoring the lines at the microphones. "Let's cut to the chase," he says sharply. "Are you gonna ride the tail of that n***** (speaking of President Obama) or are you gonna really straighten things out?"

A video of an irate customer screaming accusations and obscenities in a department store exchange line after Christmas goes viral. Not one person in the line steps in to stop the vitriol. More recently, multiple cell phone photos of a doctor being dragged off of a United Airlines flight while stunned passengers sit in silence has spread like wildfire.

Teaching Tolerance, an educational group promoting diversity, equality and justice, found in an online survey that the 2016 presidential campaign had an immediate and profoundly negative effect on children and classrooms, with hatred, fear, and bullying on the rise.[6] Washington Post journalist Petula Dvorak found the same in her reporting. In an article

6 Teaching Tolerance.

entitled "The Trump Effect," Dvorak contends that the hateful rhetoric of the Trump rallies is becoming a normal part of children's vocabularies. In the days following the presidential election, "Build the wall!" has been only one of the taunts hurled at minority students across the country. Zach, an outstanding Jewish student leader at a local high school, finds Nazi symbols and hate messages on his locker.[7] The rhetoric, which was shocking at first, has become all too familiar. What we are experiencing may have been unleashed by the relentless tone of a political campaign, but the issue is far beyond politics. It is not a partisan issue. It is a cultural issue.

"Throw her in jail!" "Kill the bitch!" (Rabid followers at a campaign rally.)

"Send them back to Africa!" (references President Obama and his family)

The Abnormal Has Become Normal

Whether we're watching a national convention on TV, checking social media or attending a live event, it's not unusual to hear or see:
- Taunting a disliked public figure.
- Interrupting a scheduled speaker with boos or cat calls,
- Posting anonymous curses and inflammatory remarks on social media,
- Bullying, and
- Threatening physical violence if certain conditions are not met.

They said what?

What, indeed. We're making noise, not music. Each person for themselves. No listening. No blending.

At the Cincinnati Zoo, a toddler breaks free from his mother and falls fifteen feet into a gorilla enclosure. Harambe, a four hundred pound silverback gorilla attempts to drag the boy around the pool, certain to cause the child serious injury, according to gorilla experts. After a frantic conference, zoo officials elect to shoot the gorilla rather than risk the life of a child. Facebook, Twitter and other social media, as well as mainstream media, are soon deluged with angry opinions. According to an account in the Detroit Free Press, hundreds of thousands of people who weren't anywhere near

---

7 "The Trump Effect," Washington Post.

the zoo signed online petitions calling for authorities to investigate the parents for negligence. A radio host who also lives a thousand miles away wanted the woman jailed and suggested she shouldn't have kids.

A starting quarterback for a major university decides to leave the school gracefully after an unsuccessful season, and is taunted for weeks with online jeers and booed by the crowd at his final game.

Multiple incidents of public vandalism and hate speech graffiti targeting San Antonio's Jewish community led the World Affairs Council of San Antonio to invite Rabbi Steve Gutow, a national figure in the interfaith dialogue movement to the city to speak. "It's our duty as Americans to fight senseless hate against Jews here and around the world," Gutow said.[8] All people must stand against "senseless prejudice" and other aspects of hate that have the "ability to destroy the fabric of our society."

Shamefully, continuing events such as the desecration of cemeteries and targeting of daycare centers happen with such regularity during the writing of this book that it is almost impossible to list them all. While active vitriol damages property and often human beings as well, passive acceptance of the inappropriate, the hateful and the destructive is equally damaging.

In a corporate venue, the discussion at a board meeting is increasingly intense. Voices are muddled, as speakers interrupt and attempt to talk over each other. The chair raps the gavel lightly, and then more strongly, to no avail. As the volume increases, a man points his finger across the table with a tapping motion, punctuating his harsh, "YOU are responsible for this mess!" before shoving his chair back and slamming out the door.

Anti-semitism, anti-blacks, anti-immigrants, anti-LGBTQ – all have raised their ugly heads in disturbing ways in recent days, weeks, and months. The vitriol is so great that often listeners and bystanders are left standing in shock, fear, revulsion – and silence. It takes an ah-ha moment for most of us to realize that silence is taken as agreement, and is complicit in allowing the hate to continue and even escalate.

Working as a consultant to an organization in conflict, I was aware that a few of the same voices spoke up on each topic. There were others in the room who never spoke at all. After rephrasing the questions several times to encourage participation ("I'd like to hear from those of you who haven't spoken", "Who haven't we heard from?"), I finally said to them, "You know, if I do not hear any voices to the contrary, I am going to assume that everyone is in agreement with those who have spoken so far." There was an

---

8 The Rivard Report, Edmond Ortiz, 13 September 2016, updated 7 October, 2016. Used with permission.

immediate shifting in chairs, an obvious discomfort on faces. Very slowly, a few spoke up. Finally, one woman said, "It never occurred to me that my silence would be taken as agreement. Nothing could be further from the truth! I don't speak up easily, especially if there is disagreement, but I am going to push myself now that I understand that my silence can be misinterpreted, or actually encourage something I totally disagree with!" Words for us all to remember.

Root Causes

Incivility and its partners, dishonesty and polarization, often hide unnamed in systems (large and small) that are not operating effectively. The solution to the perceived problem then becomes a change of leadership. The office affair between the senior and junior partners of a law firm become the reason that both are fired and quickly replaced. There is an embezzlement by a 'trusted' employee who is replaced and things go forward. The CEO of a large corporation is charged with both verbal and sexual abuse, fired and replaced. Organizations pride themselves on an efficient transition of leadership, rather than reflection on why the situation existed and possible patterns in its history that indicate deeper issues.

The solution to incivility and dysfunction has never been accomplished by a change of leadership, but by discovering and resolving root issues. And as dysfunction piles on top of dysfunction in our culture today, the root issues cannot be solved by a short-term technical fix ("we've encountered a situation like this before and have a solution that we know will work to fix things in our toolkit") but adaptive thinking, and practice of a new and different way. It calls for a time of reflection on the values of the organization, whether lived or simply espoused, and the cost and the promise of making those values the foundation of a way of life.

Here's an example of what I'm talking about. I was the consultant working with a board of directors at their annual retreat. The preliminary agenda indicated that the first morning of the two-day retreat would be spent developing norms and standards to guide the work of the organization. Of the eighteen board members, thirteen attended the full retreat. Five members elected to arrive for the afternoon "business session" only. "They're going to do all of that touchy-feely stuff in the morning," one said. "It's ridiculous. I don't have time for that kind of nonsense."

During the morning session, I provided the members with a generic set of norms and standards, reminding them that the purpose was to create a positive working environment which allowed for the most effective and productive functioning. Members divided into three groups, with each drafting suggestions for norms and standards that would facilitate the organization's work at all levels, focusing on the mission statement, goals, priorities and strategies. When the board reassembled, each small group shared their work with the larger one. The work was posted on newsprint and hung side by side on the wall, where it was easy to see the shared values for good discussion, focusing on the tasks at hand. It became clear that they had experienced previous unpleasant behaviors which had distracted them from their work, and that they wanted to change that dynamic. With markers in hand, they wordsmithed their posts until the group was satisfied.

"I think we've got a really good document here," said Mary Ann, a long-time board member. "I think it needs a name that conveys what we're trying to do with these norms and standards, so they can be quickly understood. This is how we treat each other. This is how we do business."

There was silence around the table as the board pondered the work they had done so far, and what Mary Ann was proposing. "It's a little like a mission statement," said Janet. "The title needs to convey to someone the minute they read it what the content of the document is about."

Sam had been sitting quietly during the discussion, and now he spoke up. "We are trying to create a culture of courtesy. To set out guidelines for how we are expected to behave to make that happen. And we are covenantal people. What about calling it A Covenant for a Culture of Courtesy?"

"After all," said another member, "the more courteous we are, the more work we will get done, and the more efficient and effective we will be. The bonus should be a much more pleasant environment in which to do our work, and no time wasted with petty bickering."

Everyone signed on. It had been a good morning's work. The group headed to lunch with energy as well as appetite. When they reconvened for business, they were joined by the other five members of the board. The first item of business was to place the new norms and standards—A Covenant for a Culture of Courtesy—in front of the full board for discussion and vote. Sam presented the document by title, with an explanation of how the title captured the expectations of the board. Several of the just-arrived members were shifting in their seats during Sam's presentation, and could hardly wait to pounce.

"What a ridiculous waste of time! This is a business, not a kindergarten!" said one. "I'm sure glad I didn't come for this crap – or maybe I should have," said another sarcastically. A third chimed in, "If I had been here, we would have had something much more efficient and business-like.

This is a joke! I can't believe you wasted your time on this and expect us to think it's a good idea."

From across the room, Terry spoke. "That is not the way we speak to each other here. I'm sorry you were not here for the discussions that led to the final document. If you would like to speak to specific points, please use "I" messages and a civil tone of voice."

Over the following months, similar tests of the covenant arose – interruptions, accusations, shouting. Each time, a board member spoke up. "Let's please reference our courtesy covenant so we can get our business done." As new board members were elected and oriented to the board, they were given the covenant to study. Over a two-year period, the behaviors of the group were transformed, building a practical as well as philosophical foundation for the ongoing work of the organization.

Hope Exists

Organizations that work together regularly are but one example of venues where norms and standards are needed. Public meetings, whether one time only, or more frequent, also need this guidance. I have experienced several hopeful examples of preliminary boundary setting for public gatherings, awareness that leads to positive action.

A called public meeting of anyone concerned by cuts to a state arts budget brought hundreds of citizens to a downtown meeting space well before the announced starting time. The room overflowed. Voices buzzed; tension was thick. The Executive Director of the local arts council stepped to the microphone. Calm and gracious, she expressed gratitude for the groundswell of interest in the arts, named the anxiety that was present, and outlined the procedure for the meeting. First, individuals with the latest facts would report to the assembly. Then there would be a time for questions and answers, and a time for expressing concerns. "This is not a time to push personal agendas or direct criticism of individuals," she said, setting clear expectations for acceptable behavior at the meeting.

Knowing in advance how the evening would proceed and what the rules were relaxed the crowd ever so slightly. It was clear someone was in charge. The attendees were attentive and respectful during presentations. Questions were insightful, with answers providing useful additional information. When the microphones were opened to the crowd, individuals introduced themselves as requested, and stated particular concerns and ideas. A Facebook group that had started a few days earlier grew to five thousand members before the evening was over.

Responding to concerns and negative behavior can cause anger and anxiety to escalate into an irrational response. When leaders are aware that lack of information, misinformation, and victimization are all fuel that flame frustration into something much, much bigger, positive steps can be taken instead of allowing reactivity to rule the day.

When an Episcopal church in Lexington, Kentucky was vandalized with hateful graffiti on the facade, doors, and sidewalks, the rector turned to Facebook to ask for help cleaning up. Members of the parish and total strangers arrived with buckets, power wash equipment, and energy to do the job. Instead of delivering a sermon the following morning, Mother Laurie invited the congregation to join her outside the church, where buckets of sidewalk chalk were waiting. "Let's write our messages of love. Love always wins over hate." Soon, a local television station arrived. They had heard about the damage, and wanted to film the goings-on for the news. "You are welcome to film," said the priest, "as long as the story you tell is the real story – that love wins."

I met Aliyah Levine in the Atlanta airport. Very early on a cold November morning, this child-sized African-American woman was assigned to push the wheelchair to transport my bum knee from one gate to another. Noting my New York destination, she said she was from New York and had come to Atlanta to go to school. Between gates, I learned that she was a student at Georgia State University, majoring in business with a psychology minor, to enable her to start her own business. She dreamed of creating her own after-school programs for disadvantaged youth, to offer them life skills and self-esteem as well as recreational opportunities. Her brother had been killed by street gangs, she told me, ("He was in the wrong place at the wrong time") after which she went "a little wild and crazy." Her environment was one of negativity, anger, and violence. Her life turned around when she met someone who believed in her and guided her as she turned her life around, helped her see that there were alternatives to the hate-based behavior that had killed her brother. "That's what I want to do for other people," she said.

Speaking from the Heart

While "they said what?" frequently expresses incredulity at the content, tone and volume of what is being said, sometimes it is a response of surprise at the reverse – an exchange between people that is so remarkable that the person hearing it reported is not quite sure they heard correctly. One such moment took place at a writer's conference at The Carnegie Center for Literacy and Learning in Lexington, Kentucky.

Only one sound could be heard in the room full of people – the deep, gentle voice of author Wendell Berry, reading aloud from his short story, "The Woodpile." The narrator of the story was Andy, now an adult, reflecting on life lessons learned from Dick, a black man who had worked on the rural Kentucky farm where Andy grew up. The setting for the "lessons" was the woodpile, where Dick showed the young boy how to saw wood. As Berry finished his reading, listeners mentally and emotionally shifted back into the conference room, and it was time for discussion.

Several questions into the question and answer session, an African-American participant asked the legendary writer if he had any idea of the impact the woodpile imagery might have in a black context, adding that it would be less about working together at the woodpile, and more about hiding in the woodpile. (A common figure of speech in the 1800s was "n**** in the woodpile," referring to the woodpile as a place where fugitive slaves hid during their flight north.) As Berry listened intently, the participant added, "I'm not sure if you're aware of the more contemporary meaning, that somewhere there is a black child in the white family, although I didn't hear that mentioned or implied."

The silence in the room was palpable; the author's face a study in surprise and concern. Wendell Berry, at over eighty years old, might be a basketball player past his days on the hardwood – tall, slender, slightly stooped about the shoulders. Earlier, he had shed his tweed sport coat, and, in his shirt sleeves, had bent over the elegant brass podium to look closely at the words he was reading, although certainly they were written on his heart. Now he stepped from behind the podium and moved toward the speaker. The very air stood still.

He placed his right hand on his heart, supporting it with his left hand, as if to ensure it stayed there, and that the questioner and those who were listening got the message: he spoke from that heart. "I want to thank you for telling me that," he said in his soft Kentucky drawl. "There is too little of that kind of directness, of letting someone know when something you have written or said is heard differently because of context, or experience and perspective. If we don't speak up and say these things directly, if we don't talk to each other, how can we know each other? And if we don't know each other, or about each other's truth, how can we ever be at peace with each other?"

From one end of America to the other, the discordance and reactivity to it is concerning. Two days after the conflicted 2016 presidential election, NFL Films released a short documentary entitled "Jim Brown: A Football

Life," about arguably one of the greatest athletes ever to compete. It opens with the eighty-year-old Brown speaking to a roomful of young men in his Amer-I-Can program, which endeavors to prepare disadvantaged youth for a productive role in society. "Violence is not the answer. Only love is the answer."

Visceral Knowledge

To be present during the skillful use of civility and peacemaking is to experience – to know viscerally – that it is possible in situations of polarization, high emotions and difficult topics, to be in true dialogue with others. Having experienced rather than talked about or heard about the possibility of civil dialogue, there is memory in the bones, the heart, and the soul. With a difficult conversation at home or at work on the horizon, the being part of our selves says to the doing part, "Remember? It's OK. You have done this. You can do it again."

My friend John is part of a small group who walks the streets surrounding their downtown office once a week, in an effort to have conversations with people unlike themselves. One of the men was clearly uncomfortable, and told the others that quite frankly, he was frightened. "I don't know what to say, and what to expect from them." "Maybe that's the best starting place of all," John told him. "To let yourself be vulnerable enough to begin with that. To say to a stranger, 'I need to tell you I'm feeling scared because I don't know you, and I don't have any idea how you are feeling, but I really would like us to be able to talk to each other.'"

Maybe that is exactly why the idea of civil dialogue is so hard, because it's hard to be that vulnerable. It's hard to admit that I'm scared, or unsure of what to do or how to do it. That's precisely why I'm writing this book. My work with groups across the country and the world tells me that you and I are not the only ones who desire this change. We know the reasons why it is crucial, and growing more so every day. But it is impossible to do something we don't know how to do. It is impossible to practice unless we have been given something specific to practice. That is what this book is about: learning the skills so that we can practice the behaviors that will help us talk together. It can and it will make a difference.

The fable of The Hundredth Monkey is a good reminder of how change can happen.

How Change Happens

On a faraway island lived a tribe of monkeys. This tribe of monkeys, like monkeys the world over, dug sweet potatoes out of the ground for sustenance, and ate them, dirt and all. One day, one of the monkeys washed his sweet potato before he ate it. The following day, a second monkey washed his sweet potato. Then there was a third. A fourth. No one knows exactly, but it is surmised, and the tale is told, that when the hundredth monkey washed his sweet potato, the concept jumped the waters, and soon monkeys everywhere in the world washed their sweet potatoes before eating them.[9]

Beginning where we are, each in our own circle of influence, practicing the concepts of civil dialogue, we can be the hundredth monkey.

"There came a moment in the middle of the song, when we suddenly felt every heartbeat in the room, and after that we never forgot we were part of something much bigger...."

Moving Forward to Action:
Questions for reflection and sharing

1. Describe a time when you have been surprised by the way someone spoke to you, or to a group you were a part of. What did you feel and think when it happened to you? What did you do? What did you feel and think in the group setting? What did you do?

2. How did your family of origin handle conflict? Were different opinions expressed directly, indirectly, or not at all? How have those early learnings impacted the way you deal with differences of opinion and conflict today?

3. What is your usual stance when faced with impending conflict? Do you stay put, ready to come out swinging? Do you prepare to listen for new information? Do you act first and think second? Do you stay quiet and out of the line of fire? Or another way? What kind of response has this brought you? Has it been effective? How might you stretch yourself to modify your position?

---

9 Keyes Jr, Ken. The Hundredth Monkey. Vision Books, Coos Bay, Oregon. 1982. From the flyleaf: "This book is not copyrighted. You are asked to reproduce it in whole or in part, to distribute it with or without charge, in as many languages as possible, to as many people as possible."

LOOKING AHEAD. In the world that is possible, the drama queen or king and the bully don't get to claim center stage unless I allow it.

The following suggestions and format may be helpful for use with groups.

The information from Chapter One or any of the following chapters would be presented by a team leader. Participants would be seated at round tables. It is helpful and frees people to speak more honestly if couples, families, and other groups are seated at different tables. A trained facilitator at each table is preferable, but if not available, the leader asks each table to select a leader/reporter and a recorder. The recorder will take notes on newsprint, and the leader/reporter will maintain the culture of courtesy covenant. The presenter will remind all participants that everyone is accountable for maintaining the culture of courtesy, and can call for focus on the covenant. Questions may be on individual sheets of paper, with participants given ten minutes to consider their answers prior to discussion. Or, the questions may be on a flipchart or PowerPoint, with a brief time for reflection before sharing at tables. After all tables have shared, the reporters will report out to the entire group, utilizing the notes on newsprint taken by the recorder.

EQUIPMENT: Flip charts, markers, handouts, microphones for presenter and reporters

SESSION #1. Ask participants to complete handouts with the following four questions.

1. What was the usual mode of decision-making in your family of origin (FOO)?
    _____ Discussion/collaboration
    _____ One parent decided
    _____ Parents decided together
    _____ Consistent
    _____ Always changing
    _____ Values-based
    _____ No apparent reason

2. What was the best way to get attention in your FOO?
    _____ Yell
    _____ Act out

_____ Ask
_____ Interrupt
_____ Be sick or have a problem
_____ Be silent
_____ Other: _____

3. Which of these behaviors have carried over into your adult personal or professional life?

4. Which of these behaviors have proven helpful in adult life? Hurtful?

After participants have filled out their sheets, the facilitator(s) can encourage a conversation centered on what they discovered about how our families of origin influenced what behaviors they tolerate and react to.

Participants are given sticky notes to list behaviors and practices and place them under the correct category. The facilitator will summarize the responses, and distribute a generic form of norms and standards, asking participants to relate their answers to the generic norms and standards.

SESSION #2: On Culture and Behavior

1. What behaviors are admired in our culture today?
2. What behaviors are not admired, but tolerated and accepted?
3. What kind of leadership do you most admire?
_____ Visionary/creator/prophet
_____ Good old boy
_____ Revolutionary/renegade
_____ Charismatic
_____ Differentiated/non-anxious
_____ Screamer
_____ Inspirational

As you list your preferred leadership style, please list leaders you have personally experienced who represent that style to you.

CHAPTER TWO

Shifting the Focus from Problem to Potential: Taking Back the Power

"Don't you think the world needs a great concert?" —Michael Fitzpatrick

Cellist Michael Fitzpatrick is in the musical business of tuning the planet. For the past twenty years, he has traveled with His Holiness, the Dalai Lama, sharing the stage with spiritual ease and uplifting audiences with his music. He grew up studying cello and playing soccer in Lexington, Kentucky. His life's work began through a series of coincidences, when he found himself at age thirty-one at the Abbey of Gethsemani, for a summit with representatives from the Offices of the Vatican and Offices of His Holiness the Dalai Lama. The lone lay person among the widely diverse faith leaders, he suggested that music just might set the tone for important moments of the gathering.

The resulting setting for making this particular music was at Mammoth Cave, in Kentucky, for an experience Michael says he doesn't think any of them were truly prepared for, but which "completely altered my life." He describes it this way:

"We always think of the Earth as we relate to it daily: getting to and from places, time with family and friends, special places in nature. We sometimes think of the beautiful images of the Earth taken from the surface of the moon. But rarely do we think of the Earth as having an "interior," so when we did the recording inside of Mammoth Cave, none of us were quite prepared for what we experienced: descent into the womb of the Earth itself, where we were met by immense silence and an enveloping darkness into which we sounded the most extraordinary combination of ancient sounds. Tibetan chanting. Gregorians chanting. The sounds of flute and cello commingling with 350-year-old limestone rock. The sounds seemed to penetrate into the core of our cells, yet the sounds coming through the instruments and voices seemed to be originating from the Earth itself. At the peak of the recording in the cave, it seemed as though the entire Earth itself was resonating with this newly formed music, intimately aware of our presence even as we sensed a feeling of connectedness with the Earth."

Twenty years after those momentous six days, Michael travels the world, frequently with the Dalai Lama, bringing the message of peace and harmony through his cello. Wherever he goes, "people are saying the same thing. " It's about making the kind of music of our human relationships that build bridges between people, that bind us together with common values despite our diversity. About an understanding of the nature of civility and its connection to human beings that penetrates the human spirit with the same lasting resonance that touched the historic cave recording participants.

Our conversations with each other have the potential to be a part of that great concert. To create a special kind of harmony in our world. In order to get there, we have to take back the spiritual and emotional power to make good music. Time to make good music together, instead of the cacophony we've been enduring. The good news is that we can do it. We can focus on the potential in every situation and rise above the toxic, the vitriolic, the destructive, and the depressing.

How We Do It: What This Book Is About

Attention hogs, bullies, and saboteurs take the power out of the air we breathe. The umbrella term for such a person is a squeaky wheel, someone who dominates every situation with his unhealthy patterns. And we allow it to happen, at times even enable it. Often as we excuse, complain, and worry about how to manage the squeaky wheel and its impact, the squeaky wheel gets bigger, taking up more room and demanding more attention. In our families, it might be the resident drama king or queen, who has an emotional meltdown just before the first guests arrive for Mom and Dad's anniversary party, or who seems to have a strange illness when another family member is due on center stage. Then there's the office gossip and the faculty dissident.

Every organization and system has its own version of the squeaky wheel, someone disruptive who is tolerated rather than called out. "That's just Jack being Jack again (eyeroll)." "We've learned to work around Jean (sigh)." Such people keep things slightly off-kilter and have us focused on problematic behavior, often causing serious delays and damage to projects, events, and other people. Unfortunately, tolerating such people and working around their bad behavior results in distractions, lost time, and energy drains.

All too often, individuals, families, and organizations stay stuck with the problem rather than shifting the focus to the potential for strengthening the group. The way out begins with taking the attention away from the troublemaker; to stop wasting time and energy enabling them. This, of course, means that we have to stop denying the behavior and take our time and attention back. The key is to focus on the potential for strengthening the system, and the tools are modeling healthy attitudes, words, and actions.[10]

Where Is the Problem Coming From?

In 1975, psychiatrist and researcher Dr. Murray Bowen developed what is now known as the Bowen family systems theory. Bowen's work helps us understand that organizations, from families to cultures, are emotional units, where what affects one affects all. People cannot be understood in isolation, but only as part of a group. One of the primary emotions in any system is anxiety, ranging from low-grade to intense during times of danger and crisis. Anxiety travels quickly in any system, drawing individuals closer together for protection. As we grow and develop, this kind of "herding," which is based in the dependency of infancy, lessens to more appropriate interdependency. Social regression occurs when people begin to function at a lower, more elemental, or even infantile level in an attempt to decrease the anxiety they are feeling. They react emotionally to what is going on around them. In a calmer, less anxious time, individuals are guided by the values they have developed intellectually, spiritually, and philosophically. In times of high anxiety, these values and related thought processes are less important than stopping the anxiety, which leads to fear, leading to greater anxiety and greater reactivity.

Bowen's theory states that society is more or less anxious, orderly, and organized at different times in history. When social regression is high, there is more anxiety in people, causing more chaos and irresponsible behavior. In turn, the chaos and irresponsibility create more anxiety, leading to more problems in society and an escalating cycle.[11] When irresponsible

---

10 Training session with Margaret "Peggy" Treadwell, Executive Council of the Episcopal Diocese of Lexington, 2009. The Cathedral Domain, Crystal, Kentucky.
11 Oral conversation with David Sawyer.

and chaotic behavior begins, attention gets focused on those who are causing the chaos.

We experience regression in every part of our lives, from our families to our workplaces and other organizations. As anxiety increases, people tend to take their anxiety out on each other. In anxious times, hostile leadership and poor decision-making can often occur. .Leaders in all groups are less sure of their roles, and many organizations are no longer sure of what they stand for. Long-heard stories of the Great Depression deepened anxiety in the most recent recession, resulting in hurried and often ill-advised financial decisions. Both pre- and post-Presidential election anxiety have some organizations looking for redefinition, and hastily assembled retaliatory or defensive groups springing up.[12]

Where to Find the Strength, And Those Who Have Done It

Squeaky wheels often blind a system or organization to seeing individuals with the potential to help resolve conflict and provide positive resources, because they may be quieter and less obtrusive. Someone with great potential may be overlooked because she has no need for a stated leadership position or title. These individuals are generally present and available in the ranks of an organization, quietly doing their jobs and drawing little attention to themselves. Potential is always aware, responsible, and loyal to a mission or vision, a team, and its priorities. Potential is teachable and coachable. Chances are, those with potential are already more than aware of the problems created by the squeaky wheel, and if motivated, energized by the possibility that a change can happen.

A case in point happened in a small town where I was hired as a consultant. A civic organization in the town had been terrorized for over a decade by a social and professional bully, who saw himself as superior in status and ability to anyone who appeared to gain leadership in the group. Claiming special knowledge and mission of the group by virtue of both education and longevity, Paul had been successful in maintaining control of every decision made by the organization. It took a new set of eyes in town to shift the focus.

Chuck was transferred to the town by his company, and quickly became involved in its civic life. A natural leader, he was welcomed to the civic group by the majority, yet his suggestions and ideas were always shot

---

12 Training with Margaret "Peggy" Treadwell, Executive Council of the Episcopal Diocese of Lexington, 2009. The Cathedral Domain, Crystal, Kentucky.

down by Paul. After a year went by, Chuck was aware that any idea that he or anyone else brought forward was stopped-by Paul. As a matter of fact, he was pretty sure that he was the only one bringing any ideas forward other than Paul, and that all of Paul's ideas seemed to get implemented, even if reluctantly. One evening, over a post-meeting beer with Miriam, another board member, Chuck asked, "Why does everyone put up with this bullying behavior from Paul?"

Miriam looked surprised, and hesitated a moment before responding. "I hadn't thought of it that way," she said thoughtfully, "but he does bully everyone into doing things his way, or no way. He's just always taken charge of everything in this town, and anyone who challenges him ends up being ridiculed or dropped from his list of acceptable people. We've all sort of stopped trying."

Chuck, well-trained by his company in dealing with conflict in systems, suggested to Miriam that their organization would come much closer to living into its vision and mission if it were to be open to new ideas other than Paul's, and be freed from the tyranny of one person. "There's a lot of untapped talent on this board and in this town-just sitting there!" Chuck observed. Miriam was intrigued, but unconvinced.

"Who else knows this is a problem?" Chuck asked. 'And who else understands the mission and cares enough about seeing it carried out to become a part of the solution?" Miriam named two other members of the board, both of whom who had tried without success to revitalize the organization by allowing other organizations to use their facilities. Each effort had died quickly due to Paul's resistance to any other groups using the organization's facilities.

"Are you all aware that you've been enabling Paul's behavior?" Chuck asked, listing some of the behaviors he had observed. "He is so loud and insistent that he simply wears you down. He takes all of the air and space in a room and commands all of the attention. What would happen if the attention were not focused on him? If others got some air space and time?"

With Miriam's support of his idea assured, Chuck shared his thoughts with John, whose input at board meetings had appeared astute. "You know this will get shot down, don't you?" John asked.

"It can't get completely shot down if you and Miriam both say you want to hear more," Chuck said. "And I believe that when you speak up, you will find that there are others who will, also."

At the next meeting, Chuck presented his idea to utilize their offices in the evening hours for groups in the community who had no place to gather. When Paul quickly set aside the idea and moved on to other business,

John said he would like to hear more about it before moving on. Miriam seconded the request. Another member agreed, although glancing at Paul throughout as if to check on his reaction. The idea did not come to a vote that night, but it had a full hearing.

Paul's pushback the following month was to leave it off the agenda for the meeting. Miriam called for the idea to be heard and discussed under old business. Paul attempted to set the suggestion aside for another month, but was met with the united efforts of several board members to have a motion, a second, and a vote. The motion passed, and Chuck volunteered to compile a list of those who were interested in using the building.

In the coming months, more members began to follow the model of Chuck, John, and Miriam. Firmly, but civilly, they refused to acquiesce to the domination of the squeaky wheel, opening the door to renewed energy and ideas in the organization as the focus shifted from problem to potential.

In a family situation, it was well known that Martha needed an extraordinary amount of attention. The behaviors that got her that attention were irritatingly familiar to those who knew her well. In any gathering, she would seat herself beside an unsuspecting individual and begin pouring out innumerable personal details of her life and troubles, which would end up isolating that person from the rest of the gathering. The unsuspecting individual generally had no idea they had been "chosen" to pay attention to Martha that evening, and most often, they would remain in this isolated conversation rather than appear rude by extricating themselves.

The behavior had been repeated in so many settings that several siblings decided it was time to take action. Like most squeaky wheels, Martha was unaware of the impact of her behavior on other individuals or the family system. As with Paul, Martha would not take kindly to direct communication and a request for a change of behavior. In this instance, the siblings had become practiced in not allowing their focus to dwell on the squeaky wheel. Now, they needed to empower others and free the potential in family gatherings. These men and women, unlike their sibling, had skills of self and other awareness. They noticed when a conversation seemed to be turning from social encounter to something more intimate and exclusive, as indicated when Martha positioned herself and the person with whom she was talking away from the remainder of the group. One of the siblings would then interrupt the conversation and introduce the person into another group. This model freed others to break away from the squeaky wheel.

Locating the Potential

While minimizing the impact of the squeaky wheel is important, it is equally important to locate the potential, often untapped, in the group. The way to go is to dial down the voice of the squeaky wheel, and dial up awareness of the gifts others have to offer. Invite the person who has not spoken to enter the conversation. The key questions to ask in order to locate such individuals are:

- Who seems to have a high degree of awareness of the group and its business?
- Who is loyal, dependable, and present, always at meetings, carrying out any assignment they may have been given?
- Who catches on quickly and is teachable and coachable?
- Who can command respect if and when they do speak or take a leadership role?

Once individuals have been located, ask for a particular kind of participation, and use the committee or small group as a chance to empower the voice and ideas of the person or persons,

Thought leader and Case Western Reserve professor David Cooperider, the founder of the Appreciative Inquiry process designed to locate the strength in any system, focuses on "leveraging an organization's core strengths, rather than seeking to overcome or minimize its weaknesses." The belief is that organizations "move in the direction of what they study. AI makes a conscious choice to study the best of an organization, its positive core."

As a business consultant, Cooperider often flew into different cities, being met at the airport by a representative of the group which had hired him. On the drive from the airport to his hotel, he reported, he often heard engaging stories about the entire company, with high energy and high enthusiasm. But when the entire group gathered at corporate offices the following morning, the dynamics tended to change. Problems facing the institution were named, spirits dragged, and energy disappeared. Cooperider's awareness of this phenomenon was instrumental in his creation of Appreciative Inquiry, where the focus is on potential over problems. Shifting our individual focus from problem to potential can have a similar positive impact, on everyone from titled leaders to the general population of the system. Negativity can keep a system stuck in a rut. When toxic personalities rotate out of a system, they are generally replaced by an equally toxic personality. It takes intentionality to change the behavior in the system to positive rather than negative, to focus on potential rather than problem.[13]

It Sounds So Simple – What Stops Us?

One of the ways we trip over our own feet is by focusing on what people intend when they behave in a way that is irritating, unpleasant, or downright destructive. The rationale goes something like this: "I know she meant well. She's such a good person..." or "He would never intentionally do anything to hurt anyone, and certainly not to hurt this group. Think of all the time and money he has invested in it."

But without asking a person directly what they intended when they engaged in a certain behavior or said a certain thing, it's a guessing game, seasoned with projection and wishful thinking. There's a subtext, too, which goes something like this: "This is America. We are smart people, good people with good values. We are leaders in our world community. Okay, so maybe there are a few bad apples, but the majority of people don't mean to hurt someone else. I'm sure they started with the best intentions."

In my work, I like to emphasize the difference between the words intention and intentionality. As used in this context, intent is most often considered after the fact, action, or incident, to explain why something was not well-received or was received differently than expected. ("But I didn't intend to hurt her feelings by pointing out that her skirt was too tight!") This kind of intent, from this practitioner's perspective, is not generally planned in advance with self or other-awareness. Intentionality, on the other hand, has to do with moving into a plan of action deliberately, with both self and other awareness. ("This is the timetable for the plan to build the youth center.")

One of the first steps toward health in a system is setting aside the idea of intent. Intent does not matter. What matters is impact, the objective effect on the whole. Impact happens, regardless of intent.   Every action that is taken by an individual, every word that is spoken, every behavior, has potential impact on a system and the persons who make up that system. In other words, there is an action, and it has an objective effect on the entirety of the system. It is important here to separate the objective effect on the whole from individual feelings about that effect, which are generally irrelevant. (Point of clarification, loud and clear. I did not say that feelings

---

13 Notes from lecture on Appreciative Inquiry by Elizabeth Workman, Leadership Training Institute, Dubose Conference Center, Monteagle, Tennessee.

in general are irrelevant. I said that the objective effect of an action on the system exists, regardless of the subjective assessment of it through feelings about that impact.)

There is an example from my own life that I am not proud of, but I believe it shows clearly what I am saying about impact happening regardless of intent. Years ago during one of the most difficult times of my life, I was a single, working woman, moving back and forth between visiting my daughter who was hospitalized during a very difficult pregnancy, and my mom, who was in treatment for kidney cancer. One particular evening, I was at the end of my rope from stress and exhaustion. I had stopped at the neighborhood dry cleaners to pick up some clothes I needed before an early morning work flight. I went through the drive-through, and the young woman working there informed me that my cleaning was not ready. I could pick it up the following morning at 9 am, two hours after my flight was scheduled to leave!

As I sat in the car looking at the employee, a flush of rage came up the back of my neck and out of my mouth. I yelled and berated her for at least ten minutes. Then I squealed off in my car. As I pulled around the corner of the building, I came to my senses. "Kay, what did you just do?" I knew that I needed to apologize.

When the young woman saw my car approaching the drive-through window again, terror and dread filled her face. From that day on, I never think of impact without seeing her face. Regardless of my personal issues, regardless of my apology, the impact had happened and I could not make it unhappen.

We've all been there.

Problem or Potential: The Choice Is Ours

All too often, the loud voices and shocking behaviors of those who are problematic cause us to retreat quietly. We instinctively choose a stance that is as different as possible from what we view as the problem. We do not want to be a part of that destructive way of being and doing.

But wait. There is another option.

And that option is to refuse to give the power to the problem, and to firmly, strongly, competently, thoughtfully, take the power and exercise it. Here's an example.

I had been called into a tense situation in a nonprofit organization, a conflict that threatened the fabric of the organization. The board of the organization had been meeting for several hours, with strident voices of criticism over financial issues dominating the meeting. The CEO, Executive Director, and CFO were being severely criticized by two outspoken members of the board, who were overpowering the discussion. There were moments of silence when it might have been possible for alternative views to be heard, but no one spoke. Finally, utilizing a concept first introduced in Chapter One, I said, "I am aware that there are a number of you who have not expressed your thoughts on this matter. I am going to assume, unless I hear otherwise, that your silence is an indicator that you are in agreement with what has been said."

A hand went up. "I do not agree." Another hand. "I don't agree." And then another. There were a few interruptions from the critics, who were reminded and held to the standard of respectful listening, but when all voices had been heard, it was a different story than initially presented. Said one of the reluctant speakers, "It was really important for me to hear that my silence was taken as agreement with something I very much did not agree with. I don't speak up easily, and especially not when I have experienced people's words being crammed down their throats, or the other opinions are so loud and ugly. But now I know that I have to stretch myself to speak up and be sure that loudness does not always win."

Potential is always sitting in the shadows of discord, waiting to sing in harmony. When voices are silenced, neither song nor potential can be realized.

Moving Forward to Action:
Questions for reflection and sharing

1. FOR SELF-AWARENESS. How am I building my own strengths and potential? Where have I been focusing on, and giving power to, squeaky wheels?

2. FOR OTHER AWARENESS. How is my community/organization building strength and empowering potential? Where is it focusing on or rewarding squeaky wheels?

3. PRACTICE. What one step can I take to build a strength? To be empowered? What one step can be taken in my organization/community?

A conversation with
KREMINA TODOROVA AND KURT GOHDE

Founders of "Unlearn Fear and Hate"

When and how did you hear the call to your work?

For artist/professors Kremina Todorova and Kurt Gohde, June 2015 brought a call they could not ignore. Posts from people of color, warning "don't give the police a reason to shoot you" already had brought them deep concern. The church shootings in Charleston, S.C., in which nine people were killed during a morning Bible study moved them to the realization that they had to respond in some way to the increased acts of violence in the country. The hatred that they observed around them, the inability of people to see each other's humanity placed a demand for action on their hearts.

How did you decide what to DO?

"Art is what we make," said the duo, who through the class they teach together in Community Engagement Through the Arts at Transylvania University in Lexington, Ky., were already about the business of stretching the intellectual curiosity and openness of their students, encouraging them to move beyond campus boundaries and their comfort zones to experience those unlike themselves. The 4-foot steel halo they designed is embossed with the words from Affrilachian Poet Frank X Walker - "Unlearn fear and hate," which have become the clarion call for the initiative which bears that name, bringing people

---

"We were not born with hate. If we learned it, we can unlearn it."

---

together to know and understand people unlike themselves. This effort was a natural for the collaborators, who do this work in addition to their teaching duties; Kremina teaches English, Creative Writing, while Kurt heads the art department. "We especially like this line because it emphasizes that we were not born with hatred," says Kremina, "but learned it. If we learned it, we can unlearn it!"

The collaborators have created art projects in the Lexington community which have placed handmade dolls throughout the north end of Lexington, inviting people to find new homes for them, have created projects with discarded furniture on Lexington curbs, with short essays reflecting the stories represented by the furniture.

What challenges did you meet?

Kremina and Kurt must constantly be teaching that Unlearn Fear and Hate is not about a single issue. While their work first focused on the differing opinions regarding the prominent placement of Civil War statues in downtown Lexington, which Kurt was involved with as a member of an Urban County Council committee trying to assess the pulse of the city, there were people who assumed that racial discrimination was the entire focus of their work. They emphasize that Unlearn Fear and Hate is about any kind of fear and prejudice. "We had to learn to choose our words carefully, and to be aware that every decision we made could deliver a message, whether we intended it or not." On the day that the steel halo was unveiled at a downtown hotel, the president of the local chapter of NAACP was one of the invited speakers, and was last on the program, adding energy to the assumption. There are others who made the assumption that the work was driven by the election and its aftermath, which also is not true.

The second challenge has been emphasizing that this is not "a liberal agenda." "It's an agenda for all," the duo emphasize, wherever they speak. One of the ways they have responded to this particular challenge is by speaking wherever they are invited, but particularly in churches and schools where "we're not singing to the choir; there are people hearing us who have many different viewpoints and beliefs, and that's really important."

What have you learned that you can pass on to others who want to make a difference?

"Small things matter," says Kurt, recalling a quote that has become important to him from Howard Zinn, author of the People's History of the United States who always ends his talks with "Don't let great get in the way of good," adding "A thousand small acts cause large change. It is tempting to try to start too big," he reflects, "but small is good, too." He points to small "Unlearn Fear and Hate" stencils showing up around the city — source unknown to either he or Kremina, but very welcomed.

Enveloping relationships which may have begun in public forum beyond that setting has been important to Kremina. She is enthusiastic about a yoga class she shares with new Muslim friends, and the things she has learned that they share, like a favorite spot to meet for coffee.

Her creation of cross-stitch versions of the Unlearn Fear and Hate art which she carries with her and works on are a constant source of curiosity which often leads to more new relationships.

Saying "yes" to all suggestions goes hand-in-hand with welcoming new people as initiators and thought leaders as well as worker-bees. Recently, a Syrian couple new to the community stumbled upon the candlelight prayer circle at the Fayette County Courthouse, where a group of some 60 people of diverse faiths gathered on a Monday night. Thirty-nine people offered prayers, others held candles. The newcomers were shocked to see that those from the Muslim community could pray in public and not be afraid. They quickly knew they wanted to be a part of this work, and felt welcomed to do so. Of such welcome and shared leadership is generativity born. "There are so many ripples we are not aware of," the founders say happily. "There are many ways to get involved," Kurt emphasizes.

This leadership duo hasn't "had time" to worry about roadblocks along the way, nor to fear that they themselves could become targets of hate or violence. When a roadblock is encountered, their response is to re-direct; find another way to accomplish the task.

Kurt points to the time the logo had been stenciled on the sidewalks at the University of Kentucky, after permission was secured from the proper sources. Within hours of the chalk art being competed, UK maintenance carefully power-washed it off! "I choose to try to see it from the workers' point of view," Kurt said. "If I was hired to keep the sidewalks free of graffiti and saw chalk on them, I would probably wash it off, too. It was my job. That means we have to find another way to get that message out."

What is ahead for Unlearn Fear and Hate going forward? Do you have a final word to pass on to those who are responding to their own call to change the conversation?

Plans are in the works for a 40-foot halo which can be illuminated at night to be installed in downtown Lexington. It's on hold, at the moment, as there is resistance from some who find the slogan, and the work, "too political."

Undaunted, they continue their work, speaking wherever they are invited, spreading the message that fear and hate can be unlearned. "Now is the time not to be afraid," says Kurt. It's quite clear that fear never occurs to them, as they go about their work. "We just forgot to be afraid."

CHAPTER THREE

The Why of It: Behavior Makes or Breaks Relationships

"As a society, how do we do better and stop violence happening time after time....violence is not the answer, people. Retaliation isn't the solution."
—LeBron James

William Golding's 1954 novel, Lord of the Flies, is a timeless look at the complexity of relationships and behaviors. When a group of British schoolboys' plane crashes on a remote island, they are left without adult supervision, dividing themselves into "littleuns" (around the age of six) and "biguns" (roughly ten to twelve years old). Initially, the boys attempt to establish some order, similar to the culture they have known in their young lives.

Ralph. an easygoing but responsible boy, is elected "leader" with the support of Piggy, an overweight, bespectacled asthmatic intellectual. One of Ralph's major priorities past the basic survival needs of shelter, food, and sanitation is maintaining a signal fire, hoping that a passing ship will see the smoke and rescue them. Jack is the major challenge to Ralph's leadership. He commands a group of choirboys-turned-hunters who sacrifice the duty of keeping the fire going so they can participate in the hunts. Jack draws the other boys slowly away from Ralph's influence and toward adventure.

The conflict between Ralph and Jack – and the forces of savagery and civilization that they represent – is exacerbated by the boys' literal fear of a mythical beast roaming the island. Jack forms a splinter group that is eventually joined by almost all of the boys, who are enticed by the protection Jack's ferocity seems to provide. Of all the boys, only Simon has the courage to discover the true identity of the "beast" – in reality, a dead pilot whose body had been parachuted onto the island, and symbolically, not an animal on the loose. Turning away from civilized behavior results in the deaths of Simon and Piggy. The real "beast" is the savagery hidden in each boy's psyche.

All of us have a shadow, or dark side, according to analyst Carl Jung. It's sometimes called acting out of the "reptilian brain", acting out of the most primitive part of our brain to protect ourselves, to survive. Its coping mechanisms include aggression, anger, fear, and revenge. We'll talk more about it in Chapter Five. Let us note here that the "shadow" or dark side is a little-known part of ourselves that is generally held in check by the values and guidelines of family and culture. However, like a beach ball which has been held under water, the shadow can, when a person is tired, stressed, sick, or with people with whom they are extremely comfortable or familiar, escape from constraint and explode into the air.

An example of group shadow behavior is pretty famous in my part of the world. In Kentucky, where I live, celebratory mobs take to the streets after our college basketball team wins a major tournament. Couches are set fire, cars overturned, and at times, people get hurt. It has happened with such frequency that when a big game is on the schedule, extra police are stationed near the campus. That's the shadow when the team wins. In 2017, however, the team made it to the Elite Eight, and lost. Irate "fans" bombarded one of the officials with derogatory tweets, calls, and e-mails, and even posted professionally damaging remarks on his business web site. Both the coach and the university spoke out against the behavior, but it happened! How is it possible for civilized people to turn animalistic?

It simply comes down to words and actions. They make or break relationships in households, organizations and countries. And while most organizations or systems have more governing principles than the island in Lord of the Flies, recognizing, naming, and defining healthy and unhealthy behaviors and their impact is the first step. This step is followed by being intentional about the words we use ourselves, and those we condone or accept from others in our lives. These steps are critical for returning civility to our lives. I said it was simple. I didn't say it was easy.

Subsequent chapters will delve further into naming and defining. In this chapter we want to look further at III: Intent. Intentionality. Impact. To help us as individuals unpack this in our own lives and behaviors, I want to illustrate by breaking down my own shameful story of emotional over-re-activity.

Back Story. Single working woman. Mother with cancer living with her. Bedridden pregnant daughter. Drives through dry cleaners to pick up clothes to take on a business trip. Dry cleaning is not ready.

Behavior. Angry remarks to clerk at window. Driving away in car.

Secondary Behavior. Realization that action was rude, inappropriate, Decide to drive back through and apologize.

Intent. To get my dry cleaning in order to leave on my trip.

Secondary Intent: On reflection on the experience, to express dissatisfaction that my cleaning was not ready at the promised time.

Emotional Back Story. An already stressful personal situation had just been complicated.

Impact. Expression of horror, fear, recoil on face of clerk. Despite profuse apology, awareness that no explanation of my own stress-related explosion can change her experience of me and my behavior.

Let me break it down for you in another situation. I was the consultant for a conflicted non-profit board. It was well known that Jeffrey, the president of the board, was not a fan of Adam, the CEO. Jeffrey frequently told people he found Adam "cold and distant." Off the record, other board members observed that Adam did not join the group at the local bar following business meetings, which seemed to provide further "proof" to Jeffrey that the CEO was not engaged with them. The widely held opinion was that Jeffrey, the "elder statesman" president, was resistant to the authority of the younger CEO, who was also from another part of the country, and according to Jeffrey, an outsider to their culture. In addition, the socially conservative Jeffrey had a baby boomer's discomfort with a gay man, married to his partner, in the position of CEO of "his" local organization. Although the two men were able to stay professional enough to conduct the business of the organization, things were at a maintenance level, with little in the way of creative engagement taking place.

Adam, the CEO, had invited me as the consultant to provide some much-needed team building to the board. Enraged by my presence, Jeffrey completely lost his cool at the first meeting, unleashing a string of expletives at me and emphasizing that I was not welcome at this meeting. After slinging his notebook across the table, Jeffrey walked out and slammed the door. The following day, his letter of resignation was delivered to the CEO's office by courier.

Behavior. Angry outburst at the consultant.

Intent. To run the meeting as usual.

Secondary Intent. To express displeasure at having an outsider in charge of any aspect of the meeting (an emotional substitution toward the "insult" of having a younger, gay, "foreigner" to his culture in an executive position).

Emotional Back Story. A difficult relationship between the CEO and board president that had been simmering in the background

Impact. A stunned board left without a leader, confusion, divided loyalties, loss of talent.

None of us is immune from shadow behavior; from acting out of the reptilian brain. The reptilian brain overpowers the ability to have calm and rational thoughts. The extreme emotional responses stem from a fear of not surviving. Wars, jealousy, anger, fear, hostility, worry, being stuck or frozen with fear, aggressiveness, extremist behavior, cold-bloodedness, hoarding, looting, fight-or-flight – these are just a few of the characteristics of the reptilian brain. We can be surprised by triggers at any time.

In the heated days of the 2016 presidential campaign, my teenage grandson expressed his support of Donald Trump, citing his wealth, private jet, hotels, and other material things as examples of his qualifications for public office. My response was a quick, "That's a good way to get yourself written out of the will!" My daughter looked at me in horror. "And you teach civil dialogue?"

I quickly apologized to my grandson and explained that I was not opposed to us having different views of any political candidates. What I was reacting to was an opinion based on wealth and appearance rather than policy and experience. It was a good lesson for both of us, and one which allows for real discussions on real issues going forward.

In addition to personal triggers, all of us are operating in the face of barely-masked systemic issues. Issues we considered settled and accepted, such as inclusion and gender and race equality, are rearing their heads again today. Was integration laid to rest? Do the happy pictures of same-sex weddings and families indicate across the board acceptance? What are the feelings lurking behind the slogans that look backward to a time that some seem to long for?

As a senior in high school, I was one of a group of students who walked to the corner of Walton Avenue and Main Street to welcome the first African-American students to Henry Clay High School at the beginning of the term. All was peaceful, it seemed, until time for the fall Homecoming Dance, at which time members of the football team would be honored. As President of the Dance Committee that sponsored school social events, I was asked to confer with our faculty sponsor, the principal, dean of girls, and football coach.

There were two black players on the football team. The fear, I learned that day, was that one of the black players might ask a white girl to dance. After what I remember as hours of discussion (and, I might add, where my 17-year-old voice was listened to respectfully, even as my passion for inclusion was clearly considered naive), it was decided that Coach Heber would accompany the team to the dance in time for the introduction, after which he would be responsible for leaving the party with the two players.

Such fears around many social issues still drive behaviors today. All of us can find ourselves emotionally hooked into words and behaviors, causing impact that was not our intention at all. Intervention is necessary. An important intervention model points to the relationship between attitudes and emotions to words and actions. An event or attitude directly or indirectly causes an emotion, which precipitates words, which can lead to reactive action or behavior. The intervention model calls for practicing a pause between the feeling or emotion, and words spoken. (See further discussion of this under characteristics of Emotional Intelligence and how it can be developed in Chapter Five.)

Several levels of emotional and functional activity are operating simultaneously in the situations described here, and as we endeavor to build new habits or strengthen old ones of acceptance and inclusion. Most of us tend to operate in the ways we learned from our family of origin and our current culture. Life happens to us rather than us steering a chosen course. I call it "living intentionally," and believe such living is crucial to returning civility to our culture and our world.

Living Intentionally Doesn't Come Naturally

For twelve years, I was the design consultant and primary present-er and facilitator for the Circles of Power Women's Leadership Initiative at the University of Kentucky. Originating in the Medical School as the brainchild of Edythe Tevelson Lach and eventually going campus-wide, its mission was helping women develop leadership skills in what was then a male-dominated system. One section of the curriculum was devoted to the topic of "living intentionally." Participants were all highly educated ad-vanced-degree-level professionals, who had worked long and hard to reach their chosen goals vocationally. In this sense, they all agreed that they had been intentional in setting goals and taking the necessary steps to reach them.

Yet most agreed that, in a more general sense, life had happened to them rather than having any say in it. With few exceptions, meeting a mate or partner, marrying or cohabitation, having children, break-ups, friend-ships had just happened. "I went to college because it was time to go to college," said one woman, "although I had no idea what I wanted to study, or prepare to do. But all of my friends were going and it was the appropri-ate time to go, so I did."

"That's how it was with marriage," another spoke. "I was finished with both undergrad and graduate school, had a good job, and realized that most of my friends were taking the next step, as were colleagues my age. And then it was time to have children, and we did."

Intentionality, if it set in at all, became a subject of awareness when the impact of things that happened were not the impact they would have expected or chosen. "I started to reflect on options I might have had when my husband said he wanted out – that he was choosing to do some other things with his life. I had to step back and look at how we had gotten where we were, and think about what I really wanted to do."

"That's when I became aware of the Serenity Prayer," said another woman. "Courage to change the things I can and the wisdom to know the difference."

Certainly, there are results or impacts that we may be unable to control, regardless of our forward thinking or consideration. However, being inten-tional about attitudes, words and actions can result in more positive im-pacts in all relationships and systems. It can be as simple as how I choose to speak to a service professional on the phone – whether I am intentional about speaking to them with respect. Or it can be as complex as how I go into a meeting where important decisions are to be made and opinions are divided. The words that I choose and the tone of voice I use can either assist in civil discussion or raise the heat in the room.

The harmony you want to create may be on the athletic field or court, in the orchestra or chorus, or in your own family. Or it may be, for all of us, in saving our country and our world from the terrible events of violence that are becoming too common in our lives today. For as President Jimmy Carter says, 'We must aggressively challenge our society's acceptance of violence which should never be seen as normal, or as the preferred means of solving problems…but violence is now normal in our homes, communities, in our culture, law enforcement, and in foreign policy.'[14]

Moving Forward to Action:
Questions for reflection and sharing

1. *It's really helpful to have a partner in each of these exercises, both for sharing, questioning, and discussion, and because, as we touch experiences and emotions we might not have previously processed, it's important to have support and encouragement.*

2. Have you ever been in a crowd that was having an emotional response to a sadness or loss? What happened? How did you feel? What did you think?

3. Think of a time when you were surprised by discovering that you spoke or acted in a way that caused someone else to be hurt or offended, although that was not your intent. Using the behavioral model describing the back-story, etc., see if, with your discussion partner's help, you can figure out what happened. Then, using the intervention model, discuss with your partner how it might have happened differently.

4. Think of a time that you have had such an intense emotion about something that you experienced emotional violence. What triggers that kind of intense emotion for you? What do you do with it? After reading this chapter, what choices do you think you have about 1) recognizing how everybody can have violent feelings, and 2) recognizing the fears or anxieties that cause them in order to have choic-

---

14 From both his book A Call to Action: Women, Religion, Violence and Power, and his 2014 speech to the annual Human Rights Defenders Forum at the Carter Center.

es about how to respond rather than react?

5. What are the areas for you today where it is most important for you to live intentionally rather than let them happen as they will? List them, and begin to think about how you can live intentionally in these areas.

6. Consider whether you and your discussion partner would like to be accountability partners to work on living intentionally. If you would like to do so, decide on how often you will be in contact about your goals, and how you will communicate. Be sure to pledge your honesty and confidentiality to each other.

LOOKING AHEAD. A fan once said to the great pianist Ignacy Jan Paderewski, "I would give anything to play the way you do." The artist replied, "No, Madame, I did." In the arts, and on the athletic fields and courts, we tend to think that great performances come easily to the stars. But the truth is that they understand their field, and are committed to practicing their art to achieve greater success every day. Cleveland Cavaliers superstar LeBron James says, "Every practice, every film session, every game will help our chemistry..." to which he adds these words, "Every morning you look in the mirror and you say, are you committed or are you not?" We have a game plan, a great score to read and understand for the game, the greatest concert of restoring civility to our country. The question is this: how will we answer LeBron's question?

A conversation with

CHANGE AGENT
RABBI DAVID WIRTSCHAFTER

Rabbi of Temple Adath Israel, Lexington, Ky.
Leader, Activist and Organizer

When did you feel called to make the world a better place?

From his book-lined study at Temple Adath Isreal in Lexington, Kentucky, Rabbi David Wirtschafter reflects on a childhood with parents who worked for civil rights; who "raised me with the notion of working for justice, that fighting for change wasn't easy, but quitting was not an option, and success is possible." Growing up in Minnesota, there was a requirement that teachers read the rule book to their high school students during homeroom. "It spelled out the offenses, and the consequences. This was a public school, so religion, or any supporting values were not mentioned. There was no philosophical component; not 'why' the rules existed or should be kept. I realized that day that in the absence of 'why,' there was little reason for people to change their behavior. I hoped

PHOTO BY JOHN LYNNER PETERSON

that I could make a difference helping people see the 'why'— ethically, morally, psychologically, religiously—that I could inspire and motivate others to change the environment."

Can you speak about the relationship of this awareness to the action step of becoming a rabbi?

In Reform Judaism, and Judaism in general, social justice and the rabbinate are deeply connected. One assumes the other. If there had not been a social justice component to ministry, I would not have gone into it. Dr. Martin Luther King demonstrated that one of the reasons people go into ministry is hoping that they can make a change in their country. He demonstrated so powerfully that one did not have to have lots of money or elected office to make a difference."

For Wirtschafter, the rabbinate is a way to bring several important elements of his life together under one umbrella: teaching, writing and pastoral care. All of them working together are the "right vocation" for him.

In Lexington, Rabbi Wirtschafter is well known for his Interfaith work—and in particular his stances on immigration, and his work with Interfaith and Social Justice work. He points to the history of Jewish work with these groups, as well as his own involvement.

"The Sisterhood of Salam Shalom Women's Group has been active for over 20 years," he says, pointing to the work of Nadia Rasheed and Rosie Moosnick which welcomed him into ministry in this area. His previous work, before becoming a rabbi included interfaith work wth the Jay Phillips Religious Center for Interfaith Learning. At Adath Israel, a social action committee often initiates a project, and encourages him to take stands. "The willingness to do this work comes from within the community." he says.

What kinds of challenges have you met, and how did you meet those challenges?

The greatest challenge, says Rabbi Wirtschafter, is "how to combat exclusivity, or exclusionary practices, without becoming exclusionary. "Rick Clewett, the Chair of Social Action here, says that the key question is are you ready to defend any member of the coalition; to defend their humanity and their rights. If we are not careful, we can unwittingly become participants and supporters of divide and conquer campaigns... and that kind of behavior can de-rail us."

He points to a feeding program the Temple is involved with which is sponsored by a church whose public profile includes anti LGBTQ stances. "Is it better to disappoint the gay community and feed the hungry, or not collaborate with any organization which excludes? Where do you draw the line? How do we overcome differences in deeply felt policies and form compelling and convincing coalitions that advocate for shared values?"

Wirtschafter's son Zachariah, a rising high school senior with his own passion for social justice had his own painful encounter with hate rhetoric at school. He made a personal decision, and held that decision in conversations with administrative officials and others who wanted to identify the perpetrators and see them punished, that the "teachable moment" was more important to him than punishment and consequences. In a speech at a local gathering, he stated that he wanted all of those who were concerned to help create an environment where such behaviors don't happen.

"It is my responsibility as a leader to create a safe space where people can disagree..."

"Learning how to phrase the questions that will invite people of diverse beliefs into conversation," is critical, Wirtschafter states. "We have to speak in a manner that takes the people we disagree with seriously," he said. "There's a big difference in saying 'Why are you a climate change denier?' or 'What makes your climate change dismissive?'" "Why don't you 'get it'?" immediately puts people on the defensive.

"This is something I am working on all of the time," the Rabbi concludes.

What have you learned about communicating with the "other" — people different from ourselves?

"We are living in a sensitive and fractured time. People are scared and angry. It is my responsibility as a leader to create a safe space where people can disagree." Rabbi Wirtschafter calls on his own passionate involvement in social justice work to connect with how easy it is to speak out in emotional reactivity, rather than choosing a more delayed, reflective response. "It's hard to remain rational and respectful when you've been hurt and offended," he states, clearly connecting with times he has felt the latter. "I haven't regretted what I've said (under such circumstances.) I have regretted how I've said it. I've learned through humbling mistakes that speaking in anger, outrage and righteous indignation will be perceived as labeling those with whom I disagree, and all who support them as morally deficient. And who wants to be in conversation with someone who thinks they are morally deficient?"

In both community and school settings, this father, rabbi and interfaith leader, activist and organizer works for values-based dialogue and decision-making. "We need to do a better job in creating an environment in which there is greater concern for core values — and that means teaching core values." After the school incident in which Zachariah was the target of ugly slurs, the principle of the school was asked by a concerned parent if any student had expressed sadness or fear to him. He replied that the students weren't speaking about it to him at all. Said Rabbi Wirtschafter, "We need to create an environment whose ingrained values would propel the students to say 'not in our school.'"

As an ongoing reminder to himself, he remembers an important lesson from his days as a rabbinical student: "Disagree in such a way that the people talking with you can always imagine you as their rabbi."

What advice do you have for others who would like to be a part of changing the world for good?

Let us always ask ourselves the following question:

"How can we live our lives and be advocates for the kind of country we want to be in such a way that we will be proud to tell our children and grandchildren the story of what we did."

CHAPTER FOUR

Practice, Practice, Practice: Foundations for Change

"You are what you practice most." —Richard Carlson

In the darkened room, only two images were visible: the light of moving figures projected onto a movie screen, and the silhouetted shape of a man staring intently at the screen. Will C., a college quarterback, had his eyes and mind focused on one particular figure on that screen. He was watching the arm motions of one of the all-time great quarterbacks in NFL history. Back and forth he moved the images, stopping the action to look closely at a specific angle of the arm, to observe the follow-through, before moving to the next play. Beside his chair were the round tin reels of movies of other great quarterbacks. Hour after hour Will sat in the darkened room, studying, taking the images deeply into himself as if he were on those fields, throwing the football.

Will had been drafted by a professional football team, and had excitedly reported to a preseason camp for rookies, who would have their initial workouts for the coaches before reporting for their first training camp, and having a shot at living out their dream of playing in the NFL. It was in those workouts that Will was given the assignment that led to this darkened room, the tins of film, and hours of practice. Will was endeavoring to change the position of his throwing arm.

Although he had been a highly touted college player, the position of the elbow of his throwing arm had caught the eye of his new coaches. The great quarterbacks of the league who had achieved a high degree of success at the professional level had their elbows up. Will's elbow was down. The coaches believed that if Will was to achieve success at this level of the game, and for the long-term protection of his body, Will needed to adjust the position of his throwing arm. His future in football was on the line. And so, Will found himself in the summer before his hoped-for rookie year with the man who was known as the greatest teacher of fundamentals of the game of football in the history of the National Football League. That man was Blanton Collier, my father. He was a soft-spoken man, not six feet tall, who with his glasses, topcoat, and fedora looked far more like the math professor he was than the coach of a professional football team. After his official retirement, he was still sought to tutor quarterbacks who needed special work on an aspect of their position. Therefore, the rookie quarterback found himself watching film in the Lake Conroe, Texas, study of the man who had created film studies for the NFL, and taking the images from the film onto the nearby golf course, throwing to his 75-year-old tutor with the new position, again and again. And when he thought he might be done, yet again.

My dad's belief was that in order to make the change, this man needed to:

1. Be aware that his present behavior was not achieving the success needed,
2. Be aware of the difference, the impact, the change could make,
3. Desire to achieve the different result,
4. Practice the new action over and over again until it was second nature, experiencing the feel so that his body as well as his mind internalized the new action, making it automatic.

Will had come to recognize through film study that there was a difference in the position of his throwing arm and the throwing arm of the great quarterbacks. He had become convinced that the change in arm position could have a positive impact on his potential to be an NFL quarterback, and that realization gave him a strong desire to make the change. He worked tirelessly to accomplish the change, to get his elbow up, emulating the great pros. He didn't make all-pro, but he did have a number of successful years in the NFL, fulfilling that lifelong dream.

It is not change itself we fear, it's the changes that we will have to make to accommodate the change that scare us. Even when change is desired, when I am aware that my current words and actions are not getting the results I want, something inside of me resists the work that change requires. Whatever the discipline, the change will take desire, time and effort. Practice, practice, practice.

Shinichi Suzuki, the great Japanese pedagogue who revolutionized string music education, always told his students if they had performed a passage one way a hundred times, it would take one hundred repetitions of each previous performance, executed perfectly, to build in the new habit. If a mistake was made on repetition three, or seventy-three, it was back to the beginning!

His words bring back the sounds of music practice rooms, from Kentucky to Wisconsin, Boston to Japan, over the years. Walking down a hallway near the practice rooms, one can rarely hear a completed piece of music. Excerpts. Measures. Phrases. Slowly. With varying rhythms. Back to the beginning. Repeat. Now a little faster.

This process is newly on my mind as I am attempting to live into one of my own lifelong dreams of playing the harp. In these early weeks, my fingers are learning new disciplines, both on and off the instrument. Curve the fingers thusly. Place precisely at the corner of the pad, thumb higher than the fingers. 1. 2. 3. 4. Listen to the difference in tone when the fingers are placed in waiting on the strings than when plucked individually. Repeat.

Practice. Practice. Practice. It is slow, painstaking work to move from not knowing to producing, whether the product is a professional level pass, a beautiful piece on the harp, or a productive conversation. When it comes to learning to talk with each other, the process is the same as in athletics or music: practice, practice, practice.

Not Giving Up Too Soon

When people begin to try to talk to each other, they can become discouraged way too fast. Like any other discipline, early efforts might not be the hoped-for success. And with that disappointment and the tendency to personalize failure, they simply return to their old way – a victory for homeostasis.

I was consulting with a state Council of Churches that had determined to hold a conversation regarding civil liberties, a hot button issue at the time, as several businesses were refusing service to individuals and citing religious reasons. During the preliminary conversations, I became aware of a reticence among the group, even though these leaders of various denominations met together regularly and worked well together on numerous projects. Collegiality and humor were also evident in their meetings. Still, I decided to check out my sense that there was a part of their story that was holding them back, and invited them to share any previous attempts they had made at having tough conversations.

Mike, a past president of the group, offered a bit of history. Several years earlier, they had decided to tackle this same issue when it first was raised locally. "We had three or four tables, with an appointed leader at each table. It started out pleasant enough, but it didn't take long for it to break down. Voices got louder. Tension was so high! We finally had to shut it down. People have been really reluctant to talk about anything that they know means differences of opinion," he stated sadly.

A big step toward making another effort came in having the tools to do the work differently. A precursor of every meeting when I am consulting is considering the norms and standards for our work together. What will our agreed-upon operating procedures be? The standards involve things that are required, that are essential to membership. The norms are customs, things that are desired, that develop over time. While norms are not essential to membership, deviance from them would definitely be noticed. This time, a Culture of Courtesy Covenant was put in place, outlining the norms and standards, to which everyone agreed before we began.[15]

A Covenant for the Creation of a Culture of Courtesy

I will come to the meeting on time and stay the entire time, in respect for the time and investment of all participants. If I am unable to attend, or must leave early, I will notify the leader in advance.

I will come with a sense of curiosity and openness, ready to hear new ideas from other participants, to have my assumptions challenged and to stretch my vision and sense of the possible, as I maintain personal integrity of thought and feeling.

I come with an understanding of confidentiality: I have a right to take from this room and share with others what I have said. I do not have the right to repeat outside of this place what others have said.

I come here to be in constructive dialogue for purposes of better understanding, not to critique, coerce or debate.

I will speak for myself only, using "I" messages: "I believe," "I think," "I feel," "I want."

I will listen respectfully to what others have to say without interrupting. I will not engage in side conversations or non-verbal expressions when another speaker has the floor. I will not engage in applause or expressions of displeasure.

I will not be an air 'hog,' 'bog,' or 'frog,'" speaking to hear myself speak, speaking to a point which has already been made when I have no

---

15 Culture of Courtesy Covenant, Adaptation of model originally designed by Kay Collier McLaughlin and included in the Leadership Manual of the Episcopal Diocese of Lexington.

additional information to impart, repeating myself or leaping over or ahead of the item under discussion.

I will work to build up trust among participants, looking for and expecting positive, civil interaction with each.

I understand that process (how we do things) is as important as product (the content or what we do). I will respect both and endeavor to conduct myself in a manner that respects the dignity of every person. I further understand that I am encouraged (along with other participants) to call attention to process should interactions move away from behaviors agreed upon in the Covenant, so that we can maintain the Culture of Courtesy.

As an adult participant, **I will take care of personal needs during break times** unless otherwise unavoidable, out of respect for the time and investment of all participants. I will **put cell phones and other electronic devices** on silent unless needed for emergency purposes.

An exercise on the difference between dialogue and debate was also conducted.[16]

The Differences in Dialogue, Discussion and Debate

Dialogue	Discussion and Debate
Dialogue is collaborative.	Discussion is analytical; debate is competitive.
The goal of dialogue is increased understanding of myself and others.	The goal of discussion is a decision; the goal of debate is the successful argument of my position over that of my opponent.
In dialogue, I come with an open-minded attitude that includes an openness to being wrong and to change.	In debate, I come with a closed-minded attitude that includes a determination to be right. In discussion, I often tend toward one "right" answer.
In dialogue, I listen with a desire to understand.	In debate, I listen to counter what I hear.

---

16 Adaptation of model originally designed by Kay Collier McLaughlin and included in the Leadership Manual of the Episcopal Diocese of Lexington.

In dialogue, I speak for myself only, from my own understanding and experience.	In debate, I speak from assumptions made about others' experiences and positions.
In dialogue, I listen for strengths so as to affirm and learn.	In debate, I listen for weaknesses so as to discount and devalue.
In dialogue, I approach with curiosity, asking questions to increase understanding.	In debate, I approach with self-certainty, asking questions to trip up or confuse.
In dialogue, I allow others to complete their communication.	In debate, I interrupt or change the subject.
In dialogue, it is OK to say "I don't know."	In debate, I never say "I don't know," but pivot or shift topics.
In dialogue, I respect all other participants and seek to engage, not to alienate or offend.	In debate, I am focused on my own next point and may belittle or disrespect in rebuttal.
In dialogue, I accept and honor other people's experiences as real and valid for them.	In debate, I critique others' experiences as distorted or invalid.
In dialogue, I assume that many people have pieces of answers, and that cooperation can lead to a greater understanding, possibly a better answer then that with which we began.	In debate, I assume a single right answer, and that someone (including me) already has that answer.
In dialogue, I allow for the expression of real feelings, in myself and others, for understanding and catharsis.	In debate, I express my feelings to manipulate others; I deny their feelings as legitimate.
In dialogue, I honor reflective silence.	In debate, I use silence to gain advantage.
In dialogue, I can remain open-ended.	In debate, I must produce a product.
In dialogue, the practice is the product.	In debate, winning is the product.

Some questions to ask myself if I am having trouble staying with dialogue:

Am I honoring my own experience as valid…	or am I feeling defensive about it?
Can I trust others to respect our differences…	or do I suspect others are trying to force me to change?
Can I trust myself to be permeable and still maintain integrity…	or do I fear that hearing a different perspective will weaken my position?
Am I willing to open myself to the pain of myself and others…	or am I resisting pain that I really have the strength to face?
Am I open to seeing the humanity in those with whom I hold differing positions…	or am I unwilling to see parts of myself and all humanity in those from whom I hold differing positions?

Let me point out here some of the distinctions between debate, discussion, and dialogue. The content of debate has to do with explanations, conclusions, and bias. The content of discussion deals with goals, opinions, and ideas. The content of dialogue deals with insights, intuitions, and emotions. The process of debate involves convincing others; the process of discussion involves an exploration of ideas to reach a conclusion; dialogue is an open-ended exchange which accepts the contributions of others. There are strengths to each of the three. In debate, there is a clear winner. In discussion, the people participating are able to set goals. And in dialogue, the growth of the group is fostered. There are obvious weaknesses to each of the three as well. Someone is a clear loser in debate. Some options and opportunities may be missed in discussion. And dialogue is time-consuming and not necessarily conclusive. A different kind of leadership is needed for each. Debate needs leaders who are able to articulate clearly and use relevant information appropriately. Discussion needs leaders who are able to keep an effective balance between majority and minority views and the ability to arrive at consensus. Dialogue needs leaders who are ready to remain open to everyone. There are times and places where all are appropriate. In our culture today, debate has taken over as the conversational norm.

Once a group has agreed upon norms and standards, such as the Covenant for Creating a Culture of Courtesy, and agreed to work toward being in dialogue with each other, as in this instance, trained facilitators were on hand at each table to guide the overall discussion, and participants were empowered to hold each other accountable to the Courtesy Covenant. During the discussion, there were obvious differences of opinion and experience at each table, and emotional investment from the participants. A facilitator could be heard asking, "Could you re-state that as an 'I' message?" At another table, a man addressed the woman across from him, "Jane, we haven't heard from you, and you look a little frustrated. Can you share what's going on for you?" Whenever more than one voice spoke at a table, or anyone was interrupted, a facilitator would interject, "One person at a time. Remember, we have two ears and one mouth, so let's listen twice as much as we speak," or "Please listen the way you would like to be listened to. " At the end of the sessions, participants remarked that "next time we need to be sure there are more people with strong differences to do this."

A short narrative about dialogue:

In 2009, I had the opportunity to interview Marshall Ganz from the Harvard Kennedy School while he was leading a Public Conversation Project at the General Convention of the Episcopal Church in Anaheim, California. According to Ganz, when Laura Chasin began the Project in 1989, she envisioned a civic life where it was possible to have constructive conversations and relationships among those who have differing values, experiences and worldviews. Their work, which is based in connection, reflection and mindfulness in conversations with trained leadership, was able to report on a six-year dialogue involving six pro-life leaders and six pro-choice leaders.

While neither changed their beliefs, they co-authored an article talking about the experience of developing the capacity to hold "the paradox of an irreconcilable worldview while embracing the humanity in each other." In addition, their experience altered their ways of approaching differences in other situations in their lives, and expressed their experiential conviction that dialogue can assist in decreasing violence and moving us toward a more civil society.[17]

In Lexington, where I live, a group started an initiative called Unlearn

---

17 The Advocate, Episcopal Diocese of Lexington, September 2009 interview with Marshall Ganz by Kay Collier McLaughlin.

Fear and Hate. In the early days of their efforts, the organization sponsored a forum to examine whether Civil War memorials should be taken down or moved, since many minority groups considered them offensive. According to frustrated leaders, polarization was greater after the meeting than it was before, as individuals dug deep into their positions. One group felt strongly that these memorials are a true representation of the history of this area, and should remain where they are. The other group felt that the prominence of the memorials was disrespectful to minorities today, and in order to be an inclusive, compassionate community, the memorials should be at least relocated. As positions were reiterated, the volume in the meeting room grew louder, and tones more defensive. "There were interruptions, people talking over other people, and the sense that everyone was just waiting for whomever was speaking to be done so that they could say what they wanted to say, rather than any real listening to the other person." Most felt they had not been heard by the "other side."

All too often, efforts at conversation take exactly this pattern of interaction. Politeness disappears as emotions around particular issues grow more intense. Any chance of gaining new awareness of other people in the room, new insights to ponder, are nonexistent.

Civil dialogue is the process of talking together, not at each other. Civil dialogue involves practice in attitude toward behavior and commitment, first of all.

1. Willingness to stay at the table.
2. A choice to listen more than I speak (I have two ears and one mouth for a reason).
3. A choice to believe that two people can experience the same event and be impacted differently.
4. A choice to listen to someone else's truth as their truth, not a contradiction of mine.
5. A choice to not try to defend, criticize, or change minds.
6. A choice to look for areas of commonality.
7. A choice to respect the worth and dignity of every human being.
8. A choice to be open to new insights.

The work we do in civil dialogue is something we experience together. It is based in the belief that ideal learning occurs through active participation that connects to the life of the learner.

Tell me…and I will perhaps remember a little of what you wanted me to know.

Show me...and I will remember what was helpful to me.

Involve me...and I will have a chance to integrate the experience into who I am and how I live my life.

Early attempts at civil dialogue may be difficult and far from perfect. But with toolkit in hand and heart and mind, we try again.

Three foundational concepts undergird further attempts. The first concept is known as "the provisional try" in organizational development. It is not a failure when we are trying new behavior and it is a rough version of what we hoped for. We are giving that new behavior a provisional try. We are testing to see what works. We have to tweak the behavior for a particular situation. And so we learn and improve.

The second concept is called "change back behavior" in family systems work. When we are practicing new behavior, we are stretching individuals and groups in new and different ways. Think of what happens when you stretch a rubber band. When the stretching mechanism is released, the rubber band automatically reverts to its original shape. So it is with a system trying on new behavior. It is a stretch, involving mental, emotional, and spiritual muscles being exercised in new and often exhausting ways. When the environment or leadership let up on the exercise, the tendency is to revert to the old shape or way. That is called homeostasis.

The third concept to keep in mind is called transition. The time in-between is not something we give much thought to today in our fast-paced world, where because of the influence of technology we are conditioned to expect immediate fulfillment. Not long ago it was acceptable to expect a phone call to be returned the next day, but today, we become frustrated if we don't have a text or e-mail response within minutes! The further we move away from processes in our lives that take time to achieve results, the more impatient we become, the more addicted to instant gratification in all things. Few of us these days plant gardens, and are thus unfamiliar with the process of moving through growth stages from seedling to blossom. It is not unusual for children to think that tomatoes and potatoes come from grocery stores, fully formed, therefore missing completely the process known as transition!

It's all about a process – one foot in front of the other, one step at a time, whether planting seeds in the earth, or planting seeds in the human heart and human systems. They have to be continually nurtured to grow into their potential. In this case, the nurture comes through practice. Civil dialogue, the ability to be in real conversation with people unlike ourselves, people with differing experiences and opinions, requires doing the provisional try, and not giving up when it doesn't work the first time or the second. Recognizing that like the quarterback who needs to change his arm, and the would-be harpist who needs to train her fingers, change back behavior will rear its head in efforts at conversation, and practice time is a time of true transition from one way to another.

I was asked to teach these and additional concepts to an adjudicatory staff of a faith-based organization in Chicago that was looking for a new way to work with churches in conflict. We spent two full days practicing ways of using the theories, with different participants serving as facilitators. Then we took the show on the road to one of the most conflicted congregations, polarized over a change in leadership. The head pastor had been forced out after sharp division over his stance on issues of social justice. Members of the congregation were divided into those who believed the church should focus on internal matters or worship, education, and pastoral care of members, and those who felt the institution was called to take a stand on social issues and extend their community to those who were excluded by the culture.

At the evening session, the staff divided themselves among the small groups and set about their work, beginning with a look at times people had been most energized and engaged with their mission – an exercise that revealed many shared values. Feeling included was high on the list of shared values. Feeling accomplished; respected; doing something of value. Learning something, about themselves as well as the world. Feeling connected. People who might differ on a number of issues found common ground when it came to good works such as developing a project for children, addressing the need for a new roof after storm damage, or responding to needs of people affected by a crisis like Hurricane Katrina.

In the second session, the participants shared times when they had been most challenged, hurt, or disappointed by events that had occurred in the institution. Although each story was different in impact – often due to each individual's own life story – the values that undergirded the story were strikingly similar. Some participants felt disrespected because they had spoken out about growing vandalism in the neighborhood surrounding their church and wanted to address some of the causes of the problem, and others didn't think it 'appropriate'. Others felt Ignored, or even insulted, when no one wanted to join in their work with the elderly. People spoke about losing something or someone about which they were passionate, and feeling scared, alone, or grieving because they saw worship and education as the primary work of the church, and felt what was core in their faith was being left behind for activities that could be taken care of by social service agencies. At one table, someone blurted out, "Everyone seems glad to help the poor and the needy as long as they don't live any closer to us than some third world country or New Orleans, but no one wants to see the poor and the needy right in our backyard!" Before any defensive or angry retort could come back at the speaker, the facilitator gently but firmly prompted, "I hear you have some strong feelings about your experience. Could you let us know those feelings in an 'I" message, like, 'when I see enthusiasm for helping people far away and no attention to the people in need right around us, it makes me feel…'" After a moment's pause, the first speaker said, "It makes me feel really sad and angry." Another person spoke up. "I feel that way, too, but I didn't know anyone else did." Another person added, "I want to be able to see all of these people as my neighbors, and to divide our help between the needy right here and the ones in crisis wherever they are. I feel selfish when we limit our help to our neighborhood or city." And turning to the person who felt worship and education were being overshadowed by outreach, she added, "My reaching out to others is how I understand living out what I learn in church, so for me it's not either/or but very connected." The first speaker looked startled, and then replied, "I never thought of it that way."

Similar conversations took place at each of the tables, with great emphasis on phrases such as "I was afraid to say I felt that way," or "I had no idea you felt that way," or "I didn't think it was appropriate to speak up because I might be the only one." At the conclusion of session two, there was a short ritual in which there was an opportunity to lay the papers on which the church members had written their hurts and disappointments to the side, as a gesture of putting them in the past in order that they not dominate them going forward.

Participants moved on to session three: where do we go from here? The most important statements had to do with wanting to go forward together. They recognized that there were both common values and differences of opinion among them, which would most certainly lead to disagreements over organizational life in the future. However, they felt hopeful about the future because they felt their opinions and ideas had been heard and respected in a new way throughout the sessions. Their stories, their truths, had been held carefully by others. They had found some common ground. And they had some new tools for moving forward.

I remember standing on a windy Chicago street corner at the end of the evening. It was wintry dark, with a light snow blowing, the kind of night when getting to your warm car was important. The thing that warmed the night for me was the comments from the people who had participated, as they stopped for a minute to comment on what they had just experienced. "I didn't know it was possible to agree with someone I disagree with so much," one lady said, aware that she now knew that she shared essential values with a participant with whom she strongly disagreed regarding organizational decisions. "That's the first time in my life I've ever had a conversation in a conflicted situation that didn't end up with people angrier and more divided than when we started," a man stated. "I kept waiting for someone to yell, or walk out, but starting with that Covenant for Courtesy really helped. And having people to help us stay on topic."

Experience. Practice. The process described here asks us to be aware that each of us humans have a capacity for visceral memory. For deep, inward feelings that connect not with the intellect or brain alone, but with the internal organs (viscera) of the body, especially those located in the trunk (heart, liver, intestines). It gives credence to "gut feelings," reminding us of deep, internal memories that we can recognize when we are aware of their existence.

Some people carry visceral memories of conflicted conversation that bring ghosts of yelling, broken relationships, doors slamming, objects thrown, even physical brutality. Other ghosts bring feelings of nausea, a tension in the neck and shoulders, a physical bracing, a fear of whatever unknown lies ahead. Other ghosts are blank with avoidance and accusation, and ultimately greater entrenchment and polarization, so that we shy away from any attempt to talk with an "other" so we can avoid repeating behaviors we know and have experienced, from self or others. As practice of civil dialogue adds more positive visceral memories, of being listened to, of finding commonality among our differences, talking with an "other" about any subject is less fearful. Bodies can relax; anticipation can be neutral, as in approaching a new business acquaintance, where the expectation is common courtesy as we proceed.

Learning happens in stages, whether it's physical, mental or emotional. Perhaps a powerful example that the majority of people can relate to is the learning of how to ride a two-wheel bicycle. It goes in levels like this:

- INTELLECTUAL LEVEL: This is a bicycle. In order to ride it, I will have to balance on two wheels while moving.
- FUNDAMENTALS LEVEL: As I push it, walking beside it, I can feel the weight. If I sit on the seat, and lean slightly to one side or

another, my toes can touch the pavement. If I push forward on a pedal, I move forward; push backward, move backward. The tipping point seems to be how to do that at a speed that helps maintain the balance.

- ABILITY LEVEL: I can ride! It may be wobbly, and I may have to stop occasionally, and I am very definitely not going to ride in the Tour de France, or even on a local bike hike, but I can ride a bike. I need to have my full concentration on what I am doing.
- MASTERY LEVEL: I can ride and talk with someone else, listen to my earphones, ride long distances, even, perhaps, do the "Look ma, no hands!" trick. If I go many months or even years without riding, I could easily get on a bike again and my body and mind would quickly remember.

Visceral learning. Practice rewarded. A promise for what we can do.

The Chicago experience has been replicated again and again – in upstate New York, in coastal Florida, in Oklahoma and other places too numerous to name. The e-mail updates keep me apprised. From New York, Nancy writes, "Thinking about you during our meeting as we utilized the 'provisional try' and acknowledged that it would take us some practice before change back behaviors were less frequent." From North Carolina, "Know you would be smiling to hear the vocabulary around here…particularly adept at asking for 'I' messages and calling out triangling (see Chapter Six), and what a difference that has made." From Texas, "The difference between dialogue and debate and Culture of Courtesy Covenant have totally changed the tone of our meetings, and our ability to get things done." With each experience comes a confidence that talking together is possible, for I have experienced it.

Is it a change? Yes, indeed. It is dialogue, not debate. It requires intentionality. It requires practice.

Is it worth it? It is our hope and our promise to the future of our planet.

A Cautionary Tale

There is nothing more exhausting to a person struggling with change than a change-agent who has made the change and is totally gung-ho about being sure everyone does it, preferably yesterday. Crisis response is full of such well-meaning folk. One tool for assessment of self and others is a chart based on Maslow's Hierarchy of Needs. It helps us to understand how differently people come to both thought and action, based on where they are personally.[18]

Need	Characteristics	Theme Song	Location	Projection
Survival (physiological)	Breath, food, water, warmth, sleep, sex, homeostasis, excretion	"Help Me Make It Through the Night"	Gutter	One minute
Safety	Security, shelter, job, income, protection, law and order	"Swim"	Sidewalk	Hour by hour, day by day
Belongingness	Intimate relationships, friends, neighbors, companionship	"You'll Never Walk Alone"	Neighborhood	Weeks, months
Esteem	Feeling of accomplishment, pride, prestige	"Just The Way You Are"	Community	Months, years
Self-actualization	Achieve potential, creative acts, good of others	"Let There Be Peace on Earth"	World	Future

Looking at the pyramid helps us understand the task ahead, and the various starting points for different people.

18 Maslow's Hierarchy of Needs was introduced in the book Toward a Psychology of Being, now in the public domain. This pyramid was adapted from the "Maslow Meets Jesus" pyramid created by the late Terry Parsons and the Rev. Hugh Major, Office of Stewardship for the Episcopal Church in the United States of America.

Here we can see clearly why some are vulnerable to promises to move them out of a place of hopelessness, symbolized here by the gutter and onto the sidewalk, an indication that they are out of survival mode and seeing the possibility of hope ahead; into a neighborhood and a community for a support system. Many have too many tasks to do to survive, or feel safe, or begin to belong to be concerned about world peace.

One of the changes we all have to make is to move out of our own location and begin to see and hear and experience the truth of all the lives that make up our communities, in order to begin to turn to one another, and to truly hear each other. The South Africans have a word for it: Suwa Bona, meaning, "I see you; I hear you". To them it means, only when you really see me and hear me do I exist. In this sense, to be in civil dialogue is to be in sacred, holy conversation, recognizing the very existence of an other.

The practice of civil dialogue is a bridge - a bridge from unknown (and scary) to known experience, a bridge from negativity to positivity. It is a bridge from the intellect and unfiltered emotion to the integration of heart, mind, spirit and body, where to live and interact in disrespect for the humanity of an other would be inauthentic. It is a bridge to a way of life, which has a profound ripple effect of presence, rising up wherever you go, impacting your circle of influence, and ultimately, the world. The path may be long and fraught with roadblocks to overcome, but it is a proposition of the possible.

Moving Forward to Action:
Questions for reflection and sharing

1. When have you had to make a change in the way you did something? What motivated you to make the change? How did you learn the new way? Practice the new way? What was the promise of your hard work? Impact?

2. Why is it personally important to you to begin to make this change in the way we walk with each other in our world? What of the things you have learned so far do you find most helpful? What do you need the most practice on? What kind of change do you hope to experience?

3. Please share an experience of having a conversation with someone who is in an entirely different place on the hierarchy of needs. When and how did it take place? What did you hear/learn? How could you have this kind of conversation today?

A conversation with

CHANGE AGENT
JOSH NADZAM

Executive Director of
On the Move Art Studio

**When and how did you hear the call
to make a difference in the world?**

Josh Nadzam gets up from the table at Stella's Deli in Lexington, Ky., where we are talking over lunch and faces the window. "I kept trying to move toward the goal that I could see so clearly," he says, stepping repeatedly toward the window, as if his vision was just outside. Taking a short step to the left, he points to the door. "And all the time, the door was right here." The analogy told the story of a call the young man from Pittsburgh heard in stages, beginning at an early age.

He was five years old when he knew he wanted to make the world a better place. "There was so much chaos in my family. Tragedy. Trauma. I knew I had to work as hard as I could until I was 18 and could escape. I wanted to get out of there myself, and I wanted to help other people.

"I've learned that at the end of the day, we all want opportunities, safe neighborhoods for our families, fairness and respect."

The second call came in 2012, when as a social work student at the University of Kentucky, he became involved with Bill Strickland, and the effort to bring the Pittsburgh-based Manchester Bidwell Job Training and Youth Arts Center to Lexington.

Call number three came when, after three years, the efforts to raise the money for the Manchester Bidwell Feasibility Study stalled, and Kris Kimmel, the founder of The Idea Festival, said to Josh, "Why don't you just do your own thing, and GO?" "It was as if someone gave me permission to take one little piece of this huge idea and get started," says Josh.

The fourth call happened when a professor in a graduate school social work class in non-profit management told the students, "Be the person you needed as a child."

"That was it. I was ready to go. Cathy Werking, the surviving believer from the Manchester Bidwell project, and I bought the vintage trailer, and we were moving."

How did you decide what action to take?

Of all the people who had expressed interest in the Manchester Bidwell project, Cathy Werking was the one person who had hung in there through all of the work to raise money for the feasibility study.

"Cathy was an artist, with a great interest in and knowledge of vintage trailers. I was a social worker looking for creative ways to intervene in the lives of children who might be growing up in some kind of chaos, as I did. Maybe we weren't able to raise the money for a great building with our grass roots efforts, but we could take our trailer, equip it with art supplies and drive it to places where the power of art could give kids an idea of talents they didn't know they had."

What challenges have you encountered, and how have you responded to each challenge?

1. A man whose analogies and diagrams quickly bring his listeners into his story, Josh offers a pattern of organizational life he recognized as his first challenge.

"An idea for a service project is advertised. One hundred people excitedly respond to the idea. Two weeks later, 70 people report still being on board. A meeting is called a month later. Forty people attend. Second meeting, 20 people attend. Ten core people continue the work."

"It's the battle of attrition," Josh says. "I used to take it very personally, wonder why I wasn't a better leader, why people didn't care more. My ah-ha was this recognition that this is natural. It happens in all organizations. There are so many important causes, and no way that everyone can be 100% involved in every one. A part of my job is finding those for whom this particular cause is number one. That has been my biggest challenge and my biggest ah-ha.

2. Closely aligned with this example of normal attrition is Josh's theory of the cycle of reaction/response.

3. Challenge number three Josh characterizes as "arranging bowling pins in water." "I think I have them all lined up and this one (pointing to his right) floats away. He's not a bad guy, and he's really interested, but he's got a lot of responsibilities at work, plus at home. We get him back in line, and then this one (pointing left) floats away. It's really difficult to get people together at one time and place.

4. Meeting people where they are. It's not enough to advertise. I need to engage

people around what they value, not my idea of what they value. Say there is a board member who really doesn't care all that much about art itself, or even know much about it, but he likes helping kids, so he's happy to donate art supplies. There's a person who says he doesn't have the kind of money to make a significant charitable donation but he owns an automotive shop and is happy to do the much-needed work of hauling the trailer to its different locations. Josh is looking forward to being full time with On the Move Art Studio, where he can spend more time with this issue of engaging people where they are. Vist http://www.onthemoveartstudio.org for more information.

What have you learned about the 'other' people who are different from you?

1. "I've learned that at the end of the day, we all want opportunities, safe neighbor-hoods to raise our families, fairness, respect. I don't know anyone who would say 'I don't want opportunities. I don't want safe neighborhoods. I don't want respect.' If we can start there, on this common ground we agree on, it would be possible for us to really talk to each other."

2. "If I can approach people with humility, with an interest in learning something from them, of acknowledging that I don't know it all, and I am interested in knowing how and why your experience has been different from mine, then we won't need to delete each other as Facebook Friends. If I delete you, I will never learn what I could learn from someone who has different ideas and perspectives than mine. It's hard, because the knee jerk reaction is to fire back when there are differences. I need to honor how the other person feels; honor their feelings as legitimate. They might not be factual, but they are their feelings, and I can at least say, 'that really sucks. I am sorry that happened to you.' Then I might be able to ask if they are interested in hearing my side."

"When someone says I've hurt their feelings, or what is said is offensive, I don't get to decide if that is true. If I broke my arm, and someone hit it, and I said, 'that hurt my arm.' And someone says to me, 'Oh, that didn't really hurt,' I'd be saying, "My arm still hurts. That's my truth."

Where is On the Move Art Studio headed next? Do, you have any words for people who want to be the change they want to see in the world?

"When someone starts out with a food truck, the natural next step seems to be a restaurant in a building. That was part of our early thinking, too. But now we feel like a better idea is a fleet of trailers, that can go wherever we're asked, in Kentucky and all over the place. There are several advantages. It's not us, deciding that such and such neighborhood needs what we have to offer, but groups and communities request us to come because they see a need. It's about taking the art to where the children are, and so avoiding one of the barriers of poverty — the lack of transportation, that could become an issue if we had a fixed building. Plus, our overhead is really low!

We've got lots of ideas for the future.....we'll have to see what happens......

For others who want to save a part of the world wherever they are, Josh says:

Whatever idea you have to make the world better in a literal sense is 100% possible.

2. Grit is important. One quote I always remember says you have to have passion and perseverance. Passion alone will run into barriers and setbacks and frustrations, so perseverance — good, old-fashioned stubbornness — can make a difference.

3. Ordinary people do extraordinary things. I used to think you had to be a CEO or some other important person to make a difference. Think about Rosa Parks. She was an ordinary person who was just stubborn enough not to get up when she was told to move to the back of the bus. The perseverance of an ordinary person made important things happen, which gave her status as one of the important leaders of the civil rights movement.

4. Never give up on people. My mother, a single mom, fought so hard to keep our heads above water. She worked at fast food restaurants, any place she could get a job, and she never gave up. I feel like she was given a bag of coal, and she turned it into a diamond which she gave to me to give to the world. It's like she said, "Here, Josh, spread this around." She never gave up, and everything I do I do in her honor. Because of her, I won't give up on anyone.

5. Take the passion that is in your heart and share it in ways that people can get it. Some people can get it through words. But other people won't ever hear the words. Maybe they've been talked to or talked about too often, and not seen anything happen. But passion translated into action many people can hear. Turn your passion into action.

CHAPTER FIVE

No Music is Made without Self and Other Awareness

"So war and peace start in the human heart. Whether that heart is open or whether that heart is closed has global implications."
    – Pema Chodron, Elephant Journal...It's About The Mindful Life

"So, why should I keep working to change?" the young woman demanded, standing just inside my office door. "The people around me aren't changing at all! And the more I change me, the crazier I feel when I'm around them. Who am I going to hang out with?"

After months of work to disengage from an unhealthy relationship, she had come face to face with important truths: Change begins from the inside. The only person I can change is me. If I have a complaint about someone else, I need to look at and understand myself first. I can bring my awareness of self to my experience of other people, but I cannot change them.

How Do I Become Self-Aware?

Training to work in civil dialogue always begins with exercises in self-awareness, often a surprise to people who come expecting to sit and listen to a lecture. In one training, people had gathered at their assigned tables, some with pencils in hand, or iPads at the ready, as if anticipating note taking. After a brief introduction, I issued an invitation:

"You are going to hear four sets of questions that you are going to answer with your feet, by going to the blue line on the floor at the front of the room and positioning yourself on the continuum as to what you would USUALLY do in the described situation. Don't think about it too hard –

just move in the direction your first instinct tells you."[19]

A.

You have been to a meeting, and you are so energized by the interaction that you want to go for coffee and continue the conversation.	You have been to a meeting, and after talking with so many people, you need down time and space to recharge.

B.

You have been assigned to teach a class in world history which will look at how the Vietnam War started. You will give the outline: 1 abc, 2 abc, 3 abc, and these are the reasons the war started.	You have been assigned to teach a class in world history which will look at how the Vietnam War started. You will say, "We are going to look at conditions that existed in the world prior to the start of the war, and see if we can determine how it started."

C.

You have been asked to downsize your department at work. You will ask two sets of questions. Which set will you ask first?

How do I do this so it is most logical and most fair?	How can I be most in accordance with our values? How can I keep harmony?

D.

You have been given an extra hour in the day. You are going to:

Make a list and check it off to see how many things I can get done.	Go with the flow and see what happens?

19 The Typology Continuum was created by Kay Collier McLaughlin as an experiential self-awareness exercise.

Section A refers to how we are energized in the world. Extroverts are people who are energized from the outside. When they are around people, they gain energy from the interaction. Being around people is helpful as they process aloud in order to understand what they think. In conversation with others, whether they agree or disagree, extroverts will share whatever they are thinking aloud. Other extroverts may understand this behavior, and simply be aware that the speaker is working out what they in fact think or believe, and that what listeners are hearing may not be the final word this individual has on the subject. In conflicted conversation, this may be particularly confusing to introverts, who are energized from the inside out. Introverts may like people equally well and have equally polished social skills, but after they have been around people in a business or social setting, they are drained of energy and need down time to re-energize. Introverts think things through in their heads before they respond. This internal process makes the verbal processing of every thought confusing when they are in conversation with extroverts. Because introverts do not speak up immediately, they are often assumed to hold the same ideas that previous speakers have expressed. Unless a facilitator of the group or a participant is particularly aware, the introvert can be overlooked in a fast paced or heated conversation.

Section B refers to how we give and receive information. Sensors like facts. If we can see it, taste it, touch it, smell it, it's real. Intuitors are big picture people. They see things in completed or whole images from which, if necessary, they will look at component parts. In all conversations, the sensor will want to gather and share details, often moving painstakingly from A through Z on any issue. The intuitor moves quickly from the introductory point of a conversation (A) to the big picture (Z). Sensors want intuitors to hear and value details in the way they do, and wonder how in the world they could have arrived at a decision point without looking at every detail. Intuitors, on the other hand, can be impatient with what often seems laborious to them, moving slowly from A-Z.

Section C looks at how we make decisions in the world. Thinkers' basic life questions are "Is it logical?" and "Is it fair?" Feelers' basic life questions are, "How can I hold to the values of the group?" and "How can I keep harmony?" Thinkers are "fixers" who want to find and offer solutions, and are put off by what they perceive as emotions coming at them when there is a problem to be solved. Feelers do not need or want to be fixed; they need values to be heard, respected, and included in the decision-making. When thinkers and feelers square off, they often see each other in derogatory and not completely true terms: "Those people (feelers) don't have a logical bone in their bodies!" or "Those people (thinkers) don't have a feeling bone in their bodies!"

Both types have both characteristics. It is a matter of which comes first in their process. Once the issues of logic and fairness have been decided, thinkers will move to consideration of values and harmony (although they might not be as verbal or open about them as feelers are, especially if they are introverted thinkers). Once the issues of value and harmony have been heard, feelers will definitely move on to logic. It is when their primary process is inhibited that the types become further polarized and do not move to the secondary process. The thinker/feeler continuum can be particularly difficult in times of stress or differing opinions (and processes). Thinkers often judge feelers as being overly emotional, rather than understanding that they are asking for values and harmony to be respected. Similarly, because thinkers do not deal well with emotions, they often put up a non-verbal stop sign to stop these feelings coming at them – or they attempt in some way to "fix" the issue. As feelers hear the rational, solution-type responses from thinkers, they feel that someone is attempting to "fix" them rather than accepting and valuing their emotions. The reverse can also be true, if tensions increase the emotions in the room during a discussion, and the thinkers' attempts to stop the emotions do not work.

Section D refers to basic orientation to life. Judgers (not judgmental) are people who thrive on structure and decisions in their lives. Perceivers are known as the option kings and queens. They want to leave everything as open-ended as possible, for as long as possible, because something better just might come along![20]

In addition to knowing the basics of one's personality type and how that affects interacting with others, an important part of self-awareness involves knowing that every human being has a shadow or dark side of self,

---

20 References to typology begin with the study of the work of Carl Jung on archetypes, doctoral study in psychometrics, and include selected resources on the Myers-Briggs Typology Indicator, as well as a compilation of thirty years of experiences from workshops on typology, including a week-long intensive with Dr. Flavil Yeakeley at St. Louis University, shadow workshops with Dr. Pearl Rutledge and the Rev. Dr. Paschal Baute, workshops combining aspects of typology, emotional intelligence and human relations training, and workshops with the Mid-Atlantic Association for Training and Consulting. As an experiential consultant trained to adapt resources as current circumstances require, I may have long forgotten the names and dates of particular trainers or experiences which led to the creation of exercises such as this continuum. I am forever indebted to Isabel Myers and Katherine Briggs for devoting years of their lives to creating a model that translated Jung's theories into a usable model that continues to serve human growth and development, and to other typology theorists who have added to the conceptual resources with their work in Four Temperaments, Belbin Team Roles, and other wellness instruments. There are many personality theories and models, all of which require knowledge of supporting theories for best usage. This exercise is intended to introduce or reinforce the concept of typology as important to self and other awareness, with emphasis on the fact that maximum understanding requires administration and explanation of a full instrument by a qualified practitioner of the model chosen.

as previously discussed. Perhaps the best way to think of my own shadow is to think of a picture of a house. I like to think of my house as completely clean, neat, and attractive, ready for family and friends to enjoy. But down below the house is an old-fashioned cellar. Not a fancy basement rec room, but a dark, dirt-floored cellar where everyone is scared to go, for fear of what might be lurking in the dim, hidden corners.

When I think of myself and how I assume (and hope) the world sees me, it is like the upstairs of the house – clean, neat, attractive, pleasant. And I need to own that I have my personal cellar, the dark, scary, unknown part of myself that neither I nor other people know. That is the part that can come out and surprise me and the people around me. The shadow often comes out when I am sick, tired, stressed, hurt, or just around people who are very familiar and comfortable to me.

One of the ways to get in touch with my shadow is to be aware of every time that words come out of my mouth that I would like to quickly stuff back in, or words that cause someone to say, "That doesn't sound like you at all!" This shadow part of ourselves is often called the "shadow bag" to emphasize that we each carry around this subterranean, unpracticed part of ourselves. We must practice containment because, when it does get loose, it can result in rough, impolite, rude, and often hurtful behavior.

The shadow side of self is easy to trigger in tough conversations, as people venture into unknown territory, and triggers are often touched in the process. The result can be quite the opposite of how people would normally act. Extroverts can become silent and introverts unusually talkative. Sensors fail to be aware of details and intuitors bog down in details. Perceivers jump to decisions and judgers procrastinate on closure. In all cases, the unfamiliar and unpracticed behavior is rough and unpolished, often leading to greater conflict and misunderstanding. That makes it doubly important to understand the flipside of the shadow, the gold buried underneath the roughness.

This double-faced aspect of the personality is hard for everyone to grasp. When the shadow escapes, it is a part of us that has never been allowed to see the light of day. It is not polite, or proper, or in accordance with the values we have been taught. Those observing shadow behavior often will say, "I've never seen you behave that way!" Two examples describe some of the ways shadow behavior shows itself.

Suzanne is a middle-aged woman whose stately posture and tailored outfits in quiet neutral tones seem to define the proper wife and mother with careful values and morals, but at a dinner party, she reacts to bawdy political comments with a loud and rather humorous string of expletives before marching out of the room, slamming the door behind her. Guy, a dependable, affable accountant who is known for working quietly at his desk year after year, responds to a female colleague's "see you tomorrow" with an angry 'don't go screwing around with some pickup!" for no obvious reason.

Shadow theory tells us that the more restricted an individual has been in certain areas of his life, the more the shadow is likely to emerge when triggered. Suzanne's natural responses have been carefully monitored by a strict set of values and rules from her childhood, as well as the social and moral boundaries of her adult life. She has been the responsible partner to a fun-loving husband and mischievous twin sons. Few, if any, have ever experienced Suzanne as out of control or playful in any area of her life. On this particular evening, something triggered unpracticed parts of this woman to react without monitors, surprising, perhaps shocking, herself and others.

Guy has always been experienced as quiet and even-tempered, always helpful to others. He seemingly handles the stresses of tax season and other busy times without breaking a sweat. Other than a small picture of his wife on his desk, his coworkers know very little about his private life. Behind the image of the mild-mannered accountant, stress has been building as he experiences his wife as distant and detached. Unnamed fears of possibilities he has heard about in other relationships haunt his dreams. He has pushed them down, but something in his colleague's words, tone of voice, or posture bring them roaring out.

Both Susanne and Guy reacted when unguarded emotions were touched by a trigger that set off behavior that was different from the behavioral patterns both they and other people would have considered normal for them. Reactions to public figures like Joel Osteen, the megachurch pastor from Houston, Colin Kaepernick, the football player who took a knee during the National Anthem, and Hillary Clinton as her new book hits the market, remind me of a personal experience from many years ago, and how much I learned about myself and my own super-strong reactions by applying some questions based in shadow theory.

As a religious journalist, I had the task of covering a visiting speaker at a large local church, Friday evening, all day Saturday, and Sunday morning. My job as a journalist entailed covering people with whom I agreed, those with whom I disagreed, and some on which it was easy to be neutral. My job was to report the facts and get a balance of responses. While Friday evening wasn't exactly my cup of tea theologically, the speaker clearly kept the audience engaged. As the hours passed on Saturday, the jokes and jabs increased. I was relieved to pack up my notes by the end of the evening. Arriving in time for breakfast on Sunday morning, I could hear the speaker's voice, piped into the dining hall from where he was preaching to the early service.

My visceral reaction prompted me to bypass breakfast and find a quiet spot to collect myself. I was not sure which might come first, vomiting or bursting into tears. I found an empty office and sat down. I had a job to do, so I had best figure this out. Besides, I didn't like these surprisingly out-of-my-reason feelings! What behavior is causing you to feel nauseated and sad?, I asked myself. He was getting laughs and affirmation from this audience by making fun of people and beliefs that are important to me. Have you ever, either consciously or unwittingly, made light of people, ideas, or beliefs that are dear to someone else while trying to get your point across and engage an audience when you are the visiting speaker? Everything within me wanted to say, "No! Of course not!" But honesty demanded that I acknowledge that I probably had. The "gold" for me was new awareness of myself as a presenter, and my responsibility to balance my own strong positions and means of engagement with greater mindfulness. Was I reluctant to acknowledge that the part of him that was so abhorrent to me was a part of me? You bet! The gold is to be able to acknowledge that part of me that triggered my reaction, and use it to grow myself in that area. So, my shadow questions as we head to press: what is the Joel part of those who are filled with disdain for him? The Colin part of those who would run him out of the country? The Hillary part of those who want her to shut up and go away?

The unhealthy side of shadow behavior is its continuing element of surprise, without reflection or monitoring. The positive possibility is enhanced self-awareness, calling to mind a story about a little boy digging through piles of manure, saying, "where there is this much s___, there has to be a pony!"

Suzanne's "gold", or the flipside of the shadow, is to own that there is, indeed, a playful, fun loving, slightly bawdy part of her that has never seen the light of day. If she owns that part and allows it to develop in healthy ways, it will no longer be in her shadow bag, but a normal ongoing part of her personality. The practiced part of her might have tossed off a slightly bawdy retort to the political joke, rather than using curse words that were not a part of her usual vocabulary and storming out of the meeting. In that scenario, she would indeed be allowing her own bawdiness or playful side to come out.

Guy's "gold", or flipside of his shadow, is the more forthright, bold man who lives inside the mild-mannered accountant. While his upbringing, education and adult life, inside him exists the potential for a more mature, sophisticated relationship with life where he is capable of understanding and addressing the realities of marriage directly. There is a fine line between shadow behavior and mental instability, and it is important that we be aware of what triggers our own shadow and how that works in others if we hope to have a return to civility in our world.

Mob mentality can be an offshoot of shadow behavior. This is often incited by the fervor of an athletic event, such as the ones depicted in the 1980's book Life Among The Thugs, which details animalistic behavior by soccer (football) fans in the United Kingdom and recent political outcries for assassinations, bombings and jailings.

A similar concept in systems theory speaks of being controlled by the "reptilian brain", the oldest and most primitive part of the brain, which connects to the spinal cord and controls functions basic to the survival of all animals, like heart rate, breathing, digesting food, and sleeping. The phrase refers to instinctive brain functioning that is shared by all reptiles and mammals, including humans. When someone is said to be acting out of their reptilian brain, this primitive part of their brain has overpowered their ability to have calm and rational thought. "Losing his/her mind" is a more common phrase that describes this overtake. Some reptilian brain characteristics listed include territoriality, hierarchical structure of power, control, ownership, wars, jealousy, anger, fear, hostility, worry, fear, aggressiveness, extremist behavior, competitiveness, cold-blooded, dog-eat-dog beliefs, might is right, and survival of the fittest. The reptilian brain does not like change or new viewpoints. It does not know the difference between real and imagined, so thoughts about events are just as real and significant as the real thing. The reptilian brain also does not like surprises.[21]

One of my favorite typology exercises to emphasize both self and other awareness is to post the sixteen personality types on the wall and invite participants to stand beneath their scored typology. When all are at one of the sixteen stations, I ask them to cup their hands around their eyes like blinders, and look directly at their type as posted. Then I say the following:

You are being asked to consider the topic of racial discrimination in our country. You confer with those within your view, which at this time is limited to your own small silo of life typologies. Imagine that from your position, you are signaling to everyone else in the room, 'Hey, come look out MY window. If you will look out MY window, you can see what the

---

21 Lecture notes from workshop with Margaret "Peggy" Treadwell, 2009.

world really looks like." We would not really limit ourselves in this way, assuming that we alone had the answer regarding this or other challenging subjects. But in actuality we do it all the time, rather than using our differences in typology to learn to show respect for each other.

A few years ago, I presented a workshop on Myers Briggs Personality Inventory, the "granddaddy" of all the typology assessments. I was gathering my papers at the podium after the workshop when I sensed someone waiting. I looked up, and seeing no one, went back to my sorting, and then heard a voice speaking. I peered over the podium to see a tiny, perhaps 4'8", nun, in full regalia, smiling at me beatifically. Without preamble, she said, "Do you know what I learned the first time I did the Myers Briggs Personality test?" she asked. I shook my head from side to side in response, and she continued. "I learned that I was free to be me!"

I smiled and encouraged her to continue. "Do you know what I learned today?" she said. "No, "I responded, "What?"

"Everyone else is free to be them!" With that, she threw back her head and laughed heartily. It's a great summation of concept of typology of this still-powerful tool known as the Myers Briggs Personality Inventory.

Two Additional Tools for Self and Other Awareness

During a strategic planning session for a non-profit organization, members were invited to take part in the following exercise.[22] In each of the four corners of a large meeting room, signs were posted, with a facilitator standing by each sign. The signs were rolled up and not yet visible. Participants were told: "In just a minute, the facilitators standing in the four corners of the room will reveal a description of a philosophical approach to life. When all four have been described, please move to the corner where the description best fits what drives your thinking and actions in life. You will get to move twice more: to what second best describes your thoughts and actions, and what sounds least like you."

In the first corner, Mary, an experienced facilitator, unrolled the sign. "I am a philosophical intellectual," she said. "I like to read and study about any issue. I like books and supporting materials such as music, which are rational, orderly, and congruent with the issue. I love creating position papers and having discussions based on intellectual discovery. I am a philosophical intellectual."

---

22 This experiential exercise was created by Kay Collier McLaughlin to assist participants in consulting sessions to understand the philosophical origins of their positions on given subjects.

Ken, a tall retired corporate executive, was the facilitator in the second corner. "I am a philosophical heart," he said. "I am moved by issues that touch my heart. I prefer books, poetry, music, and other supporting resources with this kind of personal, intimate connection that can move me to thought and action. I am a philosophical heart."

Julie, one of our senior trainers, was in corner number three. "I am a philosophical mystic," she said. "I am driven by internal factors which connect my daily life to my deeper spiritual self. I love silent study and retreat times when I can escape from the world and focus on how great mystics of other times have approached their worlds, which helps me develop my own writing or conversation on important topics. I am a philosophical mystic."

Matt, in the fourth corner, announced, "I am a philosophical humanist. I believe that we are here on this earth to bring justice and peace for as many people as possible here and now, and that it is my personal responsibility to do all I can to contribute to this effort. I am a philosophical humanist."

"Please place yourself in a corner," I reminded the group. After they had made their way, some swiftly, some more slowly, some stopping halfway between corners and then edging their way closer to one, I added, "Look around you, in your corner, to see who else is there. Now look around at the other corners. Wave to your family members, spouses, partners, friends, and neighbors who are in another corner. Now, move to the corner that sounds second most like you."

The exercise was repeated, and then the participants were asked to move to the corner that sounded least like them. As often happens, there was quick movement to the corners that felt most unfamiliar, or even distasteful to participants. Following the now-familiar directions to look at who was the corner with them, and who was in different corners, participants were invited to go back to their tables and answer the following four questions:

1. What did you learn about yourself?

2. What did you learn about other people you know?

3. Did this exercise reveal anything to you about experiences in your own family, office, business, or an organization you are involved in?

4. Does this exercise reveal anything to you about current divisions in our culture?

Following a recent experience with this exercise, one participant's report to the group summarized the most often-heard response when she said, "You know, it made me think how often when there are differences of opinion that are leading to polarization, with people digging their heels in and becoming more and more entrenched, we are really saying some very similar things from very different foundations. I started to wonder what would happen if we could do this exercise with Congress, or any other "stuck" group, what would happen." A good question, indeed! Each of these exercises helps us develop or strengthen our EQ, or emotional quotient.

Emotional intelligence (EI) or emotional quotient (EQ) is sometimes known as "street smarts" in human interaction. It involves both self-awareness and other awareness – the ability of people to recognize both their own and other people's emotions. It involves the ability to name those emotions, and to use the knowledge to make appropriate choices in managing those emotions. Daniel Coleman popularized the concept in his 1995 book Emotional Intelligence. The phrase has now become ubiquitous, showing up in settings as unlikely as the cartoon strips Dilbert and Zippy and art in The New Yorker. Unlike IQ, EQ can be raised to both improve relationships and achieve goals. While we might be able to get along well in life without a high IQ, we are understanding more and more how Emotional Quotient or Emotional Intelligence is essential to human interaction every day.

WHAT CAN ANYONE DO TO DEVELOP EQ?

1. Learn to recognize and pay attention to all your emotions

2. Incorporate emotions in decision making

3. Stay present without planning the future or analyzing the past

4. Be aware of the nonverbal messages you send others

5. Use humor and play to relieve stress

THE FOUR ATTRIBUTES OF EMOTIONAL INTELLIGENCE.

Self-awareness. You recognize your own emotions, are aware of physical signals that an emotion is bubbling up, and know how your emotions affect your thoughts and behavior. You know both your strengths and weaknesses, and have self-confidence.

Self-management. You are able to control impulsive feelings and behaviors, manage your emotions in healthy ways, take initiative, follow through on commitments, and adapt to changing circumstances.

Social awareness. You can understand the emotions, needs and concerns of other people, notice emotional cues, feel comfortable socially, and recognize the power dynamics in a group or organization.

Relationship management. You know how to develop and maintain good relationships, communicate clearly, inspire and influence others, work well in a team, and manage conflict.[23]

A key exercise I have used for many years to assist in the development of emotional intelligence begins with distinguishing feelings from thoughts, and giving oneself permission to own both as natural and neutral, not good or bad.

In the morning, midday, and before bed, practice identifying your feeling. Begin by asking yourself, am I glad, mad, sad, bad, or some derivative of those feelings (thankful, grateful, appreciative, angry, furious, upset, grieving, lost, lonely, forlorn, anxious, frustrated)? Then, on a scale of 1-10, identify whether that feeling is intense (7-10), average (4-7), or low (4 and lower).

Example:

MORNING: Feeling anxious, at an 8 level (very anxious). Feeling rested at a 6 level, neither high nor low.

MIDDAY: Feeling afraid at an 8 level. Feeling incompetent at an 8 level.

BEDTIME: Feeling tired at a 7 level. Feeling relieved at a 5 level.

The tendency of most people is to express a thought about their situation, rather than quickly identifying a feeling or emotion. It is this lack of

---

23 Notes from lecture by Dr. Andrew Weiner, "Applications of Emotional Intelligence to Leadership," Circles of Power Women's Leadership Session, Wooded Glen Conference Center, Henryville, Indiana, 2001

and

Notes from presentation by Roy Oswald on Emotional Intelligence, Center for Human Relations and Emotional Intelligence Executive Training, Louisville Presbyterian Seminary, Louisville, Kentucky, 2008.

ability to quickly identify the emotion that leads to feelings overtaking a person by surprise.

The narrative that could accompany this example is of a person awaking before a morning meeting in which there will be strong differences of opinion before a difficult decision can be made. The person awakens feeling anxious (the number 8 indicates a high intensity of feeling), although rested. By midday, following the meeting, the high intensity level 8 now is assigned to a feeling of fear for what lies ahead and a sense of incompetence during the meeting. The bedtime feeling of tiredness is at a 7, or just above average/neutral, while the feeling of relief is at the neutral level of 5.

A supporting exercise asks participants to identify ways in which their body warns them of emotions. What happens to your body when anger (fear, sadness, etc.) is about to be experienced? "I feel heat rush from my feet up my back and the back of my neck out of my mouth." "My shoulders tighten and my fists clench without any thought." "My stomach turns over and feels like it is in my throat."

It is important to help differentiate between thoughts and feelings, as quick identification of feelings is essential to managing emotions. Thoughts about feelings can be easily identified when someone says, "I feel that ..." and continues with an explanation rather than the quick identification.

Emotions lead to thoughts, which lead to action. Unexplored and unknown emotions fill up our shadow bags. These can be doorways to civility as they are explored and welcomed as a part of each of us that can be well used to expand our capacity for understanding ourselves, and therefore, expand our capacity for understanding others.

A recent conversation among staunchly differing opinions on the political divide illustrates the possibilities. Jan and Eric were both angry about the treatment of ten-year-old Barron Trump. Eric's anger was focused on the liberals who were "attacking a child because his father beat their candidate." Jan's anger touched lightly on this new child in the White House, but was more focused on the terrible things that had been said about the previous children to live there. "How dare anyone now speak up when conservatives have been horrible to the Obama girls for eight years because they didn't like their father?"

The good news is that Jan and Eric had a healthy respect for each other, and despite their differences of opinion, were willing to slug through a difficult discussion. "Why was it OK to talk about the Obama girls in such horrible terms?" Jan asked.

Eric sat quietly for a moment. "I can't speak for anyone else," he said, "and I didn't say things about them myself, but I didn't speak up to stop others, either. I guess for me, that family in the White House represented a way our country is changing, and it brings out all kinds of fears of loss of control. I really hadn't looked inside myself to ask those questions until you asked them."

Looking at Jan, he continued. "How about you? You seem really angry that people are trying to protect this little boy when you're still trying to protect those girls."

Jan nodded. "You're right. The part of me that wants to protect those girls really doesn't want any child subjected to that kind of treatment, but I can feel myself tempted to say, well, he is getting the same treatment they got, and that's okay. But that's not really who I am."

With the cards on the table, the two continued their conversation, each aware that a part of themselves that they did not like had been triggered, a part that they would rather not claim. Having claimed this "shadow" part, however, they were free to go beyond the polarizing anger and talk about the value that their better selves shared, the protection of the children of public figures from the angers of the political arena.

Self and other awareness – doorways to civility.

Moving Forward to Action:
Questions for reflection and sharing

1. What did you, like the nun, Sister Esther, learn about your own personality type?

2. Can you share an aha moment in your personal/professional interactions when understanding your own and others' type would have been helpful? How might it have helped?

3. What philosophical type are you? In what ways does your philosophical type best contribute to our ability to get along together in our culture? What philosophical type is hardest for you to understand and get along with? How can you strengthen a connection with this type?

4. What aspect of emotional intelligence is strongest for you? Needs the most development? What might you choose to do to improve this part of life and relationships? What do you feel would improve if you do this work?

A conversation with

CHANGE AGENT
HIROKO DRIVER LIPPMAN

International Suzuki Association and
Teacher of the Suzuki Talent Education
Method of violin

When did you hear the call to make the world a better place through teaching Suzuki violin?

Sometimes a call is clear and direct, and other times, it emerges slowly, almost unnoticed from life itself, like a flower growing steadily in the backyard.

For Hiroko Driver Lippmann, who carries the Suzuki legacy forward as teacher and member of the international organization for Suzuki education, it began in her childhood in Japan.

Hiroko grew up in Osaka, Japan, learning the violin by the Suzuki method from a teacher who had studied with Dr. Suzuki. From sixth grade on, she looked forward each term to the arrival of the great master teacher himself. In Hiroko's mother's mind, her daughter was preparing herself to enter a conservatory. But Hiroko had other ideas. She heard from her

---

"We need to show people how to be nice to others. We must take this message to the world."

---

teacher that it was possible to go to the Talent Education Institute in Matsumoto and study with Dr. Suzuki. "I knew here, " she says, pointing to her heart, "this is what I would do." Her determination led her to the life of a Kenkyuusei, or teacher trainee, with Dr. Suzuki and friendships with University of Tennessee violinist William Starr and his family which would change her life. She was in her early 20s when she moved to Knoxville and began the American teaching career that made her a household name in the Suzuki world. Several times in the ensuing years she would step back: from directorships in two programs, and into the teaching program of Mimi Zweig at Indiana University, where "no one knew my name and I could learn what I didn't know I didn't know." The answer to the call that had been shadowing the majority of her life came with the realization that she had a choice to make as a teacher: whether her goal was to produce fine players or beautiful hearts, says

Hiroko, "My goal, I knew, was to produce really good people who would work for a really good world."

How did you know what action you needed to take?

Hiroko's path to knowing the action she needed to take was one of experiencing, reflecting and choosing that led through some painful times. As one of the first Suzuki-trained teachers to come to America, she experienced not only great demand for her teaching at workshops and institutes, but also invitations to take a greater leadership role by becoming a program director.

The great ladder upward of American institutional life.

After serving twice as a program director, and with time between those stints to reflect on her experiences, she concluded that her real gift, and the one which brought her most joy and fulfillment was to "pursue the highest possibility of Suzuki teaching," and knowing, that for her, that would be in a private studio rather than in an institution. In addition, she works with The International Suzuki Association, to keep the dream of her childhood teacher alive and growing for children of the world.

What challenges did you encounter and how did you respond?

For Hiroko, the challenges were more personal and internal than external. In her own words, she tells us:

1. "If the challenge is too big, or does not fit me, I do not need to fit myself to the challenge. I must be happy within myself and how I can be the best that I can be to accomplish my purpose.

That meant taking time away from teaching to reflect on what I was experiencing, and to gradually, by going in and out of the Suzuki world, be able to see how good it was, and what my role needed to be."

2. "I have the personality I was born with. I do not feel it is selfish to cherish it, and allow it to be in the environment where it flourishes."

3. "(I am) Checking my own feelings about my upbringing and learning from that to be who I am as a teacher and a parent."

4. "I am working on letting other people know me. I am a product of my culture as well as my life in America. I don't want to force people to know my way. My way is more simple than the great busyness of life here."

What have you learned about the 'other?'

"I have lived here a long time now, and I am aware that even in the American Suzuki Movement there are many differences in the way we learned both the violin and life. My way is very Japanese. People who are close to me understand me, and my culture, as I try to understand theirs. But never force where there is resistance. I must speak from deep within my heart and let people know what I feel, and listen for what is in their hearts."

What's next for you as one who carries on a great legacy? Words of wisdom for others who would do something to change the world!

Most of Dr. Suzuki's students carry the world with them, and feel a responsibility to "Do something." For Hiroko Driver Lippmann, it is about her continuing role as a teacher.

Often aware of the difference in her approach, she is speaking up to ask those who express an interest in the Suzuki method, "why are you interested in this method?" It offers her the opportunity to talk about her lived experience of a philosophy and method which were foundational to her life, and which she works to perpetuate. She works with the world wide International Suzuki Association Board, to continue to spread the practices as well as the dream of Dr. Suzuki, for she knows in her own life, the foundation for life which it provided her. A hard-earned, mindful knowing as well as the visceral and organic one.

Her message, delivered in the low, melodious voice that those who have experienced her recognize: "We must show how to be nice to others. We need more and more people "who will carry this message to the world."

CHAPTER SIX

Every Behavior Has an Impact

"People will forget what you said, people will forget what you did, but people will never forget how you made them feel."—Maya Angelou

Mmmmmmmmmmmmmmmmmm.
Bzzzzzzzzzzzzzzzzzzzz.
Mmmmmmmmmmmmmmmmmmm.
Screech...scratch...screech.

There are sounds and senses in a meeting room that are a presenter's nightmare. The low, insistent buzz of side conversations. The sounds of metal chairs pushing and shifting across a tile floor. Feet making a constant path to the restrooms. The kind of stuff that demands more than even the best of agendas!

From my spot at the podium at St. John's Church in a small eastern Kentucky town, I was aware of the low buzz in the meeting room that was making it very hard to get people's attention and get on with the planned agenda. My leadership team and I were there to assist the congregation in gathering data that would lead to setting goals for calling a new rector (head pastor) to the church, which had a history of conflicts. Conflicts among the members, with rumors flying, folks refusing to speak to each other, folks staying away from worship and social events. Conflicts with priests, past and present, resulting in withholding of financial pledges, forming alliances for or against, constant complaining behind the leader's back (but always loudly enough to be heard by the leader in question.) Conflicts with the adjudicatory, including the latest fiasco of a priest well past the mandatory retirement age who would not willingly step down.

Leadership Team members were trained to lead the discussion in each small group. Despite a careful setting of norms and standards for behaviors during the meeting, there were side conversations in barely-hushed voices. The sounds of metal folding chairs against tile as people shifted positions. None-too-subtle-eye rolls and shrugs of shoulders. A steady path to the rest room. It truly was a presenter's nightmare!

I had to come up with something on the spot so that the team and I had a chance of getting people's attention, for starters, and then engaging them on a deeper level. Add to the cacophony by acting like an irate substitute teacher with an out-of-control classroom? Insist on staying with the agenda as planned? No. It had to be something more dramatic, and sometimes drama comes in actions rather than words.

I had been surveying the room. Now, I decisively turned my back on the participants, picked up a marker, and began to write on the newsprint. The room was suddenly very quiet. I could feel the eyes on my back, the wondering, what is she up to? It was one of many moments when I was thankful for years of training as a consultant which allowed me to make a quick assessment of a situation and shift gears as needed, knowing that the facilitators who were with me would follow along without missing a beat[24].

Sometimes, no matter how carefully groundwork is laid, old behaviors that have been repeated thousands of times continue. The norms and standards had been presented and agreed on, yet were not being followed, despite efforts by group leaders to remind participants. My "emergency" response was not to feed into old patterns, but to arouse curiosity in order to engage the group. In this case, the unexpected silence was the key. Curiosity instead of animosity took the room, and when I finished writing and faced the participants, I had their attention – and their curiosity. What was I up to and what might happen now?

Turning back to the now-attentive faces, I said, "Help me define the words," pointing to what I had just posted in large black letters on the newsprint[25]:

BEHAVIORS _____ DEFINITIONS

Triangling

Over-functioning

Under-functioning

---

24 The theoretically-based training process of presenters and facilitators is detailed in chapter notes.
25 Anxiety behaviors from notes of Stacy Sauls's studies with Edwin H. Friedman, 1990-96.

Distancing

Conflict

Sabotage

Bullying

Cut-off

A stunned silence filled the space for a few minutes, and then voices bounced from all corners of the room. Some were timid, with little question marks at the end of their definitions. Others spoke a little more firmly, as if an internal dictionary had given them the answer.

Triangling: *talking to someone else about the person you really need to talk to; indirect communication*
Over-functioning: *taking all the responsibility and all of the action for everything; overdoing*
Under-functioning: *doing nothing; failing to do what you said you would do*
Distancing: *disappearing without explanation; playing hide and seek*
Conflict: *differing from another in an unpleasant way*
Sabotage: *deliberately causing a plan or project to fail*
Bullying: *using physical, emotional, verbal, financial, or positional power to intimidate*
Cut-off: *completely leaving a relationship or situation*

I knew the facilitators were ready for the next instruction. "Let's get back in our table groups and answer the following questions. Your facilitator will record your answers on the newsprint and report out to the whole group, so you can hear what everyone had to say."

1. When have you seen these behaviors in this church?

2. When have you been sucked into participating in these behaviors, either here or elsewhere?

3. What was the impact of the behaviors on the people involved?

After sharing in the small groups, facilitators came to the microphone, carrying the newsprint from their group to read, so all could hear the findings. Reports from the groups showed many similarities. Each group had quickly been able to identify times they had experienced all of the behaviors in various projects and committees.

"Triangling is definitely the biggest thing around here. No one ever talks directly to anyone. It's always about, could you help me convince Mary to do X, or would you be willing to talk to Jack about Y."

"I don't know why I sign up for committees when I know that one person is going to do everything, even though it was supposed to be a group project."

"Bullying. Sometimes it's someone who thinks they have more information than the rest of us and uses that to boss everyone around."

The second question was addressed with a little less enthusiasm, and a touch of embarrassment, but each group admitted to, at some point, having been sucked into the behaviors themselves.

"I know I have a hard time being direct when there are decisions to be made or differences of opinion. I think it goes back to my childhood. My mom would ask me to 'sweeten up' my dad about something she wanted him to do."

"I think I distance myself because I don't like fights, so if there is conflict, I will just sort of disappear for a while."

"I tend to do everything myself because it is easier than relying on other people, and I know it will get done the way I want it done."

They were equally vocal about the impact of the behaviors.

THE IMPACT OF—

Triangling: breakdown of relationship, distrust, rumors, false information

Over-functioning: feeling like a martyr, burnout, causes under-functioning

Under-functioning: loss of talent and involvement, disinterest

Distancing: focuses the attention and energy on the squeaky wheel, loss of involvement, rumors

Conflict: distrust, anger, broken relationships, loss of energy and status

Sabotage: loss of project, broken relationships

Bullying: loss of talent, perhaps permanently, fear, enabling of bully, acquiescing, abuse

Cut-off: loss of any possibility of reconciliation and relationship

The energy rose as the answers were called out. When the newsprint was full, I asked if these were the desired impacts. In one loud voice, the group shouted, "NO!"

"It's been said that insanity is repeating the same thing over and over again and expecting different results," I said. "I don't see anyone here that appears to be insane. As adults, if we can name and define something, and know that its impact is not what we want, we have a choice. We can continue to do the same thing, knowing that we will get the same results. Or?" The question hung in the air.

"I didn't even know there was a name for these things until right now," a woman said, "and now you're telling us that we can change the way we've done things?"

"There are different ways?" another voice spoke. The voices were more hesitant this time, as if not sure that what had been suggested was possible. Now that they had named, defined, recognized, and even owned the behaviors and their negative impact, they were not too sure. After all, they had each wandered into their own experiences of behavior they had tolerated or practiced for many years.

"We do have a choice," I assured them, "and we're going to brainstorm some of the possibilities right now. You have already started by being aware that a lot of anxiety and anger come from trying to work around these unhealthy behaviors, and being able to identify what the behaviors are. The next steps are knowing and then practicing the alternatives. That makes for a much healthier and more productive organization, and a much happier way to live and work together."

Alternative Behaviors

Triangling: speak directly to the person involved. If someone tries to hook you into speaking for them, do not take that on. Tell them to go directly to the person themselves. If they say they will not or cannot, offer to go with them and support them while they speak directly, but do not speak for them.

Over-functioning: If I am over-functioning, I need to delegate more to others and trust them to do their tasks, accepting that they may be done differently than I might do them, and that's OK. If I am aware that others are over-functioning, I can encourage annual rotation, more delegation, more invitation and appointment of new and different people. Be aware of personal ownership of certain projects and check them for continued relevance.

Under-functioning: If I am under-functioning, I need to be sure I have the time, energy, and commitment for what I have signed up for, or resign. If others are under-functioning, I need to check the above areas so that people have actual responsibility and opportunity to do what they said they would do, and that relevant groups are not owned by over-functioning individuals.

Distancing: If I am distancing, I need to ask myself if I am trying to gain attention from someone, or if I am taking care of myself by stepping back for a short time and have notified someone of that choice. If I see someone else distancing themselves, I need to inquire about them, invite them back, and welcome them if they come back, but not chase after them.

Conflict: I need to name the conflict and address it directly. If assistance is needed, I need to invite another person to go with me and/or have outside, objective mediation.

Sabotage: I need to name the behavior directly in the context where it is happening so that it can be discussed and resolved. I need to be aware that objective, outside assistance may be needed.

Bullying: I need to name the experience of the bullying directly, as in "when you say or do X, I feel bullied, or I experience that as bullying." A mediator may be needed to assist.

Cut-off: As with distancing, when someone has cut off, I need to inquire, invite, and welcome if they return, but not chase. It may be necessary for me to accept that the cut-off is final for them, although it is uncomfortable for me.

In the weeks following this meeting, a new vocabulary emerged at St. John's. "Is that triangulation?" someone might ask. "Are you over-functioning?" "Is he distancing, or cutting off?" Handwritten signs listing the behaviors, impacts, and alternative behaviors appeared throughout the building. Those who had not been present at the goal-setting meeting found themselves positively influenced by the changed behaviors of others.

It has been several years since the old, disruptive behaviors of an organization in crisis and conflict played havoc that evening at St. John's. The hand printed signs identifying the destructive behaviors and their antidotes have been replaced by a single, brightly colored poster that names the destructive behaviors, their impacts, and the alternatives. Congregants' determination to turn this place around has resulted in a vestry (governing body) that took the charge put into their hand and not only worked with a new ordained leader to use the new behaviors to the benefit of the entire church community, but empowered each other to continue a productive life in their small congregation when that leader's tenure was cut short by family obligations in another state. Today the vestry is a healthy band of lay people who manage the business of the church, work well together, and provide both worship and service to the community – a far cry from the dysfunction of a few years ago.

Across the country, from north and south to east and west, wherever we do training for leaders or work in conflict resolution, this exercise is a foundational piece of the work. And wherever we may be, whether working with a group of corporate executives, government leaders, educators, or faith based organizations, reactions are the same:

"I did not know that there was a name for the behaviors that I have experienced."

"I did not understand the full impact of that behavior on relationships."

"I did not know there were alternatives."

"I did not know I had the right to change my behavior and to stand up to the behavior of others that was impacting me in a negative way."

It is hard to get a handle on that which has no name. Descriptions seem nebulous, whiny, and overly personal. All too often, a person rather than a behavior is identified, and the result is blaming and shaming. Understanding begins when there is the ability to name and define a behavior, know its impact, and be aware that it is neither desirable nor acceptable. Once identified, the behavior can be changed, changing the impact.

What Does Behavior and Impact Have to Do With Civil Dialogue?

Often, we assume that particular behaviors are simply a part of an individual's personality, rather than a pattern of behavior with a name, definition and impact. We falsely assume that we have no choice when around that person but to be impacted by the behavior. In fact, often people believe that they have no right to expect any other behavior, so accustomed have they become to the negative one, or that there are even alternatives. And considering the negative impacts listed repeatedly when working with groups on these behaviors, there is often intimidation or other form of threat that causes people to retreat from rather than engage with the perpetrator. This does not lead to any kind of opportunity for conversation, much less a positive one!

Recognizing and identifying destructive behaviors enables individuals to monitor their own behaviors in efforts to have civil dialogue, and to take steps to call for alternative behaviors from others when they experience the negative ones during conversation. Let's look at an example of how recognizing and naming a behavior helped turn a pattern of victimization and intimidation into a win-win. The problem is honestly addressed in a civil manner, and the organization is able to go forward without paralyzing escalation of the identified issue into greater conflict.

The city's youth orchestra board had been working to hire a new conductor for many months. The final candidates for the position were scheduled to arrive in town the following week, and the board and search committee had gathered for a final meeting before their arrivals. A carefully planned agenda, plane tickets, and information regarding interviews and hospitality had been sent to each of the three finalists. As the board meeting opened, the president announced that the process to select the new conductor was invalid, as a member of the search committee had not met the by-laws stipulation that each board member contribute a designated amount to the operating budget.

The board sat in stunned silence. The chair of the search committee, one of the youngest members of the board, rose from her seat, and looking directly at the president, said in a firm voice, "That is sabotage, and that is unacceptable. This process will not be sabotaged." The president, who had claimed he was "too busy" to be present for the transition/search training where the behavior/impact work was taught, appeared flustered. His strong-arm tactics had seen him control several community boards, always pulling rank and turning personal.

This time, an informed board had learned the difference between personal attack and firm but civil behavior identification. They had a name for what they were experiencing and knew the possible impact. The search chair's statement was followed by support from other members of the board. Crisis in this situation turned into opportunity.

The board members knew how to identify the behavior – in this case, sabotage – as well as understanding its impact on a system. They were no longer confusing a person's skills, prestige, or personality as a reason to excuse behavior that could have negative impact on work in progress. In this case, the possible impacts included the embarrassment to the organization of pausing the process in a very public stage of the work, the potential for losing viable candidates who would question the stability of the organization and potentially take other positions, and the escalation of conflict within the organization itself. As a governing body, they had learned a very important lesson. Destructive behavior could be identified and stopped, without loss of civility or loss to the organization.

The president completed the remaining months of his term with a newly subdued affect, then appeared to turn his attention from community boards to other pursuits. The board selected its new conductor, who, after several years' experience with the organization, observed that it was one of the most congenial and non-conflicted arts organizations he had ever seen.

Behavior. Impact. Civility. Interconnected.

Moving Forward to Action:
Questions for reflection and sharing

1. Which of the anxiety behaviors have you observed most frequently in your home? Workplace? What has been the impact?

2. Which of the anxiety behaviors are you most easily sucked into? Give an example and tell the impact.

3. Where and how will you plan to practice alternative behaviors?

A conversation with

CHANGE AGENT
EVERETT McCORVEY

Director of the Haitian Children's Choir,
The University of Kentucky Opera Program
and the National Chorale of New York City

When did you first know you wanted to make a difference in the world?

Everett McCorvey grew up in Montgomery, Ala, in the 1960s, surrounded by role models who were making
a difference. His parents were active
in the Civil Rights movement, and as
members of First Baptist Church where
Ralph Abernathy was the pastor and his
father, now 95, is still a deacon, as he
was when Everett was a boy. His round-
the-corner neighbor was a man named
Martin Luther King. "To me, these were
'regular people,' a normal part of my
life. I realized very early by watching

them that it was very important for 'regular people' to take part in making a difference in
their community and world. My entire life I was taking on a mantra that was about recognizing the importance of leadership; of not being afraid to be a leader."

How did you decide what action you would take to make a difference in the world?

"The first thing I had to do was recognize what my talent was. I believe we were each
put on earth with a certain number of talents, and it is incumbent on us each to figure out
what their talents are and then to do our work through those talents. My gift is music. My
leadership roles would come through music. I have tried to allow music to open doors, and
after a door is open, to go in and try to make a difference
in society. To use music as the key."

"More art;
fewer wars"

Using that key, McCorvey is involved on boards and civic
committees, and advises others in the arts to do the same,
not limiting their involvement to arts related groups, but
supporting other community endeavors as the arts hope to be supported. "I believe music
brings people together in a unique way. It breaks down barriers because it touches something inside of people. My mantra is 'more art; fewer wars.' When we work together we
begin to see that we all want the same things: productive work; to provide for our families;
to have friends; a decent life. Color doesn't matter. This polarization to achieve power and
control is not the way to go!" "Music breaks down those barriers. It is through music that

I met Dr. Pearce Lyon, Founder of AllTech. AllTech has teams ready to be dispatched to any country after a crisis. After the devastating earthquake in Haiti, Dr. Lyon and a team went to see what they could do to help. They had to fly into the Dominican Republic and cross the border to reach the town of Ouanaminthe. It was there as they walked through the ruined streets that they heard children singing. Dr. Lyon followed the voices, introduced himself, and was so moved by what he heard that he called me on a Sunday morning — I'll never forget it — and told me about the children and said, 'we need to start a choir.' By the next week we were on a plane to Haiti to meet the kids and meet with the school. It was one of the most disarming moments of my life to hear these beautiful kids singing amidst the desolation. There was garbage in the streets. It was like a Third World country. Yet the joy in these kids was palpable. I was more moved than I can say."

The next years would see AllTech buying a coffee co-op in Haiti, and bringing all the coffee the co-op could provide back to the states to sell, with profits going to assist the children. They would take over support of the school. McCorvey's Opera graduate students would travel in teams of two to teach the children of Haiti. For many months, there were no livable options for housing in Haiti, so the visiting teachers would stay in the Dominican Republic, fighting the challenge of border crossing each day. It took several years to find accommodations in Haiti.

But by 2009, a plan was in place to bring the Children's Choir to Lexington, Ky., for the 2010 World Equestrian Games. "Six hundred children were auditioned, "says McCorvey. "Thirty-five were chosen, but only twenty-eight were able to make the trip, due to lack of available records of any sort. The passport agency worked with us — they would take anything that could possibly provide a record of some kind, like a family Bible. AllTech sent a support person who was there for six months helping get the passports processed."

McCorvey describes the two weeks with the Children's Chorus as the "most incredible experience." One of his most unforgettable memories came as the group was preparing to return to Haiti. "It was very emotional for all of us. The teachers kept saying that we had changed their lives forever. And the thing that they said over and over again, with such wonder, was "We have passports." Little could we have imagined how empowering that was, for them to be enabled to travel if they wanted to! It was an experience I will remember for the rest of my life."

If the Haitian Children's Chorus was a mountaintop moment for all connected with it, it also is an encapsulation of the life work of this change agent. Whatever the venue, Everett McCorvey is always looking for ways to bring people together. "I want to transport them to another place — a place of beauty, grace and happiness, where they can allow barriers to fall, and commune with their neighbors. This is why I will continue to work for the Arts to be considered essential — not something frivolous that can be on the chopping block whenever a school system or community is facing budget cuts. The arts are essential."

What challenges have you encountered in your work and how have you dealt with those challenges or roadblocks?

Everett McCorvey's answer begins with this statement: "As a child, I had a problem with my feet and had to go to an orthopedic doctor." There were no black orthopedists in Montgomery, Ala., in the 1960s. Young Everett's father took him to a white orthopedist.

"We couldn't go in the front door," the famous choral director says, remembering. "We would walk around the building, through the overgrown weeds, to the back door. There was a little box on the door we would tap on. There was a slit in the box, and we would talk with the receptionist through that little window. I would always ask my dad why. Why can't we go in the front door? And he would say — without any anger or militancy — "That's just the way it is right now. It won't always be that way."

"My dad got me in to see the kind of doctor who could help me, although we had to use the back door. What it taught me is this: There is always another door. The room looks the same on the other side, no matter which door you come in. You can't always go through the front door. Figure out the other door. Look for the other door. It was another great lesson my dad provided. He was not fazed. He changed my life. Another lesson in leadership."

What have you learned about relating with people who are "other" than you are?

"I see people as people. No matter how high or low they are by society's standards, I don't see them as any different from me. I want to treat everyone as I would treat my own family, and as I want to be treated myself. I try always to relate in a personal way and hopefully that will allow me to communicate with anyone and everyone."

"There were many examples of this in Haiti. Dr. Lyon was able to open lots of doors by not being fazed by perceived 'otherness'; by looking at challenges as opportunities. It took the help of other people to get us through our work there. And that is historic. Look at the Underground Railroad. What if there had not been other people along the way to help the slaves to freedom? We can create networks of 'others' who believe that every individual should be free to live and express themselves. I try to do this in all sorts of settings."

What is next for you? What advice do you have for others who want to make a difference?

"I always try to have a 'grand' what next and a smaller what next. My grand what next is to be able to continue interacting with people to influence society through the arts as essential. My smaller 'what next' is to continue to grow the Opera program and develop new and younger audiences. We can learn from athletics. In Kentucky, it's cradle to grave love of U.K. Basketball. Babies go home from the hospital wearing UK gear. We're producing a basketball Opera - Bounce. It is to be performed on basketball courts, indoors or outdoors, not on stages. We are taking Opera, the transformative power of music, to a younger group, a group who may not be familiar with it."

"My advice for those who want to make a difference: Remember always that there is another way. Another door. Don't let anyone rob you of your dream. Know that you may have a clearer vision, see things that others can't. You can't let the naysayers try to stifle a vision. Front door. Back Door. Side door. Sometimes, even a window."

CHAPTER SEVEN

Bars, Measures, and Boundaries

"Bar lines and measures on a musical score help organize the notes and ensure you don't get lost." —Wikipedia

My Thursday night women's group had gathered at a local restaurant to meet with Dr. Nell Dunn, a specialist in women's issues. Although located in Florida, she was in town to visit family, and had agreed to meet with this group for dinner. As orders were being taken, an acquaintance of Dr. Dunn arrived. "I'm taking Dr. Dunn to dinner," she announced. Startled, the women looked at me and at the visitor. This wasn't at all what they understood was happening for the evening. Seven sets of eyes were fixed on me, waiting.

Dr. Dunn was clearly uncomfortable, aware that despite her explanation to her friend of her professional schedule, suddenly there seemed to be conflicting agendas for her time. "Dr. Dunn will be meeting with us over dinner as planned," I said firmly to the unexpected visitor. "We should be here a little over an hour. You are welcome to join us, or come back for her." Miffed, but aware it was a clear statement, not a discussion, the young woman sat at a nearby table, shaking a flip-flop on one foot as the group continued with its meal and discussion.

After Dr. Dunn and her visitor had left, Joyce, a member of the group, said, "Did you feel awkward, even rude, about what you said to that young woman?"

"Did you think I was rude?" I asked her.

"It felt...uncomfortable. Maybe rude," Joyce responded.

"I set a boundary," I replied. "It was a stop sign that said, do not go past here. It was a fence that separated her agenda from our stated plans for the evening. I drew a clear line. My line, my boundary was based in my core value of respect — respect for the time and plans of our guest, and of our group. Knowing my own core values allowed me to respond immediately and instinctively. If you are not used to setting boundaries, it can feel uncomfortable when someone sets them. I think I was firm and clear, but I didn't raise my voice. I was factual. I didn't give a lot of reasons. I just stated what was true. Dr. Dunn was our guest for the evening. It was already planned. The young woman had a need that, to her, felt important enough to override that plan. I simply stated the facts so that she would know that she could choose to join us or come back for Dr. Dunn, and what the time frame would be. She chose neither option. What did you think of her behavior in response to the boundary I set?"

"She was acting like a spoiled little girl," Joyce said. "Actually, she was the one who was rude. Assuming she could waltz in here and take our guest away was presumptuous for starters. She wouldn't join us for dinner, although you made her welcome. But she wouldn't leave, either. She just kept sitting there, where we could see her jiggling that silly flip-flop on her foot to show us how irritated she was."

"Good observation," I laughed. "And it is a good example to us to remind us all that the reaction to someone setting a boundary is not always gracious or accepting. Some people keep trying to push, no matter how many boundaries are set. If you think of boundaries as fences, for some people, chain link works, and other people need brick walls with no gates or windows."

Good boundaries have often been referred to as fences in human behavior. In music, bar lines organize the notes; in civil dialogue, boundaries create civility and ultimately a sense of harmony.

Good boundaries or organizing lines are critical to civil dialogue and civility itself. Like norms and standards, the baseline for boundaries has been ignored to such a high degree in our present culture that both need to be retaught and reset, by individuals and organizations. To do so, we must spend time reflecting on core values, particularly those that prioritize the worth of humanity and human dignity, so we can begin to organize our lives around a common narrative based on respect rather than contempt.

The most familiar boundaries are generally physical. Most people know instinctively if their personal space has been invaded, or if they have been touched inappropriately. We are less certain of verbal, emotional, intellectual and spiritual boundaries. Civil dialogue, true talking together, involves all of these, and is increasingly difficult with the advent of social media and online communication.

As discussed in Chapter One, different systems, both personal and professional, have different norms and standards. Looking at signs of unhealthy boundaries is a prelude to knowing when a boundary has been invaded, and how to stop it – and literally change the conversation. While there are many lists of unhealthy boundaries available (see appendices for resource list), the following are helpful in beginning to consider one's own boundaries.

Signs of Unhealthy Boundaries

- Giving too much personal information to a new acquaintance.
- Failure to understand types of relationships and appropriate communication at each level.
- Accepting more intimate or personal details or conversation than you are comfortable with.
- Accepting communication via social media that is crude, rude, or overly personal.
- Posting photos or commentary on social media that is crude, rude, or overly personal.
- Trusting too quickly, or trusting anyone who reaches out to you.
- Changing or adapting your attitudes, behaviors, relationships, plans, or self to please someone else.
- Extreme fear at thought of being rejected. The inability to hold one's ground and determine appropriate action is often connected to the need for approval from others.
- Allowing anyone to come physically closer to you than is comfortable.
- Accepting touch or gifts that you don't want.
- Touching another person without asking, or extending gifts or items to them without reason, or in excess.
- Stalking, or being stalked.
- Not making your limits known to people around you.
- Letting another person dictate your choices and/or determine your identity.
- Attempting to control another person's life.
- Believing that other people can and should anticipate your needs.
- Believing that you can anticipate another person's needs.[26]

The electronic and digital ages have done much to change and

---

26 Adapted by Kay Collier McLaughlin and successive personal growth groups from a handout from a workshop by Cloud and Townsend, Conference on Ministry with Single Adults, Crystal Cathedral.

expand the understanding of what is public and what is private. The ability to quickly research details of someone's life, instant communication, and reality TV and tell-all talk shows have radically impacted areas which once might have been considered private. With changing cultural norms around what is acceptable and normal as a baseline for appropriate communication and conversation, boundary invasion has reached new levels in terms of sexual predators, bullying, mean-spiritedness, and cruelty – verbally, mentally, emotionally, and physically.

The setting of boundaries, like the setting of norms and standards, has to begin with an understanding of core values. Unfortunately, sometimes we are left to "back into" discovering our own core values after we have been violated in some way. It is a part of living intentionally to identify our own core values so that we can be confident in setting boundaries for ourselves.

The following circles of core values can be helpful in coming to recognize, name, and hold to one's own personal boundaries, and to respect the boundaries of others in all interactions.[27]

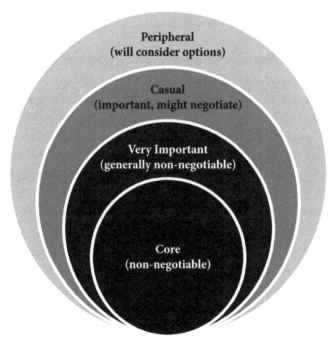

Differing life experiences will mean that core personal values, particularly of an intimate nature, may differ significantly. For example, a person from an alcoholic family might have a stronger boundary in the area of

---

27 Designed by Kay Collier McLaughlin, 1989.

association with alcohol than someone who does not have that history. A person who has been the victim of lying or passive-aggressive behavior may have a much stronger boundary regarding directness and truth-telling than others.

The following examples of core values have been compiled from numerous workshops and groups who have participated in this exercise over the years.

Core: honesty, loyalty, kindness, compassion, open-mindedness, inclusivity, directness, thoughtfulness, faithfulness, belief in something bigger than self, appropriate behaviors, respect, appreciation, steadiness, ethics, morality.

Very Important: hospitality and welcome, strong work ethic, temperance, generosity, humor, competence, education, personal growth, health, emotional intelligence, good communications, values tradition, authenticity.

Casual: adventure, curiosity, timeliness.

Peripheral: helpful, friendly, engaging.

In our culture today, one of the factors that makes the setting of boundaries so difficult is the loss of an agreed-upon narrative of who we are as Americans and what kind of society we want to be. Some people believe we are a diverse, inclusive country, living out the words etched at the base of the Statue of Liberty – "Give me your tired, your poor, your hungry masses yearning to be free." Others see a more carefully selective population that is more homogeneous. The answer to which of those definitions truly tells the American story is at the heart of our core values. When the agreed-upon narrative was the former, people tended to be more respectful of each other. While most people might not have identified boundaries as a part of either their intentionality or behavior, there was a common shock of recognition when behavior got out of line and someone experienced abuse.

As divisions and polarization have become a dominant factor in our lives, an "us and them" mentality has taken hold which has seemed to legitimize rudeness or even abuse to those who are different from us. We spend a great deal of time and energy arguing about how we want to do life without really settling on how we want our lives to be. What is our core value that sets our foundation for all of our actions and behaviors? Are we a people who live in contempt of each other, feeling that certain people and things are "worthless, beneath consideration, below one's dignity, or deserving scorn" (Wikipedia)? Or are we a people of respect for our common humanity, with a belief that each person is an irreplaceable human being whose very life is worthy of dignity? Again, once core values have been identified, it is easier to know the boundaries one has defined for their own life, or those of a system, as well as how to hold onto them.

Back to my experience in the restaurant I discussed at the beginning of this chapter and the boundary lesson lived out. The core value that propelled my setting of the boundary was respect, both for the plans already made and announced and the people who would be impacted by the change. That allowed me to put in place a stop sign, a line, a boundary that clearly said "the schedule for the evening is in place and will be adhered to." No further explanation was necessary.

An oil company was interviewing candidates for chief operating officer, an executive whose major responsibility to the firm was supervising a large staff and the facility itself. Both senior and support staff had been asked to meet individually with the candidates, explaining their work, and answering questions. When the staff gathered for review following the visit, the female staff members appeared to be reluctant to speak up. Finally a female senior staff member spoke, describing what she considered an inappropriate conclusion to their interview. "When I extended my hand to shake his hand, he pulled me into his body, put his other hand behind my neck, and put his cheek next to mine." This woman understood boundaries, and was both intellectually and emotionally astute. She pushed the man away from her and opened the office door.

After she had spoken, other female staff members each reported what seemed to them inappropriate closeness or touching in their interviews. Esther, the administrative assistant who was often the first point of contact for visitors, worked in an open and visible space, but with a physical boundary of her desk. When she extended her hand to the candidate for a formal handshake, she felt his efforts for more personal touch. Particularly protective of what she called her "bubble"- the personal space she chose to keep protected from hugs and touch that to her were invasive, she described what seemed to her an inappropriate lingering of the handshake, as if caressing her hand. The boss, who was also female, met with each staff member individually, after which she filed a complaint with the man's superior, who told her they had never had such a complaint before. While he did not get the position in Esther's company, he went on to become a chief executive in a larger corporation.

For more on issues of power differential and recognizing boundary abuse, there is no better resource than the 1991 book Sex in the Forbidden Zone. The current political climate has clearly shown this is an area that needs much further exploration and education. Recent revelations of inappropriate, explicitly sexual messaging from a United States senator to a teenage girl is but one example of how low the standard of behavior has fallen!

Bill and Sally, avid users of Facebook, Twitter, and Instagram, are disturbed by the spread of posts that contain opinions stated as facts and derogatory remarks directed at people personally. They, and many other with the same concerns, have posted statements saying they will unfriend those who make those posts. This digital boundary became necessary for countless people during and after the 2016 political campaigns and election.

The setting of boundaries, which are critical to civil dialogue, has been further complicated today by confusion around what truth is and where to find it. On both the internet and in face to face contact, boundary violation has become intertwined with opinions and beliefs that differ, and how each individual believes objective truth is to be found. As both relate to boundary setting and civil dialogue, or healthy, constructive talking together, I believe that boundary setting is most importantly about behavior, whether the boundary is physical, emotional, or intellectual.

My understanding of my own boundaries is related to my self-awareness and my core values. My respect of the boundaries of others is related to other awareness, and the understanding that their boundaries are related to their core values, which may be different from mine. The place I would hope we could come to mutual understanding and practice is in recognizing and respecting a boundary as the fence it is, as surely as if a chain link model is separating me from the other.

"Good fences make good neighbors," is one of the most quoted lines in American poet Robert Frost's poem, "Mending Wall."[28]

Something there is that doesn't love a wall,
That sends the frozen-ground-swell under it,
And spills the upper boulders in the sun;
And makes gaps even two can pass abreast.
The work of hunters is another thing:
I have come after them and made repair
Where they have left not one stone on a stone,
But they would have the rabbit out of hiding,
To please the yelping dogs. The gaps I mean,

---

28 Public domain.

No one has seen them made or heard them made,
But at spring mending-time we find them there.
I let my neighbor know beyond the hill;
And on a day we meet to walk the line
And set the wall between us once again.
We keep the wall between us as we go.
To each the boulders that have fallen to each.
And some are loaves and some so nearly balls
We have to use a spell to make them balance:
"Stay where you are until our backs are turned!"
We wear our fingers rough with handling them.
Oh, just another kind of out-door game,
One on a side. It comes to little more:
There where it is we do not need the wall:
He is all pine and I am apple orchard.
My apple trees will never get across
And eat the cones underneath his pines, I tell him.
He only says, "Good fences make good neighbors."
Spring is the mischief in me, and I wonder
If I could put a notion in his head:
"Why do they make good neighbors? Isn't it
Where there are cows? But here there are no cows.
Before I built a wall I'd ask to know
What I was walling in or walling out,
And to whom I was like to give offense.
Something there is that doesn't love a wall,
That wants it down." I could say "Elves" to him,
But it's not elves exactly, and I'd rather
He said it for himself. I see him there
Bringing a stone grasped firmly by the top
In each hand, like an old-stone savage armed.
He moves in darkness as it seems to me,
Not of the woods only and the shade of trees.
He will not go behind his father's saying,
And he likes having thought of it so well
He says again, "Good fences make good neighbors."

The opening line of the poem is hardly ever quoted: "Something there is that doesn't love a wall," or the later line, "Before I built a wall I'd ask to know what I was walling in or walling out." I believe each of these lines says something important about and to us regarding boundaries. We often resist setting boundaries, or respecting them, and then do so retroactively and reactively, rather than understanding what we are "walling in or walling out," and the type of boundary that needs to be set to maintain functionality and civility. Maybe we are a little too much like those boys of Lord of the Flies, too susceptible to influences around us to stop and check if our behaviors reflect our core values, or to even know our own core values, and to take a long hard look at how we can come to some agreement on our common values as Americans that reflect respect rather than contempt as a starting point.

Boundaries are the bar lines that help us organize according to our deepest held beliefs and respond from those beliefs. They allow for civility. Just as there were no norms and standards in Lord of the Flies, there were no boundaries. Without both, disintegration of relationships is guaranteed.

Just as boundaries are interrelated to norms and standards in our culture today, so reconsidering truth is an important aspect of the foundations of civil dialogue, of returning humanity to the ability to talk together.

Moving Forward to Action:
Questions for reflection and sharing

1. When have your boundaries been violated most recently? What boundary was violated? What was your reaction/response?

2. Fill out your circle of core values. How do these relate to the boundaries you would like to set for yourself? Do you reflect respect or contempt in your core values?

3. What core values do you experience being violated in our country today? What boundaries? How can you take a stand whenever and wherever you experience boundary/values violation?

CHAPTER EIGHT

Finding Truth

The facts were told not to speak
and were taken away
The facts, surprised to be taken,
were silent

—from "On the Fifth Day" by Jane Hirshfield,
chancellor of The American Academy of Poets[29]

As the editor of a monthly newspaper for the Episcopal Diocese of Lexington, I was accustomed to fielding questions about the current "big topic" in the news, whether I was at my desk or off duty like I supposedly was this Friday night. My husband and I were at a small dinner party, enjoying a glass of wine and casual conversation before the meal. We were the new kids on the block, having recently moved to the area. But my new zip code was well within the circulation area of my newspaper, and people often felt like they knew me from reading my by-line. The conversation turned to the news that the assistant to the bishop of the Diocese of Lexington had recently been accused of embezzlement. The story had just broken to the public; no definitive amount of money had been announced. The man accused was a member of a prominent family who had lived in the area for several generations.

The talk turned from shocked response to speculations about how much money was involved, as well as other highly publicized cases of embezzlement in the state. One person remembered a country club embezzlement; another, a small but wealthy church in the area whose treasurer had stolen funds. I sat quietly, listening and observing as the examples rolled out, hoping that my silence would make me an invisible non-presence. Inevitably, of course, the question was put to me: How much money was taken? This was a question I could answer, and had already answered many

---

29 From "On the Fifth Day" by Jane Hirshfield. Used with permission, received August 17, 2017.

times that week. At this time, I said, the exact amount was unknown. It would be announced when it was known.

There was a bit of coaxing, an assumption that I knew more than I was telling, which I didn't. Eventually, they moved on, hypothesizing about possible amounts and appropriate punishments in each case. Finally, with reference again to the country club, one gentleman suggested that if the amount was under $10,000, it should simply be dropped, as a court case would be more costly than the actual amount taken. At this point, I could no longer be silent. "So, is that what you would tell your children? If it's under $10,000, it's OK to steal?"

The conversation shifted to the importance of full disclosure – of telling the truth. There was an underlying assumption in the room that, as a religious journalist, I might believe that the truth could be softened, or that dishonesty would be forgiven completely. It was a concept I had encountered before, which seems connected to an image of a gentle, forgiving Jesus, surrounded by small children and lambs, and a misinterpretation of "turn the other cheek" as an act of allowing a behavior rather than a historical act of defiance. I informed them that our newspaper had decided over a decade ago that we were in the business of reporting the facts and telling the truth, no matter what. Earlier in the week, the current bishop (who was the publisher), the chancellor, the paper's attorney, and I had met to ensure that we told the embezzlement story responsibly, accurately, and truthfully.

Across the room from me was a man I knew from his writing, a man who would become a dear friend. That night, however, I only knew that David Dick had been an Emmy-winning correspondent for CBS News as well as the editor of a small-town weekly, and was currently the Chair of the University of Kentucky School of Journalism. He, too, had been listening and observing, and now he spoke up. "What are we about if we are not telling the truth?" he said. "What is the impact for the world – our own small worlds and the world at large – if we cover up the truth to make someone look good or to protect someone's feelings. We have to tell the truth!" I sent a grateful smile his way, and later thanked him for his strong intervention on behalf of truth. We didn't solve the problem that night, of course. The conversation moved on to things a bit easier and more social, but the topic was named, and couldn't be unnamed.

The discussion that Friday evening so many years ago was prescient when it comes to what is happening today across social media. Every time I encounter people talking about finding truth, I hear echoes of another decisive moment for me, a moment when a journalist said: "The internet has changed the very concept of truth." The speaker was the late John Carroll, former publisher of the Lexington Herald-Leader and the Philadelphia Inquirer, and winner of fourteen Pulitzer Prizes as publisher of the Los Angeles Times. He was addressing students at the annual Joe Creason Lecture at the University of Kentucky School of Communications in 2008.

Journalism, he told them, was founded on fact-checking. News coverage was checked for fact and clearly labeled as news, while opinion pieces were labeled as columns, essays, or editorials. But now, Carroll said, it is difficult to tell the difference between opinion and fact, and the instant delivery of digital communication to millions is perceived as truth. Most of this communication has not been checked for veracity. It may or may not be true. Even as I am writing this chapter, Facebook is involved in an intense study of how to manage false news sites on the internet, which masquerade as real news.

In 2016, The Oxford English Dictionary selected the word "post-truth" as their word of the year. According to Jeffrey Sherwood, Senior Assistant Editor, the word of the year is annually discerned by searching a giant database of texts looking for trends that emerge, whether the word might be new or the use of it has spiked, and how it reflects on the year as a whole. Where the use of "post" often means "after," in this case, it refers to truth no longer being relevant. According to Sherwood, Stephen Colbert scoffed that neither the word nor the concept were new, pointing to his previous coinage of the word "truthiness." To Sherwood, the difference is this: "truthiness" suggests something feels true, but no one is sure whether it actually is true. "Post-truth" says that the truth can be known, but it doesn't matter.

According to Casper Grath, the president of Oxford, post-truth was "fueled by the rise of social media as a news service and a growing distrust of the facts offered up by the establishment. Post-truth as a concept has been finding its footing for some time." Oxford defines post-truth as "relating to circumstances in which objective facts are less influential in shaping public opinion than appeals to emotion and personal belief." The online commentary on the selection of post-truth as the word of the year ends with the statement that post-truth "extends the notion from an isolated quality of particular assertions to a general characteristic of our age."[30]

The concept of "post-truth" would be startling enough by itself. But additional complicating factors exist. It is difficult today to tell the difference between real news and entertainment, as sensationalized soundbites endeavor to lure viewers, and the number of so-called "news" outlets are

---

30 Phone interview with Jeffrey Sherwood, Senior Assistant Editor, Oxford Dictionary.

sending their version of what's happening out into the world 24-7. Competition for readers and viewers and clicks has spawned a routine embellishment of fact in order to keep people interested. News is a very different animal then it was when the media had regular time slots for morning, noon and evening newscasts, with adequate time for and expectation of fact-checking. The sad story of NBC News anchor Brian Williams, who exaggerated a story about his personally coming under fire in a US Army helicopter during the Iraq War in 2003, is one example of such embellishment. Williams, the face and star of the struggling network, had to admit that he had been dishonest on the "Nightly News", but also over the years. His is not an isolated case. So who is a viewer or reader to believe?

The changing face of truth is about more than newspapers, internet, or other forms of media. The issue is deeply connected to breakdown in our culture of core values, norms and standards, and our ability to hear and receive truths different from our own. It is also deeply connected to the silos in which we find ourselves living, surrounded by people who think and live almost exactly like we do, therefore sentencing us to experience only one version of "truth." Having deep connections with people unlike ourselves is inextricably tied to the ability to interact with each other in a civil, respectful, open manner. As Wendell Berry said, "If we cannot speak directly to each other, how will we ever be able to know each other or be at peace with each other?"

Archbishop Desmond Tutu had to address this issue with the people of South Africa after the atrocity that was apartheid. With the Truth and Reconciliation Commission, he had provided a model that is at once so simple, and yet so difficult for all who want civility and peace in the world to follow. In order to come to the possibility of reconciliation and moving forward, the people of South Africa had to listen to the truth of others, without interrupting, without questioning, without trying to change minds, simply honoring and respecting their experience as true for them. The key tenets of the commission were:

- Listen to the stories of others.
- Listen not to debate, not to challenge, but to hear from the heart.
- Listen not to question or to change minds.
- Listen to believe, honor, and respect that this was true for this person.
- Expect them to listen to you in the same way.[31]

---

31 Commencement address by Archbishop Desmond Tutu, Berea College, Berea, Kentucky, May 2005.

As we learned in Chapter One, in South Africa, the words SUWA BONA (I see you, I hear you) have a much more profound meaning than basic communication, a meaning that offers a real container for our work in Talking Together. Suwa Bona means that when I really see and hear someone, I validate and honor their existence. They know that their truth has been heard, and therefore, because they have been seen and heard, they exist. The reverse is also true. When we do not really see or really hear and honor someone's truth, they simply do not exist in the concept of Suwa Bona. What a powerfully ugly thing it is to deny someone's existence – which is what we do when we do not really see and hear them!

Bishop Tutu's work in Truth and Reconciliation is a reminder of how *telling* truth and *honoring the truth we hear* are integrally connected with civil dialogue, whether it takes place formally or informally. The people of South Africa had to deal with incredible grief and loss, and the truths of their stories were often terribly painful for listeners to hear and honor… and yet that validation of the truth of another person is critically important. Many griefs are related using the Tutu model during Talking Together seminars. It is one of the most important experiences that can be taken away from the seminars into daily life.

Larry, a handsome midlife business executive, told of his pain when a man who had been tremendously influential in his (Larry's) return to a faith-based life after a period of doubt had been asked to step down from his position on the staff of a church. "To me, it was a sin of commission," Larry lamented with tears in his eyes and pain in his voice. "Everyone knew he didn't resign for personal reasons. That was just a cover-up. The truth was avoided, and then he was just gone. We never got to say goodbye, or thank him, and he truly changed my life."

Jane, who was also in this table group, had been on the governing body of the church where the man was asked to resign as his alcoholism worsened, destroying his ability to work effectively. She told of her pain and anger as the group tried to make a decision on how to best protect the man's privacy and release the necessary information that he would no longer be serving on the staff of the church. There were legal considerations, as well, she explained. Her greatest disappointment was that the potential legal ramifications appeared to win over any other consideration.

The hearing of each other's truths helps both parties deal with their hurts.

One of the things that we have learned from adherence to Bishop Tutu's Truth and Reconciliation work is the reminder that no two people will experience an event or conversation in exactly the same way, even if they are at the same place, at the same time. They bring different life experiences to what they hear, which color how they perceive what was said. Literal truth, without subjectivity, might be found if a video camera recorded the event. But individual truth as we experience it must be acknowledged and honored first, before there is a possibility of going further. And often, the very process of hearing another's truth respectfully changes everything in an almost mystical way, enabling further conversation.

Geoff, a retired executive, wrote a touching Facebook post when his former boss died, many years after his retirement. "Evan and I didn't agree on much of anything," he wrote, "and sometimes I despaired of whether we would ever be able to work together. I was headed for a meeting with him in New York when my mother became ill, and I was delayed. I phoned to explain the delay, and when I did arrive, and the two of us sat down to do business, he immediately asked about my mother, and how I was doing facing what could be a terminal illness. Weary and sad, I told my true feelings, spoke of my relationship with my mom and he, in turn, talked about his mom, and their relationship. By the time we got around to business, something had happened, that changed not our opinions, but the way we were able to work together."

When NFL quarterback Colin Kaepernick refused to stand for the national anthem as a statement of his dismay about the treatment of African-Americans in this country, the public had strong emotional reactions, both for and against. Basketball Hall of Famer and Medal of Honor recipient Kareem Abdul-Jabbar supported Kaepernick's stand, reflecting on his own involvement in a demonstration on the UCLA campus following the death of Martin Luther King, Jr. in 1968. It was a peaceful protest, with people standing along a campus walkway, for which Abdul-Jabbar was criticized. Many suggested he leave the country because he said at times the United States did not live up to its responsibilities to all of its citizens. Both he and Kaepernick were telling the story of their truth, albeit from a public platform that touches people on an emotional level. The cast of the Broadway musical "Hamilton," which tells an important story with an ethnically diverse cast, used its stage to speak directly to the vice-president-elect, Mike Pence, who was in attendance, about their truth – of fear that the incoming administration's stance on immigration would be destructive to many lives, including their own. The reactions were as swift and divided as they were for Kaepernick's and Abdul-Jabbar's views.

We may debate whether or not those in public positions have the right to use the platform of their fame to speak their truth. However, it is important that, whenever I recoil from how someone's truth is told, I ask myself if my indignation protects me from honoring the validity of that truth.

As we dig deeply into the subject of truth, we become aware how many kinds of truth there are, from the empirical, or fixed truth, to truth that evolves. There are paradoxical or co-existing truths, two things which are true at the same time, which do not cancel out the validity of each. Often with head-butting stubbornness, we attempt to cancel one of the truths with the term "but." One might say, "There are many people working hard to bring diverse populations together, but hatred and divisiveness continue." The use of the word "and" (rather than 'but') validates both truths: "There are many people working hard to bring diverse populations together, and hatred and divisiveness continue." Meanwhile, mythical truth offers a story-interpretation of an event that is about the event's meaning. Author Bennett Sims of the Institute for Servant Leadership defines mystical truth as truth that grasps the person rather than the person grasping the truth. "I might deny the impact of the Berlin Wall on the people of Germany, protected by distance. Walking along that wall, the truth of its impact grasped me at emotional and functional levels that could not be denied."[32]

In addition to these varying types of truth, people experience the truth in different ways depending on their distinct personalities and ways of processing information. A person who gives and receives information with their senses will take in what they see, hear, smell, taste and touch, and typically tell their story based on their sensory experiences. An individual who makes sense of the world intuitively may not make sense to the sensory person, as they have an added dimension of immediate interpretation of what they are experiencing. Still others make sense of the world by making connections between a current experience, previous experiences, and what the future might hold, adding yet another dimension to their truth.

Recently, my daughter and I made a lengthy car trip together. We are good friends as adults, despite the age gap and differing perspectives on many topics. I listen to NPR regularly, she to Fox News. She is a sensate, factual, detail-oriented person, while I am driven by intuition and big-picture thinking. During our trip, we were listening to a Fox News interview with a senator regarding a deportation situation. To my ears, the interviewer kept rudely interrupting the senator, with his voice getting louder by the minute. Finally I said, "Could we please turn this off? I can't stand either the volume or the rudeness!" After turning the radio off, my daughter said, "You know, if he would stop avoiding the question and would just answer

---

32 Notes from Institute for Servant Leadership Workshop at Emory University, Atlanta. Session with Bennett Sims, Marcus Borg, and Margaret Wheatley, 2004.

it, he wouldn't be interrupted by getting the question again." Startled, I replied, "Is that what you heard? That he was avoiding the question?" She nodded yes. "That's so interesting," I said. "What I heard was a person trying to set a context for his answer and not getting a chance to do so!" It was such a great example of how two people who deeply know, love, like, and respect each other can experience exactly the same thing at the same time and have different truths about it! If it is that complex in terms of how we see and hear when we are already in relationship, how much more complicated when we are talking with others with whom we have no relationship!

In another example at a Talking Together seminar, we were processing our experiences of anger. Anger can be divided into three categories. Hot anger is a consuming experience that clouds the brain and disorients people, often causing them to act in irrational ways. Cold anger is unemotional, at times even cold and calculating. Warm anger is in touch with emotion and the rational. An African-American man at the workshop told his story of being an officer on a non-profit community board that was seeking an executive director. He believed the job description was a perfect match for someone he knew whose skills would greatly benefit the organization. With a sense of confidence in the individual he was recommending, he presented her resume to the board. Not only was she not hired for the position, he told us, her application was never acknowledged, nor was she interviewed. "I was beyond angry," he said, "and left the organization."

A white woman sitting across from the man at the table looked at him and nodded. "You know, that's my story, too. It's probably every woman's story as well as every black person's story. I cannot tell you how many qualified females I have recommended, only to have their resumes completely ignored, and a less qualified person hired. You bet I understand that anger!"

The two looked at each other in silence for a minute before the man spoke. "I never knew your story and mine were the same truth," he said. "I thought it was just a black story and your story must be different."

We are, it appears, in a new and different place in our understanding of what truth is and how we can find it today. Social media is swimming in examples of different kinds and levels of truth and post-truth. The recent reaction to the New York Times best-seller Hillbilly Elegy is a good example. Author J.D. Vance grew up in both Jackson, Kentucky and the rust belt in Ohio. He survived a highly dysfunctional home life, attended Yale and became an attorney. Hillbilly Elegy is his memoir with his extrapolations of larger societal truths based on his lived truth. For instance, he refers to the loss of jobs in the rust belt leading to a pervasive sense of hopelessness.

Reactions from others with an Appalachian family background have been swift and often show flashes of red-hot anger as individuals perceive their own lived truths contradicted and jump to the defense of people and places near and dear to them. For them, descriptions, like those of joblessness and meth problems in Appalachia, lead to a fear that readers outside the region will see all of its people as jobless addicts. A more rational response to Vance's truth, carrying an important truth of its own, can be heard from award-winning Appalachian writer Silas House as he enlarges the truth of Vance's story by setting the context for the problems of Appalachia, going back to the Civil War. As a person listening and observing, and with my own close ties and experiences with the area and its people, I find that the truth revealed by the memoir, or one person's truth, and the truths revealed in House's fiction and ability to offer greater historical context, have important elements of truth, touch aspects of my lived personal and professional experiences of Appalachia, and also broaden my truth .

The Hillbilly Elegy controversy highlights, I believe, the role of emotion in both telling and hearing truth, whether that truth is conveyed in a personal narrative or a news format. Emotion is one major filter through which information will pass, a filter which can mildly or wildly distort basic facts by the teller or the hearer. At this point in our culture, emotion is driving a wedge in our ability to hear any consistent, fact-based truth on almost any subject.

Ideological polarization underlines the societal search for truth, and the great need to listen beyond our own circles of like-mindedness. Objective, empirical facts simply have ceased to matter in this post-truth culture, leaving an opening for those who are vulnerable to be manipulated into camps built on emotion, with fear being the predominant driver. Journalist Jeff Guinn's research into the Jonestown killings that took place in the jungle of Guyana in 1978 when nine hundred Americans drank cyanide-laced Kool-aid is a chilling example of manipulation of facts through exaggeration, to build both fear and a sense of urgency.

While the hopelessness of poverty might create one type of vulnerability, illness and/or aging creates another. Cleverly building on people's desire for social justice or other good causes to entice them to follow a particular "leader" and his or her version of the facts is another ploy to control and achieve power. More recently, we experienced GOP congressional candidate Greg Gianforte physically attacking a reporter from The Guardian who had asked him a question. Gianforte faces prosecution, fines, and possible jail time for his violence, but still won the election. Before the results of the election were even known, and despite the existence and persistent replay of tapes of the attack and substantiation of the attack by a Fox News crew standing by in disbelief, there were deep divisions of opinion. Springing from those divisions were accusations of a "liberal set up" to lure the candidate into unacceptable behavior, and a march to his defense with people as far away as California declaring that they would move to Montana to support the candidate's attack on the "crooked media."

At the personal level, there are situations where intense emotions blur the possibility for objective truth, as in the case of a grief-stricken family trying to make end-of-life decisions for a sister recently diagnosed with a lingering but terminal illness. The grief and fear that grip them as they move into this unknown and shattering new world have blinded their capacity to seek facts and options as they make decisions.

In late April 2017, the Annaberg Foundation presented a panel on the state of the news with recipients of the Walter Cronkite Awards for Excellence in Television Political Reporting speaking. Jorge Ramos of Univision spoke of Walter Cronkite's words regarding the responsibility of journalism: to reflect reality, not as we wish it to be, but as it really is; to challenge and to question, reminding his colleagues that the legendary newscaster saw those who reported the facts as the "allies of democracy and protectors of our freedom." In this time of post-truth and alternative facts, there seems to be an effort to delegitimize facts. Katy Tur of NBC, who traveled with the Trump campaign, spoke of posting facts via Twitter and receiving a response that said, "Who are you to decide what the facts are? We (the people) decide the facts."

The truth is not always as we wish it to be. And the truth matters. My hope is for experiences like Talking Together seminars to allow us all to not only practice telling our truth and respectfully hearing others' truths, but also to practice examining our own reactivity before we jump to the conclusion that we, or some other individual or ideological camp, hold an exclusive on the truth. With such openness and awareness, we can begin to emotionally step back from reactivity, to take time to examine what we have heard, and ask ourselves to comb rigorously through it all in a search for facts which help us discern between memoir truths, ideological interpretation and manipulation of facts and fact as if presented to us in video-ed clarity. With such clarity we can be freed to learn from each other, be in relationships which enable personal and professional productivity, and take a major step toward ending the polarization that divides us.

Moving Forward to Action:
Questions for reflection and sharing

1. Describe a time when it was difficult for you to speak the truth directly to someone. What happened? How did it feel? What did you think? Did you get the truth spoken? Directly or indirectly? What was the impact on the community? On the relationship?

2. Describe a time when you were not told the truth about something and found out the truth later. What was the impact?

3. What does it feel like to hear someone else's truth that differs from yours about the same situation? How do you react? Where does this experience fit in the hierarchy of truth telling?

4. Where do you turn for truthful information today?

A conversation with

CHANGE AGENT
STACY SAULS

Episcopal Bishop and
Founder of Love Must Act

When did you feel called to bring about positive change in the world?

"There is no particular moment in time," says the Rt. Rev. Stacy F. Sauls, an Episcopal bishop and founder of Love Must Act, an effort to bring education to children in parts of the world where it is most need-ed and least available. Grow-ing up in the south during the '60s and '70s, he was taught by his parents that he could do anything he set his mind to do. Too young to be actively involved in the turbulent times of his childhood, awareness of the civil rights movement and protest marches against the war led him to "ask questions I was not brought up to ask." "It was more about a period of growing 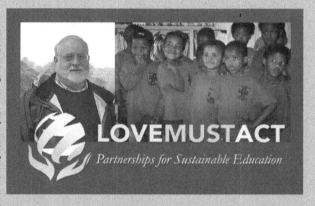 up than a moment of epiphany," he notes. "It all came together in college which changed my life in a positive way. I attended a small, conservative Baptist college in the south, removed from demonstrations about the war. My freshman year was Nixon's last year in office. A wonderful teacher and mentor, Betty Alverson, channeled my questions and ob-servations into service. I think of that period as the most spiritual time in American life in my lifetime — and wonder if we are approaching another one."

How did you decide what action to take?

The work of Love Must Act is currently focused in Grahamstown, South Africa. The foun-dation for the work — for putting love into action — began with the influence of his college professor and mentor. "She always told us that we could not do everything, but we could do something — and we needed to do the something we could do. She was such a major influence on the formation of my thinking," Sauls muses. Over the years that formation has translated into his belief that "For most of us, it is lots of people doing little things that add up to positive change." "Energy can be wasted thinking about what change theory can affect the entire system. I'm fairly suspicious of big things, which end up being more 'talking about' than 'doing.' The little efforts might not change the whole world, but they will change some part of the world, and will definitely change the self."

From this foundational thinking, and the experience of his long relationship with Brother Timothy Jolley of the Order of the Holy Cross in Grahamstown, South Africa , and through him, increasing involvement and deepening relationships with the people there that Love Must Act moved from a long-evolving idea to action.

"There are two different sides of the same coin," Sauls stresses. "It's all about the importance of bringing education where it is most needed, by building holistic schools of excellence, one place at a time. And, it is about affecting the lives of affluent people by offering them the opportunity to build relationships in these contexts. The 'change theory' involved here is about conversion — not in the religious sense, but in the sense of what can be done. Once you get to know and love a child in one of these poor communities, have made a commitment to them, an investment in them, you can never walk into a voting booth again and act like that child doesn't exist."

He pauses — as if picturing the children he already knows, and their counterparts waiting to be known. "Love is a pre-condition to justice. You can try justice first, but it's not the same thing. It may be altruism. But love means doing something you don't have a duty to do."

The 15 years when the idea that would become Love Must Act was brewing involved the years when as Bishop of the Episcopal Diocese of Lexington (Ky.), the innovative diocesan Reading Camp program took wings and spread far beyond diocesan borders, including connecting with the school the Holy Cross Brothers had built in Grahamstown. "It might be considered a little thing," Sauls says, "but it was an ingenious, transformative, revolutionary endeavor, impacting not only the 60 students, but their families. And that's where it makes such a difference —- recognizing that the unit being dealt with by the school is the family, not just the student. That opens the way to affect the life of the family, through support groups, medical and social services. It occurred to me that this could be duplicated elsewhere. The starting place had to be expanding and securing what already exists, and then replicating it." The work will be done by partnering with groups in the United States who commit time, talent and money to the work.

> "Once you get to know and love a child in one of these poor communities, to commit to and invest in them, you can never go into a voting booth again and act like that child doesn't exist."

What challenges have you experienced and how have you approached them?

Stacy Sauls is a leader for whom challenges create interest. "I don't ever think of roadblocks. I think of challenges. There are few challenges that can't be overcome. It's like a game to overcome whatever challenges appear."

Sabotage and emotional issues are two of the challenges he names which often appear as "roadblocks of some kind." And overcoming them brings the naming of an additional, and often unidentified challenge — outside perception of the stick-to-itiveness that is perseverance.

"A fundamental quality of leadership is perseverance," he states firmly. "Without perseverance, nothing can be accomplished." An additional challenge for leadership, he acknowledges, is that perseverance can often be viewed unfavorably by those with a low tolerance for dealing with the inevitable challenges that would block accomplishment, or the completion of tasks. "People can confuse perseverance with bulldozing," he warns. An additional challenge is staying clear of emotional reactivity that can distract and de-rail efforts. As a leader, he must be aware of, yet not sucked into emotional quicksand. "Personally, I hate for people to be mad at me. I want to be kind and fair. I never want to hurt anyone's feelings. The other side of that coin is that I cannot control or take responsibility for anyone else's feelings or reactions. This is a constant challenge for leadership."

Another challenge specific to the culture in which he is working has to do with the deference to white leadership despite the black majority of the culture. The universal tendency to sabotage strong leadership of any kind is exacerbated by the forces of sabotage to undermine any Xhosa leadership, and "get rid" of them, always replacing with a white leader. Sauls reflects, "I have believed that the work of the Truth and Reconciliation Commission in South Africa had them far ahead of the United States in dealing with issues of racism. It's not that simple. For now, I must continue to observe and learn."

What have you learned about being in relationship with people who you experience as "other?"

"The more 'other' someone is from me, the more I can learn from them. And a good leader likes to learn," says Sauls. "I am often asked 'why Africa?' My answer is because the Africans are definitely not us. When we are faced with the experience of a culture and people entirely different from ourselves, it disrupts every preconceived notion we ever had, and offers the greatest potential, the maximum opportunity for us to learn to see things differently. I have found that the more 'other' I encounter, the more liminal the experience of opening up the world of fundamental differences. Sometimes it is easier to gain new insights into how the world is when I am completely out of my comfort zone. The more I hold onto the familiar, the less likely I am to learn. There is less incentive in 'sameness.'"

For Sauls, a white, American southerner working in an entirely different culture, he must:

- Communicate with the people on their own terms.
- Try to learn Xhosa. In this multi-lingual country, Xhosa reinforces an appreciation of the native culture, while English is primarily the language of economic opportunity.
- Demonstrate respect
- Understand that this is language-based culture and I can't fully learn unless I connect to the culture.
- Continue to learn the parallels in U.S. and African racial issues; to recognize that there are not easy answers, no simple solutions.

What's next for Love Must Act? What words of advice do you have for those who want to work for change in the world?

- The lessons of long ago run deep. Attend to the little somethings rather that grow big. Love Must Act has just entered into a contract with the Order of the Holy Cross in Grahamstown for a 6-1/2-year partnership that will bring much greater involvement with the school. "We want to stabilize the school. Expand it into a full primary school. Enlarge the facilities and be sure what we do is sustainable. It would be easy to be distracted by other things. Already we have inquiries from Israel, Palestine, The Dominican Republic, Myanmar, and others. And that is our eventual goal — to take the model and replicate it. In order to do that, we must stabilize; enlarge; sustain — then replicate."

For those who want to bring positive change, and have a dream, the founder of Love Must Act has this message:

- "Believe in yourself. Believe in your dream. Plenty of people will say you can't do what you believe in. You can. You will face challenges. You can overcome them. Try a different approach. Try again. Persevere. If the results are good, count God on your side, even if not everyone else is."

CHAPTER NINE

Good Grief, Charlie Brown

"The whole world can become your enemy when you lose what you love."
– Kristina McMorris, Bridge of Scarlet Leaves

Good grief, Charlie Brown. Those familiar words from the oracle known as the comic strip "Peanuts" sound a little like an oxymoron, but good grief – doing grief fully and well – is a component of the lack of civility in our world that is too often ignored or bypassed with tokenism. The ability to be rational, reasonable, and civil is deeply connected with the management of one's emotions around loss. Grief, and its close ally, fear, are too often stored up, unidentified, and unnamed, much less experienced and processed in a healthy way. They can be masked by silence and pent-up rage, and flares of anger and acting out. Our culture struggles with grief as an enemy of happiness, more than many societies. The good fortune of our country through most of our history has led us to believe that we have an inalienable right to happiness. Therefore,we are miffed and continually shocked by the ups and downs of life, much less its major losses. Despite the fact that hunger, poverty, and homelessness are regular struggles for innumerable people around the globe, along with discrimination and fear as a daily reality, the myth of the right to a happy, burden-free life persists in the United States, and grief is the antithesis to that myth.

The subjects of death and grief have been less taboo since the publication of Elizabeth Kubler-Ross's groundbreaking book On Death and Dying in 1969. Yet despite numerous subsequent books on grief as well as conferences and documentaries about grief, the American way of dealing with loss remains minimalistic. A couple of weeks off from work for the death of a member of the immediate family, civilized rituals of flowers and food, and life should be back to "normal." The further removed the loss is from the death of a close family member, the less able we are to acknowledge that there is something to grieve about, and to walk through that grief for ourselves, or to support someone else's painful journey.

And so the losses mount up over a lifetime, unnamed, unattended to, yet living somewhere inside us, waiting for someone to notice that something sad or bad happened and a life was changed. We tiptoe around the truth of our stories which might come too close to the loss for comfort. Next to dealing with conflict in a straightforward way as a normal part of life and communication, dealing with our own or someone else's sadness, especially their tears, calls for extra bravery.

What Does Grief Have to Do With Civil Dialogue?

When people come together to talk, in either structured or unstructured situations, especially around issues where there are differences of opinion, grief is like an iceberg, with only the tip visible to the eye. And that tip often reveals as anger. Under the waterline lie a myriad of other emotions that have not been explored: embarrassment, guilt, shame, and so on. Like the Titanic, the ship of conversation can unknowingly plow directly into the dark hulk under the waterline. The subsequent result is that efforts at dialogue are destroyed.

In Talking Together seminars, one of our practice conversations invites participants, seated in small table groups with a facilitator, to name hurts, disappointments, and losses they have experienced during their lifetime. They begin the exercise by writing down what they are naming, and then choose whether or not to share what they have written aloud with the small group. As the leader reads out the question, and passes out the papers on which answers will be written, the atmosphere in the room changes. The friendly buzz of chatter that normally occurs between presentations and exercises dies down. People stare at the blank pages with great intensity, as if some answer is written there for them to discover. In the silence offered as time for reflection, some eyes are focused on some far away point, outside the window, or on the ceiling. Others close their eyes, or even bury their head in their hands. Then, without fail, out of the silence emerges the quiet scratch of pen on paper, growing louder as it is multiplied by the number of participants.

Writing continues for many past the two-minute warning. Yet others make no mark on their sheets at all, the losses too painful to think about, much less write about. After participants have shared at their tables, the facilitators summarize what they heard. Again and again, regardless of what part of the country the seminar is in, regardless of whether the participants are members of a faith-based group, a civic group, or are a diverse group coming together around this training, there are similarities when the losses are shared. Some date back to childhood: the memory of seeing the lashes on Kunta Kinte's back in the TV series "Roots" as a small child, and being terrified of the dangers in the world revealed in that moment, the loss of innocence, starting a lifelong journey of activism. The death and funeral of John F. Kennedy, and the loss of a sense of safety. An abuse of power towards a young volunteer youth worker by wealthy members of a non-profit board. The stories go on and on, often with apologies that "this happened so long ago, it shouldn't even matter anymore."

While physical deaths and recent losses may be included in the sharing, more often, three types of grief are represented:

- **Marginalized grief.** Grief over losses which the culture has not recognized, such as the loss of a close non-marital relationship, the loss of a pet, loss of a job or a home, loss of faith or innocence.

- **Delayed grief.** Grief which was not identified and processed at the time of the loss, and re-surfaces at a later time, often triggered by a newer loss.

- **Anticipatory grief.** Grief at the knowledge that a loss is coming, or the fear that current behaviors, attitudes, etc. are leading to a loss of something tangible or intangible that is of great value.

Don found himself unable to focus on his work or find pleasure in any of his normal activities for months following the death of his closest friend, Burt. During the long months of Burt's battle with cancer, Don had been a part of the response and support team for Burt and his family, driving to medical appointments, and later taking his shifts at the hospital, comforting the teenage children and the overburdened wife. He had been included with the family during the funeral, and was still in close touch. To the rest of his world, it was time for Don to be "back to normal." There were no notes of sympathy, offers of food, or acknowledgment that his life had changed completely with this loss, which left him reeling. There are no formal rituals for the loss of a friend, through death or other departures.

Martha was in divorce recovery following the ending of her nineteen-year marriage. During an evening session as she was working with her therapist on feelings of abandonment, she began to sob, crying out in a childlike voice, "They should not have done that to me!"

"Who?" the leader queried.

"My father!" Martha replied, sobbing even harder.

"My father shouldn't have..." the therapist prompted, leaving a space for Martha's pain. The story rolled out of her mouth, tangled with her tears. Martha had been sent to a prestigious boarding school when she was in the seventh grade. Just after Christmas her first year there, her mother died quite unexpectedly. Martha was brought home from school for the funeral, and quickly returned to school, supposedly so she wouldn't get "too far behind." When she came home for the summer, not only was there no mother there, but her beloved dog had been sent to a farm to live because her father couldn't take care of it. While the adult Martha knew in her head that her grieving father had coped as best he could, the child Martha whose dual losses had never been recognized or grieved was triggered by the losses of divorce to deal with this delayed grief.

Often, inside the average, "normal" adult is a grieving little person, who in our bootstraps culture has stuffed such hurts and losses. The uncensored grief of a child contain truths that help us understand the complex ways in which the painful situations of life can show up in a casual encounter as anger.

Five-year-old Alicia was not only grieving over the death of her father, she was holding her entire family hostage with her anger and acting out, months after his death. A look at her work with a bereavement specialist is helpful for people of any age struggling to deal with their own losses and truths[33].

Therapist shows Alicia several drawings of faces: a crying face, an angry face, an anxious face, a smiling face. Alicia, do any of these faces look like what is happening inside of you before you hit your sister?

Alicia: points to teary face

Oh, there was a very sad person inside of you! Did she talk to you?

Alicia: She went POP! (stomps her feet, claps her hands and makes a big face) inside me and turned into this (points to angry face).

Are these scary faces to you?

Alicia: nods yes

---

33 Verbatim client notes from Kay Collier McLaughlin's personal files.

How big are they?

Alicia: spreads her arms as wide and tall as she can

Would you like to try to make them smaller, so you can have them come out just when you need them, not to surprise you?

Alicia: nods yes. Her expression is a little doubtful, as if wondering if such a thing is possible.

Therapist shows Alicia a paper bag, and a basket full of Styrofoam teary faces. She asks Alicia to fill the bag up, closing it tightly each time, until it finally gets so full it goes POP! Then she says, "So, if the bag gets too full of teary faces, it pops and then this (shows angry face on Styrofoam ball) shows up?"

Alicia: nods yes.

What if you had a sad bag, and if you feel like crying, which is an OK thing to do when you're sad, you can say to someone "I'm sad" AND you can put as many of these teary faces in the bag as you need to. They understand and are with you. The trick is this – keep watching the bag, and if it, or you, gets too close to the popping point, what might you do?

Alicia: nods. "I could cry with somebody. But I don't want to make my mommy more sad. Or my sister. And talking and crying won't ever bring my daddy back. And it's scary without him coming home, even when he was sick. At least I could sit beside him on his bed. I feel scared. And sad. And mad."

I know it feels sad. It is sad. It makes me sad with you, and your mommy and your sister. I am so proud of you for being able to tell me how it makes you feel. I feel really proud that you trusted me with those feelings. After the angry face comes and you hit something, do you feel better?

Alicia: shakes her head no, and then says, "Maybe just a little, because the sad face stops getting bigger when I do it (makes a hitting motion) and then everybody is mad at me and it's all really big and I'm really little and I can't make anything stop or be better."

Alicia's five-year-old description of her internal process of coping with the immensity of her loss and her overwhelming sadness and fear has remained with me over several decades in its stark truth.

For many, grief threatens to overwhelm us, either consciously or subconsciously, with its paralyzing intensity. If the fear of being eaten alive by something keeps growing larger and more out of control, the result is often POP!, an active and spontaneous expression of anger, manifested in words or actions, as a way of controlling the uncontrollable. The anger provides momentary release from the shame of losing control and the overwhelming pain of the emotions no one really wants to experience. And the cycle begins again.

Not everyone expresses their unresolved grief in this way, of course. But unfortunately, our culture's way of dealing with grief, whether that be the loss of a job, home, friend, physical health, or anything else, is to medicate rather than doing the hard work of moving through what Freud called "mourning labor." It is hard, courageous work-and, unattended, it hangs around, waiting to surprise at the most unexpected times.

The ability to understand and begin to name and deal with our own losses is closely related to the ability to have civil conversation. This means recognizing that grief is a normal part of life, not an aberration, and that we cannot ignore, overmedicate, or deny until the big one comes along.

Dr. Burrows, an academic administrator, became fully aware of how this played out in his life after his wife's death from cancer. He was participating in a departmental personality assessment session where he had previously tested as a Thinker, a person whose basic life questions are "Is it logical? Is it fair?" He had brought an earlier score sheet with him, and pointed out to me that it showed only a point or two on the feeling dimension on the earlier indicator, while the more recent one showed a more balanced score on the Thinking and Feeling continuums. "I didn't become a feeler," he said, "but I am sure that the reason I showed more feeling points this time was that I had never before encountered any situation in my adult life that I could not move through with reason and logic. But Carolyn's illness was simply too big. My emotions were bigger than my thoughts, and I had no practice with that at all. It made me so angry that I started to lash out at people, people who didn't deserve it. I finally realized that I had to own what was happening, whether I liked it or not." The adult exegesis of the five year old words: truth from the opposite ends of the spectrum.

Grief is not selective about whom it hits. But we can be selective about how we choose to deal with our own losses, and how we respond to the grief of others, even when we encounter it in its rawest form.

Suggestions For Dealing With Your Own Grief

These suggestions are not a separate exercise per se, but can be used when needed to deal with grief new, old, or delayed, large or small.[34]

1. Develop the practice (see Chapter 5) of locating and naming emotions on a daily basis: glad, bad, sad, mad, or derivatives thereof.

2. Once the feeling has been identified, use the Schneider grief model.

3. Give yourself permission to talk about losses in your life, whenever they occurred, choosing a person who you consider safe and confidential to hear your stories.

4. If you are in the anger stage of grief, or recognize residual anger, which is authentic and valid in the grief process, find a person trained to walk through this with you. Check with your local Hospice, even if the loss is not a physical death, for resources. Do not try to do this alone or with someone who simply feeds your anger.

5. If anger heightens or persists, despite this intentionality, please see your doctor or a therapist.

Suggestions for Responding to Others:

1. In situations of collective or communal tragedy/loss/crisis, such as in Columbine, Sandy Hook, Orlando, or the recent political crisis, respond to accusatory anger, blaming, or personal attack by something like "I hear you are in a great deal of pain" or "I know you are really sad and I am so sorry." Do not attempt to "fix" that person or diminish their feelings.

2. If you know the person well, you might add (only after speaking to their sadness, as angry reactions are often pushed by the need for someone to notice they are in pain), "I am sad, too. We just express

---

34 Suggestions created by Dr. Kay Collier McLaughlin for Grief and the Holidays seminars, sponsored by Hospice of the Bluegrass and Milward Funeral Home.

it in different ways and sometimes for different reasons."

3. Realize there is no time table for grief. It takes as long as it takes. We don't go around it, over it, or under it – we have to go through it. And each loss remains a part of who we are currently.

4. It is possible that a recent incident has triggered grief over an old loss that may have been unresolved or has simply come back for a short time in a milder form.

Civil conversation in the early stages of any grief process is difficult, perhaps even impossible, as so many aspects of the body, mind, and spirit are working overtime for pure survival. This is one of the reasons that angry, often confused, and almost incoherent words get spoken during a crisis or under extreme stress. And in the strange way of grief, it can surprise us at any time, playing havoc with uncontrolled emotions that can lead to uncontrolled words and most uncivil conversation.

During a Wendell Berry reading and lecture, I was seated next to a young woman who had driven to Kentucky from North Carolina for the event. During the question and answer session, she spoke, in a trembling voice, about being the mother of young children, and her fears for their future on an unstable planet. She asked him how, in the face of so much horror and sorrow in the world, he always managed to write with hope, rather than anger or despair. Her fear for her children in this chaotic world was palpable. Her hands twisted in her lap as her voice broke; tears coursed down her cheeks unchecked.

Berry's answer stays with me. "I cannot avoid the world's pain in my writing," he said, "I must write in faith that there is something greater than myself." After the session concluded, I asked the young woman, "Was it worth the trip to come here?"

"Oh, yes," she responded, softly but firmly. "He validated the sorrow that so many people deny. And he told me how he keeps going in the face of that sorrow without telling me that was the way I needed to do it. I still feel sad, I still feel fear for my children and their futures, but I don't feel alone."

Moving Forward to Action:
Questions for reflection and sharing

1. What loss and grief are you holding inside that you have never shared or has never been validated? What triggers this loss for you today?

2. What are you grieving most today in the world? What do you fear losing?

3. What are you doing with your grief?

A *conversation with*

CHANGE AGENT DONALD LASSERRE

Executive Director of The Ali Center

"Mohammed Ali looked for what unites us despite our differences. We all stand on someone's shoulders...the legend of Mohammed Ali and what he represented must not be lost."

Donald Lasserre grew up on the South Side of Chicago, a young African American man who was a "huge fan" of Mohammed Ali — particularly outside the boxing ring, where the champ's stance for "black is beautiful" as well as his work for peace and justice inspired a journey out of the south side, through Harvard Business School and Georgetown University Law School.

Five years ago, Lasserre heard that the position of Executive Director of The Ali Center in Louisville, Ky., was open. He had only lived on the west or east coast, and he knew nothing at all about the Center.

What he did know was that "the legend of Mohammed Ali and all he represented must not be lost in the annals of time." Already he was noticing the contributions of people such as Ghandi, Golda Meir and Nelson Mandela fading into history, their impact unknown to younger generations. "Mohammed Ali looked for what unites us, despite our differences. I thought about the capacity for sharing his important work through the Center. We all stand on someone else's shoulders. I knew that I wanted to continue his legacy in a way that

---

"We all stand on someone's shoulders. You owe it to your community and self to always give back, and inspire others to be the best that they can be."

---

could touch other lives the way he touched mine. I had to answer the call."

How did you decide what action to take? In your particular situation, you were called to continue the legacy while the legend himself was still alive when you first arrived.

When Donald Lasserre arrived at The Ali Center, the champ was still alive, although his ability to speak was greatly diminished by Parkinson's disease. "I learned so much by seeing him around others. He loved being around people. He lit up around people, and his joy in being with them shone through his eyes and his very presence with them, in such a powerful way that the lack of ability to speak was hardly noticed. I think of the time he met with a young man who was struggling with cancer. I watched them sitting with their heads together, Mohammed's eyes looking deeply into the young man's. At the end of their time together, the young man said, 'I'm going to keep fighting and win this fight because of you.' Mohammed simply inspired people to do great things, to be the best that they could be. I wanted to facilitate the cascading of his legacy to the next generation."

The initiatives for creating that nexus between Mohammed and the next generation have included:

- The annual Mohammed Ali Humanitarian Awards.
     √to six young adults under the age of 30 who are serving as advocates, activists and role models in ways that will ultimately bring about positive change in the world, and represent Ali's core principles of confidence, conviction, dedication, respect, giving, and spirituality.

     √to "seasoned humanitarians" who are making significant contributions toward securing peace, social justice, human rights and/or social capital in their community and on a global basis.

- The encouragement of archiving "red bike" transformative moments. When Cassius Clay was 12 years old, he was the proud owner of a red bike — a bike which was stolen. A furious adolescent, he was prepared to go after the thief, and might have done so in ways which could have made a bad situation worse but for the intervention of a man named Joe Martin, who asked Cassius if he knew how to fight, should he find the thief. Young Cassius admitted he did not. Joe Martin took him to his gym and introduced him to boxing, and the rest is history.

Who is your Joe Martin and what was your transformative moment?

On the third level of The Ali Center, recording booths are provided where young people archive their answers to two questions, which can provide inspiration to others.

What was your red bike moment?
What are you fighting for?

The Center is now creating an app which will give those outside the Center an opportunity to listen to the inspirational answers.

What challenges have you encountered and how would you respond to them?

1. The location in Louisville was an initial challenge, as perceptions of outsiders did not encourage visitors to the state. A major shift in attitude occurred after Mohammed Ali's funeral, when leaders of many faiths came together in Louisville, were treated so well, and were seen on Cable TV that there was a real spotlight on the city. That gave the outside world a different perspective of the city and the state, which encouraged more people to visit.

2. The absolute "bigness" of Mohammed Ali, and how to synthesize all that he did so that the important contributions can be grasped. It is NOT enough to say that he fought for social justice. It was the way he fought that we need to highlight. He was able to help

people find common ground, that the Center must continue to do. He was adamant that not listening to each other is a mistake. Once, when a journalist had been particularly brutal to him, he was asked if he was mad. His response was that to be angry would be hypocritical. That the journalist was doing what he thought was right. It is the ultimate respect to listen, he emphasized, not to ignore. He gave us examples time and again of taking down barriers to relationships, leveling the playing field by leaning in and showing respect for others' experiences and opinions … not because he agreed with them, but out of respect for their common humanity.

3. The non-profit speed bump of money. How to reach as many people as we can to help us spread the message that, inspired by Mohammed, we do not have to be Mohammed to accomplish great things.

4. Technology. How to utilize technology most effectively to take the work of Mohammed and the Center out into the world.

5. It's a lot harder than I initially thought. "No matter how open I may be, people come up with their own perspectives, communication difficulties get in the way, and we unintentionally erect our own barriers, I must think about Mohammed's respect for the other, and be as agnostic as I can possibly be to get people to really understand his message. My basic response to these challenges is to look for the Ali in all of us. To inspire people to do acts of kindness and service, to touch one person at a time. I think most people want to give back to society, but aren't sure in what way.

Where I encounter differences in perspective, it's important for me to ask questions, to share what I just heard the person say, and see if that is what they intended to say. I use my experiences growing up in Chicago in the '70s, where I was assaulted three times, to say that many of the problems we have facing us today, such as the issue between the police and the black community are not new. There are myths we need to cut through, accountability that needs to be owned on all parts and recognition that there is always more than one way to address any issue or problem. We just have to work together and talk together to find the best way.

What's next for The Ali Center?

The Ali Center is continuing to develop its technical platforms and extend its global reach. It has expanded into Africa, and has a pilot program in a school in Manchester, England, only a few blocks away from where the suicide bomber attacked. "This is a community in real need of the message we bring — in need of a way to believe they can accomplish, and make a difference," says Lasserre.

"We will continue to develop partnerships. We have tried to do it alone, but we know that that is an impossible task. We need to create partnerships with others who share the values that we stand for, and together we will reach even more people."

"My message for others who would try to make a difference in the world. " You owe it to your community and yourself to always give back, inspire others to be the best that they can be."

CHAPTER TEN

Daunting Duet

"A duet is a composition for two performers in which the performers have equal importance to the piece." — Wikipedia

In 1960, Cassius Clay, an eighteen-year-old from Louisville, Kentucky, traveled to Rome to participate in the Olympic Games as a boxer in the light heavyweight division. He won all four of his fights easily, defeating the three-time European champion in the final to win the gold medal. Returning to Louisville, he was presented the key to the city by the mayor, who told the young champ that it entitled him to go "anywhere he wanted to go" in his home town. Taking the mayor at his word, Clay and a friend soon entered a hamburger stand where they were promptly refused service because they were black. Clay then walked to the middle of Louisville's Sixth Street Bridge, which overlooks the Ohio River, and threw his cherished medal into the water. It was his way of protesting the systemic roadblock of non-possibility that he had encountered.

Recently a friend and I drove the River Road into Louisville. Turning onto Sixth Street, we were immediately captivated by The Muhammad Ali Center, its name marching across its facade in bold green, red, and blue letters. The building looks down on the city, the interstate, and the Ohio River.

Inside the center, a young guide walked us to the large window overlooking the Sixth Street Bridge and told us that the building is oriented to face the bridge to honor the long and often difficult path Ali—Cassius Clay—had walked as he held up the ideals of a peaceful world. A replica of that segregated hamburger stand is also inside, complete with its chrome and red vinyl swivel stools. Nearby are glass cases that house the champ's boxing medals and many humanitarian awards. The hamburger stand and Ali's awards are not only a reminder of the determination that steeled a young man to wage a lifelong fight to change the institutional and systemic wrong of racial discrimination, they stand as a metaphor for our own commitment to learn how to change the polarized conversations in the world that threaten our freedom and democracy, and as a reminder of the roadblocks that we,too will face along the way.

The truth is that there are systemic and institutional practices – gender bias, racism, the legitimization of alternative facts – that have become normalized and accepted over the years that are just as problematic today as the institutional and systemic discrimination Ali and others faced. Even as we strive to learn how to interact with each other, we run up against these ingrained structures.

There is the personal – what you and I as individuals can do to create change if we choose to do so. And there are institutional and systemic problems – things that are a part of something larger and more complex than an individual, and rooted below the issues we hear about every day. These daunting duet partners are coexisting truths. We limit our response to them with the word "but."

"I am committed to practice civil dialogue, but people aren't willing to talk outside of their circles of likemindedness," says a frustrated citizen.

"As a physician, I have discovered a new and different way to approach the pain and inflammation of arthritis," says an internist, "but I am being ridiculed by skeptical colleagues in the profession."

It is important to consider how many things we take for granted today would never have happened if the word "but" had been the roadblock. The physician in New Orleans who discovered that his treatment of kidney patients was also relieving their arthritis pain and inflammation was respected by few in the wider medical community during his life, and he successfully treated and made life more manageable for hundreds before his death. On a larger societal scale, if those who fought for fair labor in the 1930s had listened to "but"s instead of "and"s, there would be no weekend, minimum wage, or the forty-hour work week most in the United States take for granted today.

All of us who take up a cause, who feel called to a particular fight, will, like the young Cassius Clay, face our own moment on the bridge. Both personal and systemic change must take place for our world to become everything we want it to be. This coexisting truth creates a paradox that is difficult for the mind to hold. It endangers the pursuit of our dream. So as we learn the new skills of civil dialogue to create change, we must not let the discouragement that surfaces when we face societal roadblocks discourage us.

It is part of the present chaos in our country that these institutionally and structurally ingrained dysfunctions as well as personal dysfunctions have been building for decades politically, without attention to repeated patterns, or the naming of the impact of behaviors in a bipartisan rather than partisan manner. Most recently, this pattern reared its ugly head again in the blaming of the shooting at the Republican baseball practice on the hateful rhetoric of both the right and the left, and again following demonstrations and death in Charlottesville, Virginia. Not even the humanitarian efforts to aid after Hurricane Harvey were immune to this vitriol! The flood waters were still keeping the shelters full in Houston, yet the shaming and blaming, the finger pointing and name calling continue, giving rise to acting out of that hate by reactives waiting for a trigger to propel them to insane acts. While there have always been incidents of politically induced anger in this country, never has there been such a continuous public adversarial period, with tragedy following violent, senseless tragedy. The masks of the KKK have been removed to reveal fresh young faces as well as older ones, spewing venom for all to see and hear. Accusations are personal rather than behavioral. There's been a "blame and shame" game going on rather than a unified effort to analyze what has been happening, how it started, how it repeats itself. It is part of the role of personal change to model a stop to the blaming and shaming as a first step toward addressing systemic issues. There are responsibilities enough to be owned on all parts. The bigger question looms: who will take the first step to working in harmony? And how can we endure to do the work?

The particular issues all have familiar names that fill our news outlets on a daily basis: climate change; renewable energy; refugee crises; terrorism; the failure of public education; an aging infrastructure…the list goes on and on. Underlying the list, however, are conflicts if not caused then perpetuated by people's behaviors, the patterns that hold us in dysfunction. These behaviors repeat themselves in conflict and dysfunction, again and again throughout the system that is life in these United States, with the same negative impacts. They include:

- adversarial thinking and decision making; contempt for those whose beliefs and perspectives differ from our own
- the impact of an unhealthy focus on ego and personal legacy
- the things not said
- prioritizing personal power over systemic growth
- unacknowledged racism and white supremacy
- systematic inequality in education, health care, employment, housing, life expectancy, poverty, a lack of public safety

- ecological change
- political stalemates that create winners and losers
- isolationism
- the dangers of magical thinking and subconscious myths

It would be almost impossible to create a hierarchy of these issues, so I am addressing them alphabetically.

Adversarial Thinking and Decision Making. We have become a country of enemies in different camps. We make decisions from those camps, to defeat other camps. We are so busy defining ourselves by the perceived failures of others that we rarely articulate what we stand for, much less continue to stand for it. A glaring example of adversarial thinking came from Speaker of the House Mitch McConnell. In February 2017, at a gathering of protesters at the American Legion Hall in Lawrenceburg, Kentucky, McConnell proclaimed, "Winners make policy; losers go home." The pride of democracy has been the willingness of individuals and ideologies to fight hard for their program, policy or point of view, and to come together for the good of all when a decision has been made. The growing adversarial rhetoric and behavior has changed this value, to the detriment of all.

Ego and Personal Legacy. It seems today that achieving personal power via position and wealth and the drive to create a personal legacy for one's self have become more important in this country than developing and sustaining organizations made up of good people working for the good of the community. As I travel the country as a consultant, I too often see the impact of this pattern in people who have been damaged by a lack of values in their workplaces, or lack of alignment of decisions and actions with a stated mission. This creates a lack of congruency that is confusing to both those who work for an organization and its constituents.

A conversation with one organizational head shed some light on this issue. David is the CEO of a one-hundred-year-old family-owned construction company. "I have a question for you," I said to him. "In your opinion, are there foundational characteristics that sustain the healthy functioning of an organization? If there are, can and should those characteristics be maintained across leader tenures? If they can and should be, why aren't they?"

David didn't miss a beat. "That's an easy answer," he said. "If you have the good of the company or organization and the people in it as your priority, you will look carefully at the guiding principles, the characteristics, as you say, that are foundational and allow the healthy functioning of the business. Foundational to me means that they are in place regardless of who is in charge, because without the foundation, the organization is weakened. If you take a chunk out of the foundation, or ignore it, because you just don't think it matters, then the whole foundation is weakened. You build on the things that worked, the things that are consistent with the values and mission. If the leader is driven by ego, rather than the good of the organization and its people, he will be more concerned with building a personal legacy and drawing attention to himself rather than the good of the company, its people and its role in the community. He may even be so threatened that previous successes diminish his own that he does away with things that are essential for the long-term success."

My questions were based on observations made consulting in various systems transitioning from one leader to another. An example close to my heart is my beloved Cleveland Browns. My dad was the team's Backfield Coach from their inception in 1945 through 1952, and its head coach from 1963 to 1970. The Cleveland Browns were known as one of the classiest organizations of professional football. There was a values-strong congruency from front office through football performance. When the franchise moved to Baltimore and took the name the Ravens in 1996, Cleveland fought long and hard to keep the name, the colors, and the logo. After five years, Cleveland was granted an expansion, or new team. The current team wears the name and the colors of the "old," historic Browns. A revolving door of personnel have failed to return a championship to the city. Meanwhile, the values-driven culture of the historic franchise lives in Baltimore, under a different name, and with continuing success. In Cleveland, it appears that any awareness of the values that shaped the "old" Browns has disappeared completely, and the few individuals who understood the value of passing on core values as a foundation to the future don't stay around long.

This is a familiar institutional story – fear that a former personal legacy will overshadow the new leader or will prevent new ideas from taking hold, or simply not understanding the importance of foundational values, strips away any opportunity to retain and build on what was good in the previous regimes. In fact, one of the major trends to be observed in organizations focused on solving all issues through changing leadership rather than focusing on the core beliefs of the organization is the hiring of leaders who are the exact opposite of the predecessor, usually with the same kind of gathering dissatisfactions haunting each new regime.

Sitting in an Oklahoma City hotel room on the May weekend of my granddaughter's college graduation, I had one of those moments of sheer gratitude that I had a glimpse of someone not only espousing values, but living them out, when I tuned in to get the weather and instead heard part of an interview with a man named Anthony Tjan, who was talking about writing a new book entitled Good People: The Only Leadership Decision That Really Matters. In a city whose TV stations and programs were not familiar to me, headed to a most important family occasion, the title clicked. (Later, I would order and inhale the book – and at publication time, am still endeavoring to get an interview with the man who believes that the world, as well as his business, can be a better place if good people with high values are in place.)

A few hours after that a-ha moment in my hotel room, I experienced a living example of what Tjan was talking about in the person of Celin Romero. I, of course (says proud grandmother), was present when my granddaughter was graduating from college, but was fortunate that my presence at that graduation allowed me to see the great Spanish guitarist awarded an Honorary Doctorate of Musical Arts by Oklahoma City University in May 2017. Romero, known for his virtuosity and elegance on the instrument, has been performing publicly since he was seven years old, and is perhaps best known as the driving force behind the Romero guitar quartet, known widely as "The Royal Family of the Guitar." His brother Pepe delivered a few words about his sibling prior to the presentation of the honorary degree. Pepe spoke of the famous agent who wanted to represent Celin, believing that fame and fortune were in the future for the gifted guitarist. Celin invited the agent to the Romero family home and introduced him to his talented father and brothers. For Celin, it was a natural consequence of his core values to think of his family rather than to focus solely on himself and opportunities he might have available as a soloist. For the agent, the values-driven meeting and a brother's concern for family over ego opened his eyes to the possibility of a unique performing ensemble that eventually became world-famous. The quartet regularly perform for presidents and royalty across the world, and its members are sought to teach their art. They have been knighted by Juan Carlos, King of Spain, and received the Gran Cruz la Orden d'Isabel de la Catholica, the highest honor that Spain can bestow on a civilian. "You see, what was important to my brother was family, and what was best for them," said Pepe.[35] "Family, the promise of making music together, and giving back to others was more important than fame or money."

Extraordinary values as well as extraordinary music.

---

35 Commencement at Oklahoma City University, Oklahoma City, OK, May 2017.

Ecological Change. An oft quoted fable says that the Emperor Nero played his fiddle while Rome burned in the great fire in A.D. 64, thus demonstrating his total disregard for the people of his country. It has been said that the ignoring or disclaiming of ecological change is our contemporary version of "fiddling while Rome burns." Scientific evidence is unequivocal; climate change is behind our rising sea levels, melting glaciers, more extreme heat events, fires and droughts, and extreme events like hurricanes and severe storms. While doubters will argue that climate change has always been with us, the speed of current changes indicate that human action is greatly impacting what is occurring today. I do not claim deep scientific knowledge on this subject. I do have a deep respect for the mounting evidence that human behavior is behind climate change, and we must take steps to alter that behavior to prevent ecological disaster.

Isolationism/Siloism. While we have more communications tools at our disposal and greater capacity for global interaction than ever before, we have become more isolated personally while simultaneously more prone to groupthink. We interact within silos of perspectives. All of this contributes to our political stalemates and adversarial thinking. During the recent presidential campaign, the Lexington Herald-Leader editorial page featured an archival photo of the young President-elect John Kennedy and his wife Jackie at dinner with Republican Senator John Sherman Cooper and his wife Lorraine in 1961. The accompanying editorial focused on the need for politics that enabled such across-the-aisle connections rather than the divisions which are present today. While this isolationist trend is experienced every day in the lives of American citizens, the aftermath of the shooting that took place at the Republican baseball practice has led Washington veterans to speak out about the increasingly adversarial atmosphere that is their lives. It is life in an echo chamber, where anyone outside is seen as the enemy, and post-debate friendship across partisan lines an act of disloyalty to the "brand" that must ultimately "win", for the good of the party, rather than the ultimate good of the nation and humanity.

In the late 1980s, I attended a national communications conference where the keynote speaker was a member of the Futurists organization. Two of his researched forecasts stayed with me. First, as technology advanced, the use of computers would change our lives beyond our imaginations, and second, over the next twenty years we would find more and more people working from home rather than gathering in office spaces, thus totally changing the face-to-face interactions long associated with the working world. I remember the follow-up discussions with colleagues, as we saw our floppy disks mounting up and worried about what degree of trust we had in the backup systems for our data. More importantly, we wondered about the alienation of working individually from personal spaces, without both the challenge and the creative and intellectual energy of daily interaction with associates both like and unlike ourselves. The poet John Donne wrote the words "No man is an island" four hundred years ago, comparing people to countries and speaking out for interconnectedness. In the face of the creeping isolationism of today, Donne's words might have been written in and for the twenty-first century.

A new awareness of the degree of isolation and siloism that have overtaken America has been growing steadily as the reality of divisions in our country stands on opposite sides of a new issue every day, from local elections to border walls, immigration, charter schools, and Confederate statues. The outing of intense hatred aimed at different ethnic groups in Charlottesville and its aftermath has spoken clearly of systematic online organizing among like-minded, for their time to "march on the world." It is a far cry from the vision we have carried as a united people.

Personal Power and Greed Over Systemic Good and Empowerment of Others. In one of my Talking Together seminars, an elderly gentleman appeared disturbed as we discussed the question "When have you been sad, angry, irritated, or disappointed to be an American?" When the facilitator at his table asked if she might help him in some way, the man replied, "It's just that my pain is so old, it hardly seems worth talking about." "If the question brought it to your mind, I'd suggest it's worth talking about," the facilitator said encouragingly. The following story emerged from the nearly 90-year-old's memory.

As a young man raising a family in a small town, he volunteered to work with youth in his community. The community had a youth room above the fire station, and the kids loved the space, but Russ had some concerns about the stability of the old building. In particular, it seemed to him that the floor was rotting in several spots. He shuddered to think of what could happen if the floor gave way while a youth meeting was going on. He spoke to the head of the community organization board, who took a look at the situation and invited Russ to speak to the board about the need to replace the rotting boards and shore up the subfloor. The board heard Russ's presentation, which included cost for the project, and said they would study the proposal and have an answer at the next meeting.

When Russ arrived at the following meeting, an uncomfortable chair and one board member were in the room. Turning to Russ, the lone board member said sarcastically, "It is interesting how easily the have-nots want to spend the money of the haves." The answer was no. There would be no new floor in the youth room.

In the seventy-some years that had passed since this incident, Russ had himself become a "have," a man of some wealth and prestige who never failed to share what he had and to empower others. And the bitter learning of that long-ago time had never left him. He told the Talking Together group that part of his continuing sadness was that he believes people in our country are focused far more on personal power and greed than on empowering others. "I am old," he said. "I've done what I can and I can only hope and pray that the trend I see in the country today will be stopped, and we will again become a nation that empowers and shares."

Magical Thinking, Inappropriate Optimism, and Subconscious Myths. I believe that, as a people, we are living with levels of magical thinking. First, we tend to see people and situations as we would like them to be rather than as they really are. Second, as a country and a people, we live with the subconscious myth that anything is possible. Another layer of that myth is the belief that America is a Christian country. The current polarization in the United States is due in part to reactive responses to these unconscious structures. It is easier to engage in the magical thinking that we are moving steadily forward.

The issue that we must face first is moving beyond this magical thinking to accepting the reality of the present, rather than the utopia of which we dream or the dystopia we fear. While the old way of viewing the world may have worked in the past, it is not serving us well today. It drags us into a victim state where we see ourselves, the "good people of the good society", unfairly and shockingly encountering the bad. It completely ignores the coexistence of good and evil, within ourselves and in the culture. As victims, we may flail about in our despair too long, stuck in the quicksand of shock and disbelief. This stuckness keeps us from accepting reality, grieving the reality, and dusting ourselves off to choose a response that accepts our individual responsibility for changing that reality.

Change is hard. Perhaps my mind is attracted to the new first, or I have an emotional response that engages my heart. Both of these elements are critical, but the third tells the tale. My desire to make the change – my will – must be engaged sufficiently to do the work that is required. Like the quarterback determined to change the angle of his throwing arm, or the violinist doing the necessary repetitions to change a finger pattern, without the will to follow the mind and the heart, the new way will remain an ideal rather than an action.

During the twenty years when I served as a teacher trainer in Suzuki Talent Education, I taught the introductory unit to violin teachers who were in the class because they had a desire to teach this new approach to playing the violin. Presumably, then, they were present with head, heart, and will ready to learn. Each, however, came from a traditional method of instruction in their own lives which lived at a subconscious level inside them, so ingrained that it was an automatic filter for new information – a filter often stronger than the stated desire to learn the new way. During the introduction to each teacher training session, I would ask that the teacher trainees frame their experience with two ideological concepts. First was the literary "willing suspension of disbelief," that essential ingredient of storytelling that allows the listener to suspend their own judgment about the implausibility of a situation. In other words, I asked them to be willing to hold their previous training and experience to the side during this training, while they engaged with something new and different and allowed it to add to their previous experiences. The second concept was the Zen idea of beginner's mind, which says to the experts, there are no options because they already know all that can be known. The eternal beginner is always seeking more information to add to their reservoir. In civil dialogue, and in our ongoing lives in this day and time, both concepts would be truly helpful in moving past magical thinking, inappropriate optimism, and subconscious myths to a new reality.

Systematic Inequality. Much lip service has been given over the years to America as the "melting pot;" the land of equal opportunity. In truth, story after story, both biographical and fictional, tell another tale of dreams and lives shattered by the reality of life in the United States. Data reveals there are inequities in all major areas of life: education, health care, employment, housing, security, life expectancy. The equality thing is a better story to tell than a life to live, and as the melting pot has grown larger, the fear of losing control of the system has strengthened resistance to all efforts for equality. While the election of Barack Obama was a high point in the lives of many Americans, it struck a huge fear in the hearts of others, a fear that has seen an acting out of unspoken racism, and a return to a fierce re-engagement with white supremacy behaviors.

This spring and summer of 2017 has seen white supremacy unmasked, and the voices of those who live with inequity demand to be heard, whether by marching, by protesting or counter-protesting, or by taking the knee at football games. It is almost impossible for those who live with privilege to truly understand the passion behind the voices. There are equal frustrations over what many name "political correctness," saying "we've gone too far." The thing I can say is this: I have lived with privilege most of my life. It was becoming a single-again adult in a world geared for coupled and married people that gave me a tiny taste of inequity, and led me to twenty years of advocacy geared to opening the eyes of a system. I will never forget leading an awareness training for a group of professionals in North Carolina. We were engaging in an exercise about the number of chairs arranged at tables in public places, and particularly in churches. (Even numbered.) As I floated by a table, I heard one man say to another, "She's asking us to believe that being single is normal." The tone of disbelief said that he wasn't buying it. His comment also spoke to the lack of awareness, the inability to see the preferential treatment given to the coupled and married. As I said, this is but a minuscule taste of what minority groups have been experiencing throughout their lives. One of the things I learned in those years of working with and for single adults is that reaction was related to fear – fear that somehow normalizing singularity would be detrimental to marriage and family. I believe that those same kinds of fears – fear of losing something important, like control and/or domination – drives the resistance to normalizing equality and working together to achieve it. Watching multi-ethnic groups braving the flood waters in Houston in rescue after rescue, someone said, "There is a true depiction of who Americans are. We can accept their bravery; we just can't admit that we are all equal when we're not saving lives in an emergency."

The Things Left Unsaid. One of the huge patterns in our country is the inability to tell the whole truth and nothing but the truth. We leave things unsaid, disguising truth with abstract language, thus creating anxiety in those around us. The excuses for doing so are usually personal privacy and a fear of legal action. Just as equal opportunity and racism are carefully walked around, so too are things left unsaid. A long-time employee has "elected to resign" or "chosen to take another position," while the real reasons are guessed at, adding to the general anxiety in the system. In the South, it's the "bless their heart" syndrome, a tag line that means, "you have no idea how awful this really is." In polite Southernese, it is said with a charming smile and a chill in the eyes that belies the words. For Southernness in action, watch The Help.

As a cross-country consultant, I have learned that every area of the country has their version of the things left unsaid, and what is said to avoid the truth, although friends from other sections of the country believe themselves to be much more direct than their Southern counterparts! My observation is that it is more about systemic patterns than geography. We do not know how to speak directly, clearly, and honestly, nor do we know how to deal with the people who do, so accustomed are we to verbal manipulation.

Two book titles by sociologist Stephanie Coontz, *The Way We Never Were* and *The Way We Really Are*, encapsulate a big truth that has us in its grip. We are living in a big sprawling country that is radically different from the "new world" to which many of our ancestors brought their hopes and dreams generations ago. We are living in a time of not only unprecedented change but unprecedented speed of change, with no time to assimilate, to grieve that which is inevitably left behind in the wake of progress, or decisions that don't feel right for my particular part of the country or seem to respect my belief system. It's easy to feel nostalgic for something slower, more familiar, less challenging.

What Coontz points out to us is that when we become nostalgic, we tend to remember only the good parts of a time long past, and not the minor inconveniences or the major difficulties. Each of us, in looking back, look through our own lens of experience, a lens which brings back the strong emotions of situations and events that benefited us personally, but blurs the images of ways in which those same situations and events caused great pain to others. So the question becomes, exactly what period of time are we nostalgic for, and what parts of it would we be willing to relive to get the feelings of comfort or privilege we remember? A child of the 1950s, I might think fondly of the telephone operators who, when I called home, would say, "Honey, the line is busy," and the downtown merchants who knew I was "Dr. Jo's grandchild." But do I really want to give up my cell phone or laptop? Certainly, I recall a sense of security, but as an adult, I must acknowledge that part of that sense of security had nothing to do with technology or the size of my hometown, or who was in political office, and everything to do with a kind of innocence and joyful lack of responsibility that can only be truly ours in that one time of life. And even then, that sense of security was only available to for those privileged to live in the abundance that allows it, rather than the scarcity or poverty that brings early recognition that the world, for all of its possibility and beauty, can be an unforgiving place.

So there's the truth, stark and unvarnished. We have come a long way, and we have a long way to go still. It is hard not to personalize the struggles that are our roadblocks on our way, particularly when we, or people we know and love, are impacted by them. When the work we are doing may not show results in our lifetime, we must choose to fight in faith that the change will happen. When the ideas and actions for which we stand, and our role in working for change are questioned, ridiculed, or worse, ignored. We each have our own examples of giving our heart and soul to a calling, and running smack dab into institutional and systemic roadblocks wherever we turn.

In the late 1960s the Suzuki Talent Education method for string instrument instruction was new to the United States and certainly new to Lexington, Kentucky. Traditional music educators and professional musicians tended to look skeptically at the young students carrying their tiny violin cases, performing credible renditions of Vivaldi and Bach without reference to musical scores. There were devoted parents attending lessons and supervising at-home practice, and there were those who looked at pioneers and, like one Lexington attorney, asked bluntly, "Are you sure you really understand what Dr. Suzuki is doing?" For every skeptic, there was a Harriet, mother of a young violinist, who as both a parent and a pre-school teacher had heard the song deep in her heart. Her youngest child was still in the early stages of learning the violin when the Suzuki Tour Group came to Lexington, ten young Japanese students, ages 5 to 12. On stage, the young virtuosos played music that transcended language; off the stage, they formed friendships with the Lexington children that were beyond any language barrier, playing games in the autumn-hued neighborhoods like the normal children they were. Their laughter, as their music, was universal. One father, looking at the symbol of the rising sun on the luggage tags of the children, said pensively, "And to think we once shot at that flag!" Reflecting on the experience of cross- cultural connections, Harriet wrote of a new and visceral understanding that had come to her as she experienced the visit of the Tour Group children, and her awareness of how easy it is to simply believe that we in America have a handle on it all, and everyone wants to be just like us. Instead, she had her eyes opened to an "other" culture and its people, and found her own small world broadened, expanded, and changed forever. She could not go back to what she had been before; only forward to integrate and pass on what she had experienced. None of us knew what was to come, only that we were called to something more.

In 1966, Jim Brown, the greatest running back the game of pro football had ever known, hung up his cleats. He was 31 years old. The occasion was not marked by a $1,000-per-plate dinner, but by an evening at the Cleveland Arena to benefit the Negro Industrial and Economic Union, which Jim had founded to support black businesses. In 1988, he founded the Amer-I-Can organization, a program to teach life skills to young men whose backgrounds might prevent them from finding a productive place in American life. On Thanksgiving Eve of 2016, he and LeBron James were feeding the homeless in downtown Cleveland. In an interview on CNN, Jim Brown was asked why he had stated that post-presidential election, he was hopeful for the country. His answer was vintage Jim Brown, straightforward and to the point, underscored by the still-massive figure of a great athlete, wearing a Cleveland Browns sweatshirt as he dished up turkey and dressing for the homeless: "Now we know where people really stand, and people know that they have to get out and do their part. Everybody has to do the work." At the age of 81, he's still pushing through defenses in his fight for justice and equality.

When the young Cassius Clay stood on the Sixth Street bridge, he could not really see the other side when he chose to stay with a fight that was greater than any match that ever took him into a boxing ring. Still to come were the criticisms of his choice of a new name and a new faith; the stripping of his championship when he chose not to go to war, but to honor the principles of peace of his chosen Muslim religion; the support which dropped away; the facing of a possible prison sentence; the years away from the ring. As we face our roadblocks, we remember that when the chips were down, support for Ali came in the form of relationships – the gathering of some of the professional sports world's greatest athletes, who heard his story and stood with him, regardless of the risk to their own reputations or careers. These were not relationships based on thinking exactly alike on every subject, but on core values from which thoughts, decisions, and actions are formed. Relationships in which questioning and challenging each other, and telling hard truths to each other, is the norm. Such was the group who assembled to ask questions of Muhammad Ali, and then to stand with and for him.

In order for us to sustain our efforts to make the individual changes that will allow us to talk together with respect and civility, to negotiate and compromise so we can progress toward the larger systemic and institutional changes, we must each find a way to sustain ourselves physically, emotionally and mentally for the long haul. When change is on the horizon, there will always be skeptics and resisters, as well as the roadblocks of the institutions and the system itself.

The group of supporters who came together to support Ali became known as the Cleveland Summit, gathered by the Cleveland Browns' great running back Jim Brown in the city of Cleveland. From the time I first heard the call of the song for freedom and peace, my work has been sustained by the knowledge of a far-flung ever-evolving group of others who continue to believe and work as well. The power of such a personal summit group is collective sustainability, as some will carry on while others are exhausted, allowing time for each to rejuvenate in turn, whether it is the body which must recover in order to continue, or the soul.

My "Cleveland Summit" has never been in one geographic location at the same time. They have entered my life at different times, and we have recognized each other. I held the door of a conference center for a man carrying an armload of newsprint, and shortly thereafter we found ourselves in the same staff orientation meeting. Strangers until we entered that building, by the end of a weekend's work, we were, without invitation or articulation, part of something bigger than either of us. The leaders of those long ago, back to back, life-changing experiences of music and human relations have all finished their earthly lives, yet they are actively with me every single day of my life. There were the Harriets in Lexington, and literally across the world, who caught the dream of one Japanese violin teacher. Across the country, a long-ago journalist colleague's newest book *Meditations in Times of Despair* grabs my weary spirit and lifts it up, and I pass it on to others who are tired, so tired. And there are those with whom the initial connection was an experience of disagreement or frustration, strengthened by honest confrontation and working through.

It may sound like a simplistic answer, but I believe it is an essential part of sustaining the work that must be done to address the institutional and systemic roadblocks to live in the knowledge of such support. As the numbers grow of those who have learned to speak with rationality and civility, and to listen with respect, so too will our capacity grow in our willingness and ability to negotiate, to compromise, to change. It cannot and will not happen in the midst of polarization and division. It is both/and, the individual and the systemic, and a team to support our work for the long haul. There is only one way to cross the bridge, and that is by coming together.

The young man who stood on the Sixth Street Bridge had no way to know that on the other side of the bridge would be his greatest achievements, after he left the ring for good, or that his magnificent body would be ravaged by the cruel forces of a Parkinson's disease that respected no champions. Neither could he have known that weakened by illness, he would carry the Olympic flame into the stadium in Atlanta in 1996 as people around the world cheered. That his funeral would bring together interfaith leaders from the Muslim, Christian, and Jewish faiths, kings, former presidents, celebrities from many life platforms, thousands of onlookers who lined the roadsides chanting his name. His wife, Lonnie Ali, said that her husband wanted "young people of every background to see his life as proof that adversity can make you stronger. It cannot rob you of your power to dream, and to reach your dreams."

There will not be another Ali, but his story reminds us that even in the face of systemic and institutional roadblocks and the sadness of horrific illness, much that is good can happen when there is persistence.

Martin Luther King, Jr. said, "The moral arc of the universe is long, but it bends toward justice." Sometimes it appears to bend away, and our passion is dimmed by disappointment, tarnished with discouragement. The music may be more difficult to hear at such times, but it is still playing, sending its call to all who would hear and compelled by the music, fling their own songs into the brokenness. As we stand on the bridge, we, too, are called to keep on singing, keeping on for justice and peace, gathering others to travel with us as we go.

Moving Forward to Action:
Questions for reflection and sharing

1. What systemic issues are of most concern to me? Who do I know locally who I can speak to about my concern? Nationally? Have you spoken out about your concerns? Why or why not?

2. How might you speak up and out now? Detail your action plan. Who might you include to work with you? What is your time frame? What is your backup plan?

3. Who are the people in your Cleveland Summit? How are you taking care of yourself to empower the long haul?

CHAPTER ELEVEN

Where Do We Go From Here?

"There came a moment in the middle of the song when we suddenly felt every heartbeat in the room, and after that, we never forgot we were part of something much bigger." – Brian Andreas, contemporary poet[36]

Juxtaposed against the modern high-rises in the main shopping district of Berlin is the bombed Gedächtniskirche, the Kaiser Wilhelm Church. Built in 1890, it was heavily damaged in the 1943 bombing raids on Berlin. In 1959, new church construction began surrounding the damaged old spire, the base of which has been transformed into a memorial hall. I walked the ruins in 1987 while in Berlin for a Suzuki Talent Education worldwide conference. As I traversed the church, the absolute devastation of war hit me in the gut, as though physically assaulted. I remember the silence among the crowds of people moving slowly through the memorial hall, staring at the symbols of war and peace, the panels depicting the history of the church. Alone yet strangely unified with hundreds of strangers, I stood looking at the damaged figure of Christ which had once stood on the high altar of the church. On its right was a cross of nails, made from nails from the roof timbers of Coventry Cathedral. To its left, an Icon cross, given by the Russian Orthodox Church. The haunting specter of war hung over me like a pall as I made my way out of the church and back into the busy city.

Later, I walked for miles along the still-intact Berlin Wall two years before it would come down, accompanied by my daughter Diane, a violin teacher, and our colleague Joanna. We read the poignant, often desperate messages on the wall from family members, separated from each other on either side. We talked quietly together about the contrast of being in that city while about the business of creating harmony in the world through

---

36 Andreas, Brian. From Story People, 2017.

music. In 2014 I would experience the same kinds of surreal feelings as I sat beside the reflecting pond at the National Memorial in Oklahoma City, listening to the horrific story told by a park ranger of how one man's hatred was the cause of unimaginable death and destruction. I was in Oklahoma to present the work of Talking Together at the "Reclaiming the Gospel of Peace" conference, and as in my experience in Berlin, the contrast between the hope of many people years after the devastation, and the reminder of where hate and division can lead us was terrifyingly, tangibly real.

And so today, as we face another period in our history when divisions in our country are tearing at the very foundations of our democracy, leaving holes as gaping as those open to the elements in the ruined church spire in Berlin, and erecting walls as ugly and impenetrable as the one which physically and ideologically divided Berlin for twenty-eight years, I believe that it is imperative that we take action, to ensure that the escalating slide in that direction stops now. In the wake of the most contentious presidential election of recent years, sales of the dystopian novel 1984, written by George Orwell in 1949, hit a new high. The rise of new dystopian fiction predicting dire consequences that are both similar to and more chilling than 1984 is a warning to us. Danger! What are we going to do about it?

I received another wake-up call recently from another piece of fiction. It was an early April Sunday morning in Kentucky. The air was balmy here, and the sun tipped the redbuds dotting the new green leafing on my drive to Lexington for a writing retreat. It was a gentle sort of morning, no ominous skies predicting storms, no driving rain or wind or ice. As usual, I was accompanied on my hour's drive by my local public radio station. On this Sunday morning, "Weekend Edition" was airing an interview that so "ungentled" my day, that as soon as the writing retreat was over, I hurried to the bookstore to get a copy of Omar El Akkad's novel American War, a dystopian telling of a second American Civil War, a devastating plague, and how one family became caught in the middle. According to a blurb by the book's publisher, it is a story that asks what might happen if America were to turn its most devastating policies and deadliest weapons on itself.

I plunged into the book and found myself pulled into a dark narrative that bore down on me with such ferocity that it seemed as if I was caught with the characters in a series of life circumstances that take Sarat, the main character, who is six years old when the story begins, and her family to a Mississippi refugee camp where unspeakable horrors form her growing up years. As a result, all of Sarat's love and curiosity are sucked out of her, and her life is redirected toward hatred and revenge. Throughout the reading, I had to remind myself that it was not some third world country the author was writing about, but America. America!

Each time I paused in my reading, I could not shake the feeling of returning from a visit to a grim place, filled with warning. Images of Berlin and Oklahoma City flashed through my mind. There are places we must not go, now or ever again. Words that the author had spoken on that Saturday morning returned to me now with dark intensity: "Once the switch of hatred has been turned on, almost nothing can turn it off again."

Writing in his seminal work Generation to Generation about what we can learn from considering observable patterns in history, Rabbi Ed Friedman's voice echoes in my brain as he points us once again toward paying attention to those patterns in our human systems: "the most immediate threat to the regeneration and perhaps the survival of American civilization is this…we are polluting our own species."[37] So, where do we go from here? What will we choose?

The message of this book is about closing the door on hate and instead, choosing respect, kindness, civility, and love. It is about being intentional about switching off hate so it does not destroy us. Our current reality requires that we choose now, with great intentionality, to act. We cannot afford to wait, to think that someone else will do it.

It is my hope that, as you have read these chapters, you will have begun to consider how you might be called to be a change agent, both in your immediate circle and beyond. Perhaps you are starting to see opportunities opening up for more civil dialogue. Whether a clear call has come to you or you are looking for signposts toward action for yourself, or to offer others, here are pointers for the way forward.

One. I believe we must choose to leave whatever our place of comfort is, whether emotionally, intellectually, or physically, and in so doing, learn how we react, what behaviors we exhibit, when we are not in our comfort zones. For to seek a change in the conversation in our world, to seek civil dialogue, is to be with others, those unlike ourselves, in places we might not normally choose to be. I remember when my excitement about my first trip to Japan was interrupted by my horrified awareness that I would be unable to even figure out basic signage done in Japanese characters. I would be traveling for five weeks with my eleven- and fourteen-year-old daughters, and I was determined not to show them how uncomfortable I was in this anticipation. My discomfort led me to a general grumpiness and displacement of anxiety on everyone and everything around me! Similarly, the girls' father was definitely out of his comfort zone when exchange

---

37 Friedman, Edwin H. Ibid.

students from Japan or France came to stay at our home. His "I'm feeling uncomfortable in this strangeness" behavior was to SPEAK AS LOUDLY AS POSSIBLE as if the foreign visitors were deaf!

During a recent Talking Together session I gave these two examples to participants as I asked them to consider when they have been called to leave the familiar and comfortable and be in an environment that is strange to them, or with people unlike themselves. Those sharing at tables concluded that often they had been called to the unfamiliar by life itself, finding themselves unexpectedly out of their comfort zones, while not geographically far from the place they call home. One participant described the ethnic mix in her class when she went to nursing school as her first experience of diversity. Raised in a small, sheltered community, she had never had contact with people from other countries or backgrounds. "Unsettled and uncomfortable" in the beginning, over the months she discovered commonalities with those who initially seemed very different from her. She found they were not only aligned by their commitment to the caring profession, but that her classmates possessed qualities such as integrity and humor that laid the foundation for forming deep friendships. Another participant told of finding herself in an unfamiliar part of the city she had lived in her entire life during a local leadership course for civic leaders. "Part of my discomfort was about myself, feeling shocked and finally a little embarrassed at what I didn't know about this city I professed to know so well. The other discomfort was in simply not knowing how to respond as we were meeting the people of these neighborhoods—that is, what should I say? And thinking ahead, what can I do now that I am aware of my discomfort?"

Participants summarized their reactive behaviors as follows:

1. Acting inappropriately in the new setting, i.e. talking too much, too little, too loudly; trying too hard; making awkward, clumsy, socially unacceptable blunders.
2. Withdrawing from encounter with new environment or people.
3. Returning to the safety of one's own environment and like-minded people.

Most of us can identify times that when in an unfamiliar situation, we have reacted in similar ways. Once we are aware of our own response to being out of our comfort zone, we can imagine how others might react when they are in the unfamiliar, like when someone new comes into my own familiar and comfortable circle or environment. As we practice being out of our own comfort zones, we develop more empathy for others when they are out of their comfort zones, as well. With such awareness, we can become more confident about stepping out of our own safe places in order to encounter the "other" and open ourselves to new relationships. We understand that this discomfort is a short-term thing, and something that everyone goes through.

A starting point might be a Christian-Muslim-Jewish dialogue, with a time for mingling afterwards. Or a community discussion group around a topic you know is heated for many. Let me emphasize it is a starting point only, albeit a good one. It is an introductory step that allows for the possibility of entering into a relationship with an "other" in an ongoing way. True dialogue becomes possible when we participate in events where stories are shared, perspectives are broadened, and true dialogue becomes possible. One model to emulate comes from the work of Unlearn Fear and Hate in Lexington, Kentucky, a project designed to promote public dialogue and civic engagement, created by Transylvania University professors Kremena Todorova and Kurt Gohde. Public sessions, such as an evening prayer circle where people of all faiths surrounded their Muslim brothers and sisters with candles while they prayed, have led to smaller, more intimate gatherings including a yoga group. In such settings there are opportunities for real learning about each other, and the development of relationships. "When a new Muslim friend and I were making a plan to meet for coffee, I found myself surprised when she suggested Starbucks," says Kremena. "I had to ask myself why I was surprised, why I thought our differences might lead us to different choices for something as simple and ordinary as a favorite place to have a cup of coffee. Yet our choice was the same."

Two. A commitment to learning the skills of civil dialogue. The next step is taking the time to participate beyond get-acquainted sessions. It means attending a session of Talking Together or any other training which has such skill building as its purpose. I recommend a commitment of anywhere from fifteen hours to a week of your life. Consider this question: what is the cost of investing fifteen hours, the cost of investing a week, as opposed to the kind of world El Akkad depicts?

Training takes time. A consequence of our too-fast-paced world is that we have forgotten that real learning does not happen overnight. The speed of technology has given us the expectation that a message sent will not only be delivered in seconds, but an answer will be forthcoming in just a few seconds more. That information can be accessed just as rapidly by the push of a button. Impatience is not an ally when it comes to building skills in any medium, and not an ally in learning the skills of civil dialogue. Recently, Cynthia, an elementary school teacher, told me that she was requiring her fourth- and fifth-graders to use dictionaries and encyclopedias in the classroom, rather than relying exclusively on their smart phones and computers. She said, "The easy answer to their 'why?' is that they need to know how to access information when their fancy gadgets lose power. But the more important answer, to me, is that they need to experience how information becomes a part of them – not a few words to plug into a report and be forgotten, but something of value that impacts how they see the world, and how they behave in that world. That takes time, and it can't happen with a simple click!"

Training and practice in the skills of civil dialogue are like that. Remember the analogy of learning to ride a bike. Remember the work of changing the way of doing something to a new and better way. And ask yourself this question: how many hours am I willing to give to work that will stop us from sliding into another civil war? Stop the building of more walls of division? Stop the acts of hatred?

A reminder of the good news about the promise of committing time to training can be found in the name given to the work "Unlearn Fear and Hate." The words come from the poem "Love Letter to the World" by Affri-lachian poet Frank X Walker:

> We can't pass the course on humanity
> if we keep failing the lessons
> on harmony
> and until we unlearn fear and hate.[38]

The good news, says founders of the Unlearn Fear and Hate organization, is that we were not born hating, but learned it somewhere along the way. What we learned, we can unlearn. And that surely makes it worth the commitment of time and effort.

Three. Create a follow-up group to the training and this book for continuing practice, feedback, and support as you model civil dialogue in your circle of influence. Changing old behavior, as we have stated, is hard, and those familiar old habits of behavior loom ready to drag us back to the way we've always done things. We need other journeyers for support and feedback and for helping us get back on the path when we might falter by ourselves. Individuals who attend Talking Together seminars can opt

---

38 Walker, Frank X. Love Letter to the World. 2016. Used with permission.

to participate afterward in quarterly check-in sessions, where people who have attended the training can spend an hour at a local coffee shop or restaurant, sharing with each other their attempts to practice their skills in their families, workplaces, or elsewhere.

Four. Invite others, particularly those you know who have different perspectives from you, to go with you to a training and a follow-up group. Encourage them to pass it on. Remember the monkeys whose new practice of washing their sweet potatoes became a new normal across the world when the hundredth monkey took up the practice. When enough people adopt a behavioral practice, exponential growth can happen.

Think of a time when you were invited to attend an event where you knew no one, and perhaps had never been to the particular building where the event was taking place. Maybe you did not know the neighborhood. Perhaps you were fortunate and had a friend or acquaintance who not only invited you to attend the event, but offered to drive you there, and introduced you to people when you arrived. Then think about a time when you may have gone to an event in an unfamiliar place by yourself, where you knew no one. Contrasting the two experiences may be a good reminder that including an invitation for a ride and introduction to a few people as part of your invitation to a person to join you in civil dialogue is a really good step toward building bridges!

Between Talking Together sessions, I make it a practice to have lunch or a cup of tea with someone in my life who views the world from a different perspective than I do. Not only do I want to encourage the relationship itself; I also want to build on something I know we do share, namely, awareness that there needs to be a change in the conversation in our future. Despite our differences, I want us to be able to talk honestly about uncomfortable topics. I want to share my experience with Talking Together and invite them to take part. All too frequently, what I experience is fear that this is one more situation of political divide, where partisan opinions and emotions will preclude any real dialogue.

My answer is always the same. Talking Together is not about political parties or particular individuals. It is about going deeper, under what divides us to look for possible areas of common concern. Over lunch with a dear friend who truly fits this description, I asked what might keep her from joining in this effort for changing the conversation, knowing well that she was as concerned about the hatred and violence as I was. "I am tired of being judged as uncaring when my views differ from someone else's," she told me. 'I care about people a great deal. I may have a different opinion on how to live out that caring in terms of policies and allocation of funds than some other people, but I don't want to be in a roomful of people who are judging me in that way." It is the hardest area of all, inviting people different from ourselves to join in the training. There will be those who turn down any effort – but we must keep asking.

Five. There are many voices taking to social media and other ways of communication to express their desire for ending hatred and violence, for creating a world where kindness, compassion, and respect are the norm. The important question is this: if this is your goal, where are you personally putting these characteristics into practice? Where are you actively sharing your beliefs with others? Are you taking your practices into action groups where your voice and modeling can be seen and heard? You are the alternative to hatred and vengeance. And those alternatives must be seen and heard in order to change the conversation as widely as possible. None of us can wait for people to come to us, or isolate ourselves with our individual passions. If your passion is the arts, hopefully you are using your skills for civil dialogue in every arts-related situation. But please remember not to use those skills exclusively in arts-related organizations. Step out to learn about other aspects of your community which are less familiar to you, passing on your skills and broadening your relationships. (Hint: your willingness to look at community gardens, Little League sports, or other fields of interest will, in turn, cause people from those groups to look with new or renewed interest at the arts, or your particular passion, as well as spreading the practices of civil dialogue wherever you go.)

One of the strengths of social media is sharing acts of respect and civility. Recently a woman and her son were seated behind an NFL star on an airplane. The ten-year-old boy watched every move the player made, noting the healthy snacks he ate and the extreme politeness he exhibited to everyone with whom he came in contact. The mother quickly wrote a thank you to the young man, and handed it to him as she left the plane, thanking him for being such a great role model for her son. As the story has circulated online, people have taken note of how what we do impact others, whether our behavior is a positive model or a negative one. In addition, several posts have indicated people deciding to carry pen and paper with them so they can express their thanks to those who are modeling civility and respect!

Six. Take your practices to the next generation. We know that the model of hatred and violence has invaded our classrooms and homes, indoctrinating the next generation in destructive ways. It is crucial that you – yes, you, and you, and you – take steps to influence our educators at every level of every school to teach and model civil dialogue. Introduce your resources to people you know. Go to school board meetings. Talk to teachers. Offer to volunteer to help train our youngest now. We cannot wait. They are the present and they are the future, and we must not enable a future of hatred and vengeance that robs them, like Sarat, of their curiosity and love, but empower them for a future of respect, kindness and civility.

When my granddaughter Virginia was about eight years old, she asked me if I thought there would ever be a woman president of the United States. I told her that I believed that in her lifetime, if not mine, we would see it happen. "It could even be me," she said. I asked her what she would like to see come to pass if she was president. She told me that she had a dream of a "School for Listening." It would be mandatory in the United States, and someday, everywhere in the entire world, for people to attend the school. She told me, "They would learn how to really listen to what people were saying to each other. Not just what they think the person is saying, but what the person really means. What they believe with all their heart. Because they'd be listening with their hearts, so they could really hear. That's what we'd teach them to do. Then people would be able to understand each other better, so there wouldn't be so much trouble in the world." How old would you have to be to go to this school, I inquired. Virginia thought a minute and then answered, "Five, I think. By the time you're five, you know when someone is sad, or when they're hurt, or when they're angry. So you could start to really learn to listen. It's hard to really listen if you don't know the difference. But when you know the different feelings, you can learn to listen. And Gamma, we could be in the same class, because no one is too old to go to the school for listening, and the ages would all be together, so everyone could learn from each other." Listen up, educators. It's an idea whose time has come!

Doris, a second grade teacher, made it a practice to have a special session with the girls in her class to talk about how to treat others. "This 'mean girl' thing starts early," she said, "and I want to nip it in the bud. These early years are when habits are formed, and we have to let them know what is acceptable, and what is unacceptable."

Jessica, a first grade teacher in a low socioeconomic environment in Lexington, Kentucky, attended a Talking Together seminar out of her concern for the hatred, disrespect, and ugliness with which her students spoke, both to her and to each other. Afterwards, she said, "Talking Together was a great training for me to attend as an elementary school teacher in the public schools. So many people could really benefit from learning how to talk to each other in a respectful way. I strongly believe that the earlier we teach children how to do this, the bigger difference we will see in our world in the coming years."

Seven. Do not stop and do not lose hope. Stay connected every day to those in your local circle and those you connect with globally who are determined to change the conversation. It will not be a quick or easy road, but we must not ever stop. When asked if they had been discouraged by roadblocks to their work along the way, Kremena Todorova and Kurt Gohde, founders of Unlearn Fear and Hate, responded that when they encounter roadblocks there are three things that keep them going. First, they work as a team, and when one is discouraged, the other is the encourager. Second, says Kurt, when he steps back and de-personalizes, he is aware that what he considers a roadblock, if not a deliberate attempt to sabotage, may simply be someone doing the job they were hired to do. He cites the time the logo of Unlearn Fear and Hate was chalked onto the sidewalk at the University of Kentucky, an act that required extensive steps for permission. The image lasted only a few hours before it was power-washed off by university maintenance. "I could think of it as deliberate," said Kurt. "I prefer to think of it as people hired to keep university property in good condition, and part of that would be free of graffiti. If I was paid to do that job, I might not even be aware that this was different, and there by permission, I would simply be doing my job." Third, not stopping often means redirecting efforts, for perhaps the one hundredth or even one thousandth time. A redirection can seem like a step backward rather than forward motion. Yet, all those interviewed who have worked for civility, peace, and justice in our world for decades say that the key to holding hope in the face of obstacles is about how one chooses to respond. If response includes the openness to information and experience in the redirect that might have been unavailable in the original effort, there will be pieces of the puzzle to be found along the way. If the response is to add to the vitriol by blaming, the gifts to be found in the redirect will be missed in the blindness of frustration.

Bill Strickland, founder of the Pittsburgh-based Manchester Bidwell Corporation, walked a long road from the poverty of his youth to a degree from the University of Pittsburgh, the MacArthur Genius Award, and the 2011 Go! Peace Award. One of his most important contributions to societal change is the clarity with which he shares the relationship between the "depressing extent of corruption and decay" that dominates his memory of the ghetto that was his neighborhood as a child, a neighborhood that was shaping his outlook on life, and the awareness of beauty which opened his eyes to the possibility of a different, better life. "It was as if some meanness had infected the neighborhood at its very core, and was killing off Manchester from the inside out." He tells how his life was turned around by an art teacher who introduced beauty into his young life by using Bill's fascination with the teacher's work at the pottery wheel to help him see beyond the limitations of his environment and give him hope for something better. His creation of job training and youth art centers across the world always begin with the establishment of a beautiful environment, which in itself, stimulates learning and provides an experience of beauty where there had been none. Strickland believes the exposure to such an environment is the key to opening the path of hope and aspiration for a better way. But carrying those values with him did not shield Strickland from roadblocks that might have killed both his spirit and the work. The death of Martin Luther King, Jr. and the anger and violence that followed; a fire at his school; the slashing of federal funding for social programs in the 1980s – time and again there were circumstances that brought Strickland to a sense of despair at ever seeing his dream realized. He is clear about the setbacks that he experienced along the way. He is equally clear that with each setback came a redirect, and each redirect led him to a connection with a person who would later have great impact on his project and his life.[39] For Bill, the connections go out from him to others who stepped in to introduce him to a local change-maker, or point the way to granting possibilities. He is also aware that he, like each of us, may also be the point of connection for someone out there who is searching for an anchor to keep them grounded in their dreams.

Josh Nadzam also grew up in the inner city of Pittsburgh. Running track became his way out of a life of poverty, broken family, and tragedies. The numerous letters he wrote to college track coaches brought only one response, from the University of Kentucky, who offered a scholarship to the field and cross-country runner. It was while earning a master's degree in social work in Lexington that Nadzam heard of the man with whom he shared a hometown, and traveled to Pittsburgh to meet Bill Strickland. Josh became one of the lead figures in the efforts to establish a Manchester Bidwell project in Lexington. Falling short of its funding goals, the original project was not finalized. Today, however, Josh Nadzam is the Executive Director and Co-Founder of On the Move Art Studio. In a renovated 1969 Airstream trailer, Josh, Cathy Werking, the artist who partners in the work, and a passionate crew of volunteers take opportunities to go into neighborhoods where disadvantaged kids live and offer them the opportunity to create art, and through art to be empowered by talents they did not know they had. Josh, like each of the change-agents who shared their stories for

---

39 Personal conversation with William Strickland in Lexington, Kentucky. 2015.

this book, never stops, never gives up hope that what he is doing will contribute to the building of relationships and conversations across the deep divides in our country, and to peace and justice for all.[40]

Eight. Refuse to be sucked into partisan myopia that leads to further polarization. Instead, take a stand for all of us who are united for the good of America. We must ask ourselves, "What do I have to lose by truly listening to those who have different experiences and perspectives from my own? To listen to them with a desire to really hear and understand, not simply to debate with them. Is it possible I might gain some new information? Is it possible that I might not be 100% correct and could learn something that enhances my own life and beliefs, if I simply give myself permission to listen wholeheartedly?"

People who have lived the path of polarization and dictatorship in other countries know the impact of divisions on their lives. Neighbors spying on neighbors, fear of voicing our opinions, normalizing of the unacceptable, such as limiting access to communications, dividing people into fear-based factions to limit power bases, restriction on artistic and literary expression, a diminishment of curiosity and wonder about anything or anyone "other", a growing contempt of anyone who differs in appearance, perspective or behavior. Fear and compassion cannot exist together.

Dr. Jennifer McCoy, Distinguished Professor of Political Science at Georgia State University in Atlanta, has studied polarization and done mediation in such divided countries as Venezuela, Turkey and Hungary. I spoke with her by telephone on the Monday following the violence in Charlottesville. Having heard her briefly on the radio, and familiar with her writing in the Washington Post, I know her to be a big proponent of depolarizing by any way we can come together to tap into our common humanity. On this day, when the country was still reeling from the deep hatred and divisions revealed on that Saturday when death, injuries, and the rhetoric of hate ran rampant through the Virginia college town, I wondered out loud if we have already passed the point of being able to find that common humanity. In response, Dr. McCoy shared the things that she had seen happen in other countries to exacerbate polarization, that are really warnings to our own.

1. The "In" and "Out" divisions, where people lose contact with anyone outside of their own group of like-minded people with whom they communicate and associate. This leads to what she called the "Big Sort," with segregated social as well as political identities, lead-

---

40 Personal conversation with Josh Nadzam, Lexington, Kentucky. 2017.

ing to an "us vs them" mentality where it is easier to dehumanize. She has been observing this process in Venezuela for over twenty years, noting that it impacted not only political parties, but also media, student groups, and human rights organizations. The radical extreme voices begin to so dominate public discourse that they drown out any voices that are more moderate or close to the center, any who want to build bridges. In Venezuela, those who would try to find commonalities across divides are considered traitors or sell-outs. "You have to have real courage and be aware of the risks to be willing to form a bridge," says McCoy, "because you will be attacked."

McCoy sees many examples of this "in" and "out", us vs. them behavior in Congress, with many members no longer moving to Washington but commuting on long weekends, resulting in a lack of no kids in school or on ball teams together, no running into each other in the grocery store. Without social contact, our senators and congressmen and their constituents are following the patterns she saw among the pro- and anti-government forces in Venezuela. Those on "our side" are considered trustworthy, intelligent, hard-working, and honest. The "other side" is considered less trustworthy, less intelligent, lazy, and arrogant.

2. From this position, says McCoy, it is easy to fall into the "conspiracy trap," attributing most of the actions of the other side as intending to harm us, the good guys, although these theories have no basis in reality. People who have been sold on the conspiracy theory can be presented factual information which they will simply bypass or ignore, because they already believe what they had heard previously. Her words reminded me of a conflicted church with which I had been consulting, which was angry with "that bishop" (the one presently in office) who had "changed the rules" and "called them out" in an "unfair" disciplinary and personnel matter. Letters from two previous bishops stating the rules were shown to the group, but no number of facts could dissuade them from their previous position.

3. Third is "tit for tat logic": if one side is exclusionary, we will be too. Again, the Senate was a prime example, looking at the stated refusal of the Republicans to cooperate in any way with President Obama,

in an effort to see his presidency fail, and their refusal to hear the nomination of Merrick Garland for the Supreme Court. Since that was the stance of the Republicans, the Democrats assumed an identical stance against Trump's Supreme Court nominee, Neil Gorsuch. The result, as it often is in tit-for-tat thinking, is the loss of something good for the future of both groups – in this case, the exercise of the Nuclear Option, leaving the Senate with the requirement of only sixty votes in the future, rather than sixty-two.

McCoy is well aware of the state in which we find ourselves in the United States today, with the country so polarized that her strongly recommended "coming together to tap into our common humanity" is difficult. Research from social and political psychologists in this area can be discouraging in their negativity, as there is much motivation to support pre-existing beliefs. When these beliefs are contradicted, people reassess and often reject the new information and fall back to old beliefs in a more deeply entrenched way. Her suggestions for moving toward depolarization include:

- Social contact theory. The kind of contact matters. How can we look for intergroup situations where we can view our common, shared humanity? Levels of common interest that are "moved up" beyond the level of divisive subjects might include a shared interest in common patriotism on holidays such as the Fourth of July, when people are more receptive to engage with the other camp around a larger social construct.
- Common, neutral projects, such as a community park clean-up, playing on an athletic or other kind of team made up of diverse people, or working on making a decision. Diversity among decision makers has been proven to be stronger than silos of decision makers.
- The venue matters. In Venezuela she experienced groups who refused to go into certain parts of a city or certain buildings. Neutral sites are important.

We discussed briefly the situations each of us had encountered which have run counter to those suggestions, before I asked the hard question: "And if we can't, or won't, go there?" The consequences for democracy are terrible, McCoy said sadly. There is gridlock such as we see in Washington today, where there is no ability to compromise or negotiate and nothing gets done. There are examples overseas which the United States needs to look at, where the party in power swings back and forth, careening between extremes, voting each time for the opposite of what has been in power, resulting in severe instability. And there is the example of one side staying in power, excluding opposing voices, passing laws to change the constitution to achieve more power and authority and exclude whole segments of society. McCoy's work is moving to the evaluation of different efforts to move beyond polarization, looking for models with prove helpful in different locations and situations.[41]

Two novels sit side by side on my nightstand, constant reminders that this kind of world has happened before, and could happen again. The Nightingale, Kristin Hannah's story of two sisters coming of age in France during World War 2 and their efforts to resist and survive the German occupation, is based on a true story of what did happen. American War is a warning of what could. Once again, it is a choice. Choose to Talk Together, and take every opportunity to listen more than you speak.

Nine. Let your vote be a clear message to those who govern our cities, our states, and our country that you insist on a new and functional model of behavior from those who call themselves leaders. A father who was an activist in the sixties was in conversation with his son about the state of the country and the apathy that he perceives. "We are probably better informed than you ever were," the son protested.

"That may be," said the father, "but we did something. And you will have to act, also, if things are to change."

The winds of activism are stirring, in many forms and many forums. Perhaps we are undecided at this point what kind of action we want to take. Perhaps we are even bothered by the term activist or activism, as if it belonged to another time, and is limited to one end of the political spectrum or another, acceding activity on behalf of our country to extremists and fundamentalists of all stripes.

On Mother's Day, 1985, I was sitting in the amphitheater at Randolph Macon Woman's College in Lynchburg, Virginia, for my daughter Laura's graduation. The commencement speaker was Ellen Levine, at that time the editor of Woman's Day magazine, the only female editor at that date of the top seven women's magazines. It was a beautiful May day. The graduates and families were in a mood for celebration, ready to move on to the next chapter in their lives. Levine had a message for them.

Leaning over the podium, she told the story of receiving the invitation to be the graduation speaker, and turning to her staff, saying, "What does

---

41 Telephone interview with Dr. Jennifer McCoy, August 14, 2017.

the graduate of one woman's college (Wellesley, 1964) say to the graduates of another woman's college on Mother's Day in 1985?" Before anyone else could speak, a man responded, "Give them your favorite recipe for quiche."

"That toothpaste has been out of the tube for years, and it's not going back!" was her reported response to the male staffer. To the graduates, she said, "It's easy for you with your new leather briefcases and your three-piece suits to think that all of the battles have been won. To make fun of the bra-burners, the foremothers who made possible the opportunities you have today. But know this. There is still work to be done, and you must find your own way to continue to pave the way for those who will come after you, to work for the kind of world you want to create for your children."

It is a call that goes out, generation to generation. It is not an option of whether or not we will act to create and sustain the kind of world we dream of, but of how we will act in our time to be the change we want to see in the world. My encouragement is this: may we each find a way to carry the values of civility and respect that lead to the ability to listen, to negotiate and to compromise forward in our own circles, and from those circles, move out to insist that we will accept no less from those we elect at every level of our common life.

The stakes are too great for partisan blaming. We have all been guilty of allowing the untruths and the lack of civility to grow and undermine our way of life. For the sake of our democracy and the future of our country, we must, in unity, rationally and firmly stand together now.

A recent roundtable discussion from reporters who cover the Kentucky legislature found a disturbing trend. In the just-completed "short session" of the first Republican-controlled legislative and executive branches in the history of the state, statements of both the legislative agenda and decisions were heard not as matters of policy but of dominance. More recent health-care debates in the Senate are drawing public ire because of the lack of willingness of the legislators to listen to the people, and to work together for a bill that is reflective of more than partisan dominance.

If Professor McCoy's observations hold true, that when the country is badly polarized, there will be a veering back and forth of parties in charge, with each imposing their beliefs on the other in turn, we have reached a frightening impasse. My mind hears playground echoes: "You are not the boss of me!" "I'm the boss and you have to do what I say."

Even more recently, the brief coming together of elected leaders in a show of unity after the shooting at the Republican baseball practice quickly returned to a partisan blaming and a continuing stubborn standoff on issues impacting the country. It is now time to demand by our voting power that those we send to state and national positions behave in an adult manner, rather than resorting to the behavior of playground bullies.

Ten. In a world that has forgotten to sing, those who hear even the faintest echo must never stop hearing the music. Wherever there is music, there is a blending of individuals and differences into a ensemble that is more than any one individual can be alone, a knowing that you are a part of something bigger than labels and partisan politics. Let the music swell your capacity to be filled with curiosity, respect, wonder, and courage that will enable an expansive embrace of the adventure of living and growing in a time of unprecedented possibility as well as unprecedented division. The current discordance in our country has brought uncertainty about the narrative of who we are as a people and what kind of country we want to be. When there is discordance and uncertainty, the music falters, and can come dangerously close to ending. Without the music of civility, the possibility is diminished, the deadly division heightened.

It is time to begin again. Time to remember that we are part of a big, crazy, fascinating family, who may be far bigger and more sprawling and diverse than our founding fathers envisioned, or for which they planned. Like any family, we have disagreements, ups and downs, yet each of us has come here with hope for a better life in a democratic system, and have moments when we know that it is worth every effort it takes to sustain it.

Moving Forward to Action:
Questions for reflection and sharing

1. When have you personally been deeply aware of the fragility of life and the possibility of destruction of our culture? What happened to raise your awareness? What was your greatest fear? What did you do? Has there been a lasting impact from that experience? Please share it with others.

2. Think of a time you have been most out of your comfort zone. What did you feel? Think? Say? Do? Do you stay in comfortable circles the majority of the time, or have a cultural, ethnic, and racial mix with whom you work and socialize? What have you learned from being outside of your own comfort zone? What do you still fear or find uncomfortable?

3. What does activism mean to you? Who are the activists or change

agents you most admire? Least admire?

4. Have you ever run into a problem in life for which you had no previous examples of answers or solutions? What did you do? How did you find a way forward? Was it transactional (related to a previous solution of answer of some kind) or transformational (brand new uncharted territory)?

A *conversation with*

JIM BROWN
Founder of Amer-I-Can

**When did you hear the call to make
a difference in the world?**

Picture him. Jim Brown. Arguably the greatest running
back in the history of football, streaking through defens-
es of every opponent on his way into the history books of
American athletics. Picture a little boy, growing up on St.
Simons Island, Georgia, cared for by a grandmother who
overcame alcoholism to raise the boy and became in his words, "a great human being."
Picture a little boy who, in the words of Jim Brown, the very adult, very human being, the
founder of Amer-I-Can program for the teaching of life management skills, "knew when
I was eight years old," he says. "My mother was too young to raise me, and I had no relationship with my father. I had to develop independence, and I knew that I needed help...
which came from my grandmother, and from people in the community, like Mr. Willis at
the convenience store. When I was eight I moved north with my mother. She worked as a
domestic, and we lived in a suite over the garage. I was alone much of the time, and lonely,
but she did all in her power to keep me in a good school, Manhasset. It was there I started
to meet great people, and became determined to keep going, to someday help others."

"There may be short cuts to material success;
it takes change of attitude and
spiritual change to make a lasting difference."

How did you decide what action to take?

"I believe we live in the greatest country in the world," Jim says. "But the right education
has not been made available to African Americans. I watched acts of self-destruction, and
knew that something had to be done to help educate people." As an athlete, Brown had
come under the influence of many coaches. "I realized that the really successful people
taught about family, and education; African Americans did not. That kept the population
going in circles. I realized what was needed was life management skills."

Immediately after retiring from professional football at age 31, Jim Brown had started
the Negro Economic and Industrial Union, which emphasized economic development for
minority groups. "It was successful with people at the top of the totem pole, due to their educational degrees, and innate life management skills." The resources and expertise did not
speak to the group that he was now trying to reach — the disenfranchised youth. "We had

to develop a curriculum that taught life management skills; that taught people how to take responsibility for their own work habits, their successes and their failures. As the program developed, we would take the brightest participants and train them to become facilitators, to actually make a living as professors of Amer-I-Can. They did not have to have a college degree, and it brought economics into the community. "

It was a message that resonated with the communities Brown and Amer-I-Can were trying to reach. "Many had given up trying to be useful," Jim reflected. "But they heard the message: 'you are responsible for you. If you learn these life management skills, and apply them properly, you will be successful.' It sold itself. It was a real self-esteem boost."

Like Mohammed Ali, you interact successfully with people from all walks of life. What have you learned that you can pass on to others who are attempting to work with those both like and unlike themselves?

From the beginning, Jim Brown's wife Monique has been figural in the program, along with friends, many great athletes and former gang leaders, who the Browns have become friends with as they invited them into their home to tell their stories. "If I had not met Monique..." The great man pauses, clears his throat and continues to describe the dedication and caring his wife has brought to this work. "All of these people have come to our home, which has always been the base of our operations," he says. "They see us — not me — US; and they receive the greatest respect and caring." He pauses, and then continues. "In my life, so many individuals, so many successful people went out of their way to help me. They didn't want anything from it in return, except for me to become a decent human being. Monique and I want to do that for others. She is a great humanitarian, a true participant in this work. Together we have built trust with people. People pay attention to others' relationships. We hope that as they know us as a couple and experience the way we treat each other that they will pay close attention to their own relationships. The way they treat others. There are special people in all walks of life. I have made mistakes in life and I admit those mistakes. I believe we were each put here to show man's humanity to man. If we will respect ourselves and respect others, and reach out to help others in need — it doesn't take money or power or position to do that. And there is no higher contribution any one of us can make. The world emphasizes trophies, physical accomplishments, money, jobs. I believe we each have the responsibility to be in touch with our spiritual self, to carry ourselves in that spiritual way, and to treat every human being with respect as a human being — that this is what God intended for us to do in relation to others.

What challenges did you encounter on the way to becoming a change agent?

"If you study our society," says Brown, "the people at the top with big money and power want to control what is taking place, any changes that might happen. The biggest challenge is to stay free of that control. Free of people who don't want the work to succeed unless they control it. The people I am working to reach need me to be who I say I am, who I represent myself to be — not controlled by someone else whose money or power tries to influence who I am or what I do. And that kind of control, which can result in an influx of money, can be seductive, and hard to resist. It takes extra hard work to stay free. There may be shortcuts to material success, but for lasting change, it takes a change in attitude and spiritual change."

He sees a challenge in the attitudes and behaviors in our country following the presidential election. "People call the president names, and take positions Democratic or Republican, and stick to those positions regardless. There is nothing people will work on together. It's an opposition position. If the candidate I support in an election does not win, it does not mean that my participation is going to stop. I am going to let the person in the elected office know that I am going to continue to try to work for the betterment of people in this country.

What lies ahead for Amer-I-Can and what message do you have for those who would be change agents for our country?

"Amer-I-Can will continue to spread education, create peace, stop violence. To turn negative communities into safe communities for our people."

Jim Brown is aware that as his work in providing the fundamental life skills for a safer, better life transforms African American communities, other communities in our country are dealing with increasing vitriol and violence. His is a voice asking people to consider if perhaps they have been emphasizing the wrong things.

"We must meet at a spiritual level where we can come together for a better life for all," he says. "We are one step away from the bomb, as we consider what is going on in our own country, in North Korea, Russia, and other countries. One step away from extinction. We have to realize we are talking about the conditions of our very existence. We have to get away from bullying, from negativity, from disrespect and submit ourselves to develop as human beings."

"Every human has to make choices. It is simple; it is profound. If we look at our country today, we see confusion and division. The one thing that we can and must do is to be a decent, caring person and give a hand to someone who is less successful by our culture's standards, or doesn't have the basics of life."

"Our achievements, and possessions are things man has made up. Man did not create man. The power that created us charged us to live in right relationships with each other. That is the higher level we have to achieve. To do what we know is right, every day."

Writing a New Song

"You have never been in this exact moment before, so you don't have to pretend like you know exactly what to do." – Brian Andreas, Bring Your Life Back to Life: A Guide to Effortless Joy[42]

We can all feel that we are in a time of rapid and unprecedented change. Every morning seems to bring with it news and images we do not want to believe are of America and Americans. Last week, North Korea and nuclear warheads; this week, hate-filled action in the streets of Charlottesville, Virginia, which left three dead, numerous injured, and a deeply divided country outraged, and as divided on the cause of their outrage as on every other issue. Today, as we struggle for relief for those devastated by Hurricane Harvey, we are staring again at North Korea, at Russia, and at deep concern for the Dreamers, those undocumented young people who arrived here as children. We claim the "real America" as Katrina, Harvey, Orlando, Oklahoma City, Boston, and other disasters briefly unite us. Their names remain with us, reminders of what we have the capacity to be, while all too quickly we return to our separate corners.

Fear walks hand in hand with weariness over this divide. Keeping on living in this tumult brings three types of observable response:

1. Denial. I will not watch the news. I will not engage in conversation about the world. I will continue to live the life that is familiar and comfortable.

2. Righteous indignation and blame. Ain't it awful? They are terrible. Someone must do something to stop them. (The identity of "they" and "them" varies according to the speaker.)

3. What can I do to change my part of the world? I don't know the answer, but I know each one of us has a share of responsibility for

---

42 Andreas, Brian. Bring Your Life Back to Life: A Guide to Effortless Joy. A Hundred Ways North, Deborah, Oregon. 2016.

where we are, and for stepping up to find a way to be the change we want to see in the world.

As words about North Korea and the threat of nuclear war swirled, I found myself viscerally a young mother, gut-clenching, fearful that my infant daughter would not have the chance to live to wear the tiny blue coat I was stitching. As scenes from Charlottesville streamed across the internet and television, I felt the night when Lexington's East End businesses and homes were devastated during racial conflict, and black and white hands grasped each other in church pews across the city, singing "we shall overcome." The feelings compelled me to the Courthouse Plaza in Lexington to join others in peaceful but adamant solidarity against all forms of life-threatening hate and discrimination. Before these pages are in the hands of readers, and predictably, as long as human beings endeavor to live and work together, other moments will arise to viscerally haunt as each generation faces its own storms. Is it possible that what we are seeking is not answers to specific issues, but a process that can evolve with us as we live across the years?

The polls continue to indicate the divide on the current question of removing historic Confederate statues in Lexington and other southern cities. Are the statues a painful reminder of slavery, those who fought for it, and those who supported it? Or are the presence of the statues a daily reminder of both our heritage and where we must never go again? The argument itself seems stuck in the transactional, seeking solutions in actions taken before, while the moment is calling beyond where we have been and what we have done before, to the transformational. Meanwhile, as we leave the Courthouse Plaza, a white-haired man muses, recalling the challenge to his fraternity pledge class to paint the balls of John Hunt Morgan's statued horse a bright Tennessee orange.

The transformational does not pretend that we know what to do in a moment in time that has never been before. Unlike the Cuban Missile Crisis or the riots in Lexington's East End, these moments of crisis are fueled by global technologies that have taken us far beyond the dystopia of Brave New World or 1984. We are called to stretch the imagination; to walk on the edge of a world that has constantly changing demands and fresh possibilities.

This book is about one portion of those demands; one new possibility, new ways of communicating that create and further civility. Those who are in denial will continue to ignore the swirl around them. The blamers may continue to blame, simply abdicating all responsibility for making personal changes or working for societal change. Those who are willing to walk on the edge of possibility will step forward to listen and respond to the demands of an unknown future.

Opening ourselves to a message from an unknown future begins with one statement. "I will." This is a declaration of the most important change of all, a personal, individual commitment to move from the debilitating "I won't" that has paralyzed us in bitter divisions to a receptive "I will" posture that allows a clear-eyed awareness of who we are and a recognition of the nostalgia that would keep us clinging to the familiar, to times we felt comfortable and in control. It will take the courage of every person to will themselves to be in a radically different place – a place called civility. We have strayed so far from the knowledge and experience of civility that it will take this hard first step of releasing ourselves from the stubbornness of an "I won't" that is carrying us to the brink of self-destruction to both a frontier mentality of "I will" and new practices to go to it. But without civility, without the willingness to come together in the practice of civil dialogue, we cannot go to a place of creative possibility.

There have been other times of dramatic change in our history when we have needed to come together in new ways to move forward. When brother has fought against brother in the Civil War, in the aftermath of Vietnam, following the struggles for civil rights, and the Black Lives Matter movement. Not everyone has been willing to come together. Each time, however, there has been sufficient willingness to step to a middle ground where listening is possible, reason is possible, and therefore, moving forward is possible. That willingness is more crucial today than ever before. Never have the words we say and the actions we take been able to reverberate so swiftly across the world, for good or for ill. A strident voice on the radio announces that "we organized online and we're coming into the world in real time to let everyone know that we're taking back this country." A local rabbi is verbally attacked on Facebook as a "libtard" and told "you will be replaced." I wake up to a message from a trusted friend in another state informing me that the GoFundMe page for this book has been labeled "malicious." Pictures and messages of peace and hope aim to utilize the same rapid transmission without being swallowed up by the vitriol which has been building in anonymity. Never before have the distractions as well as the polarizations which keep us locked in the struggle been more real. We live in a world so cluttered with possessions and busyness that it is difficult to breathe, much less allow the winds of imagination to blow through us, blowing out the detritus and opening us to the clarity we need to hone our skills.

In my days of training in Japan, two practices became formative in my life: centering in quietness and stillness, and the Zen Beginner's Mind. Centering is not a concept familiar in our culture, yet I have used it with students from ages two to eighty, from young musicians to corporate boardrooms. It's a quieting of both body and mind in preparation for what will come. A small child stands with feet on a cardboard circle and pretends he is a tree, digging a pretend hole and planting his feet deeply in the ground. Standing tall, breathing deeply, the "wind" of a teacher gently pushing cannot blow him over. From this quiet, grounded place, even the youngest child is open to learning. An anxious adult stands, quieting her body, allowing each muscle to untangle, breathing in power, breathing out all that is toxic. Like the young child on the foot chart, the stopping of usual activity, the focus on breathing, the allowing of the things occupying and cluttering the mind to slip momentarily away, like a heavy backpack sliding down the arms to rest on the ground, allows the mind to empty and clear in order to be open to new thoughts and connections.

A circle of men and women sit with their backs to the center of the circle, eyes half-closed, fixed on a spot on the wall, hands open, palms up to receive what will come. A quiet voice gently reminds them, "Thoughts will come and thoughts will go; let them go." In western culture, to stop, to be still, we often focus the mind on a problem to be solved or an inspirational phrase. Seldom do we allow ourselves to let go of whatever we have been carrying around in our minds and hearts until we are empty. And until we have cleared ourselves, emptied ourselves, we cannot be ready to receive what is coming. The continual releasing of the thoughts that float across the mind develops a practice of emptying and clearing that is the prelude to receptivity of the new and previously unimagined.

The second concept is the Zen Beginner's Mind. To the expert, there are no options, for the expert knows it all; to the eternal beginner, there are always new things to learn, new possibilities. Again, this is a foreign concept to the western achievement-oriented mind, where being the "expert" is highly desired. The possibility of learning new things is always with us. The attitude of the beginner's mind provides a model which allows us to open ourselves more completely to all there is to learn.

After stopping and emptying, opening to what may come to us is an important next step. Like civil dialogue itself, this is a process that cannot be rushed. Our American way takes us straight to goals and action plans, often moved into without time for digesting and reflecting. A current case in point would be the controversial health care plans, the one created behind closed doors, with efforts to push votes without the usual public hearings, the other the signature act of the previous regime and the target of this one from campaign days forward. Right now, there is no outcome. By the time this book is published, there may be. I wonder what would happen if the Senators were to stop. Empty themselves, of party names and ideologies, of agendas and lobbyists, resentments and fears. And open their hands and hearts as they sit quietly, with the eternal beginner's mind. We have all experienced times when we went to bed struggling with a troublesome problem on our minds and awoke surprised to find an answer had arrived in the night, from who knows where. Perhaps the mind at rest is more open to the transformational?

For a little over a decade, I was the design consultant and principal facilitator for a women's leadership initiative at the University of Kentucky, preparing women in junior leadership roles for senior leadership in a male-dominated culture. One of the sessions in our ever-evolving curriculum was a session on utilizing intuition in decision-making. This process involved selecting an object from hundreds displayed, and sitting quietly with it to see why it symbolically spoke to the person who had selected it, and what it had to say to them regarding their work. The program began in the medical school, where scientifically trained women went from skepticism to interest and belief as they used the exercise. Their experiences mirrored those of corporate executives who, when introduced to intuition and quiet reflection, found their way to decisions which had previously eluded them.

The transformative answers, the new song we are called to sing, will not be found in the usual ways or usual places, for these are not usual times. Contemporary poet Brian Andreas offers these insightful words to remind us[43]:

> You have never been in this exact moment before
> so you don't have to pretend
> like you know
> exactly what to do
>
> when you quit defending
> the stuff you think you know
> there's a lot more room
> to simply be there fully
> with all the things you don't

---

43 Andreas, Brian. *Bring Your Life Back to Life: A Guide to Effortless Joy*. A Hundred Ways North, Deborah, Oregon. 2016.

Listen quietly
when you don't know
and wait
to act
until you do.

I stumbled on such a moment recently when my friend Carolyn and I went to a bed and breakfast tucked back in the rolling hills of Kentucky for our annual May birthday getaway. It's not something easily worked into busy schedules, but we are intent on making it happen – on getting out of our usual locale where we have time to simply be, together. In the comfortable dining room of Snug Hollow, we sat down at the table with folks we had never met before. Our only known commonality seemed our arrival at this time, in this place.

We hailed from Utah, Tennessee, Washington DC, and various parts of Kentucky. We ranged in age from a young couple having their first weekend away from their almost-two-year-old to two mothers and daughters spending time together to a couple both struggling with catastrophic illnesses underneath their smiles and warm personalities. We were corporate, government, education, banking, food service, rehabilitation, psychology, and retired. Somehow, we had each found our way to this isolated place. Our dinner conversation began, quite naturally, with "how did you find this place?" It could have ended there. We might have gone back to our rooms and cottages and easy conversation with our own.

But the conversation continued, moving from one fascinating subject to the next, working with spinal injuries, needle arts, the beauty of Kentucky and misconceptions about the state from outsiders, travels in Thailand and other exotic locations, the teaching of Suzuki violin. Occasionally, someone would say, "I don't know anything about that. Could you explain more of what you're talking about?", and the attention of the table would turn toward the answer, riveting their attention as though expecting an exam on the subject the next morning. One woman told of her family's experience of camping in their pop-up camper, which led to their experiences of watching the sunset in a community of strangers beside Lake Michigan. "I had never experienced anything like it before," the grandmother of the family added. "I'd seen many sunsets in my life, but to sit with so many people you don't know, who had all come to this one spot to watch the sun set was amazing!" Around the table, heads nodded in affirmation, and one by one, the members of this temporary community, gathered around a common table, told their sunset stories. There was a sense of consensus that we all knew and valued our own sunset moments and all the peace, the hope, the possibility they held, and in that short time and place, we knew the heart and the values of others.

We lingered long over coffee, in some unspoken reluctance to break this moment of at-oneness. It seemed a glimpse of the narrative we must begin to re-write.

This new narrative will have a strange, perhaps disparate cast of characters, whose geography, psychology, culturation, educations, socioeconomic statuses, and ways of living every day may vary widely. Some will bring a touch of wisdom from experiences of the past. Others carry visions of a future that is for those who will live it to imagine. There will be words that release bits of the old story, the old song, to make room for the new. The narrative will be dependent on each of us for what is to be lived and told. We have not walked this particular path before, and so the answers will not be found behind us, but in gathering the propositions of what is possible for the future. Like sunsets, shared values, and answers yet to be conceived are all around us, waiting to be recognized and given some music we can all hear and sing. We have an opportunity to begin to sing it now. To offer new and greater harmonies to the world. The music that emerges, that moves and touches the human spirit, is not of opinions and ideas, but of values and purpose; a sense of emerging together into something new.

On a recent talent show, a young girl named Mandy took the stage with her ukulele. She had completely lost her hearing at age 18, and stopped singing. At age 29, she stood barefoot on the stage, preparing to sing a song she had written herself, entitled "Try." "I didn't want the kind of life I was living," she said. "I had to try to sing again." And sing she did, before an awed and tearful audience and judges, the vibrations of the music infusing the beat through her bare feet to join her visceral knowledge of pitch and tone and color as a new song emerged.

She tried.

And a new song was born.

It is our time to try. And it may take some risking something strange and new, like standing in our bare feet and allowing the beat of the universe to pulse through our being with a new message, a new way, a new hope.

Stop. Open yourself. Wait quietly. Listen. Gather around tables with people wherever you find them. Ask about their lives, their stories, their jobs, their battles, their dreams, and their sunsets. Offer yours in return. Hold the moment, know it fully, and go out to make more. This is how our story, our shared narrative, is transformed into music. Forget to be afraid. Embrace curiosity about the human condition. Approach with respect. Talk together. Listen some more. Learn something new, no matter how small. Say I'm sorry. Say I'm wrong. Give yourself permission to change your mind. To begin to be open to the humanity in someone you have only seen on the periphery of your world, if you have even seen them at all. To live and advocate for our country in such a way that, as Rabbi Wirtschafter said, we will be proud to tell our children and grandchildren the story of what we did.

This is our song, the song we must begin. We must sing it every day, wherever we go. We must listen for new harmonies to blend the voices who choose to join the chorus, adding to the harmony that will build as we go, soaring beyond where we can name or imagine. We can, we will, we must lift every voice and sing.

Once there was a girl and a boy who wanted to change the world, and at first they thought it'd be easy, because if everyone could see how beautiful it'd be, it'd take about a minute, but all the people they talked to were too busy to stop and listen. So, they went off and did beautiful things all on their own, and pretty soon people were stopping and asking if they could come along and do it, and that's how they figured out how worlds change.

—Brian Andreas, contemporary poet
Story People

Moving Forward to Action:
Questions for reflection and sharing

1. What are you holding onto that needs to be released so that you can be open to new, transformational answers? Are you willing to release it?

2. What is the song that you are hearing that will inspire you to work for talking together to move beyond polarization to really see and hear each other?

3. What is the song you are uniquely called to sing? Who are you called to sing it to? How can you equip yourself to sing this song?

4. List specific places where you plan to sing your song in the coming year. List three points that you want to make. What will you need to change or let go in order to live into this goal?

Of course, I want to change the world, she said,
but I was hoping to do it from the comfort of my regular life.
                                        —Brian Andreas, Traveling Light
                                                Used with permission

COLLECTIVE WISDOM OF OUR CHANGE AGENTS

The major impetus for writing TALKING TOGETHER was to provide hope that each of us can make a change in our world, and a guidebook for ways to begin the change from mean-spirited interactions to civil, respectful dialogue. As I spoke with people about the book and the process of talking together, it became clear to me that many people wanted to be agents of change, but were not sure that changing the world is something that ordinary human beings are called to do. If indeed, ordinary humans were called to this work, how would they know how to begin? And once they had started to work toward change, how could they persevere as resistances to change came at them in the form of challenges and roadblocks?

It occurred to me that by the time we learn about those who are thought leaders and change agents, they appear bigger than life. Some have had extraordinary platforms from which to begin. Others have begun from baby steps, with no legacy behind them. Seldom do we know the back story or current thinking. I decided to ask eight individuals who are making positive changes in the world to answer the same five questions – questions I believe anyone who wants to make a difference in the world will need to consider for themselves.

The five questions are:

1. When did you hear the call to make a difference in the world?
2. How did you decide what specific action to take?
3. What challenges or roadblocks have you encountered, and how have you managed those?
4. What have you learned about interacting with "otherness" – with those who are unlike you; with the diverse people who make up our world?
5. What next? And what words of advice do you have for others who want to make the world a better place?

The conversations with change agents represent nine men and women ranging in age from twenty-something through sixty-something, and organizations as diverse as music, art, education, life skills management, immigration, interfaith relationships, and changing the attitudinal and behavioral dynamic in our country from fear and hate. While the stories and the individuals themselves are very different, the answers to the five questions asked each person showed connecting principles that suggest a message larger than any one story.

As you go forward in your journey to make a difference in our world, may these collective thoughts go with you.

1. The lives of "regular" and "ordinary" human beings are filled with people, places, time in history and events that are forming our thinking, often at a subconscious level. The impetus to build on that formation to make a difference in the part of the world to which we are called may come with an epiphany, a life crisis, a disappointment, the influence of a significant connection, or a gradual growing into action that wants to happen. The individuals interviewed all paid attention to the "action that wants to happen."

2. Little steps that lead to action are more important than big visions without action. This reminder was expressed in different words by our change agents, but the message was the same. "Don't let great get in the way of good," says Kurt Gohde of Unlearn Fear and Hate. "A thousand small acts cause large change." Take a "little piece of this huge thing," says Josh Nadzam of On the Move Art Studio. "If the challenge is too big or doesn't fit me, I don't need to fit myself to the challenge," says Hiroko Driver Lippman of the International Suzuki Association. Stacy Sauls says, "Attend to the little somethings that grow big."

3. You may not have a perfect product or all of the answers when you begin, and must be able to receive feedback and adjust. In organizational development, this is known as the "provisional try." In various technical fields, it is called prototyping. It demands self-observation and awareness, and willingness to adjust and correct course. It is about transformational work, where answers are not available from the past but are gleaned from reflection on present experience. Perceived failures are simply another opportunity for another provisional try, a better prototype. Going where the energy is rather than against it is important, even if it is not the direction or in the time frame you had been going.

4. Openness to "otherness." Each individual's life was expanded and

enriched to the degree they had opened themselves to getting out of their familiar, comfortable environment and connecting with people who are different than they are. Jim Brown reminds us that it does not take money, power, or position to reach out and treat others like we want to be treated ourselves. Stacy Sauls says that the "more other" the people with whom he is in conversation, the greater the learning opportunity for him.

5. Each leader was a self-defined life-long learner, as aware of what they didn't know as they were of their area of expertise. They were willing to have preconceived ideas and assumptions challenged and changed; curious about how different cultures and environments, within and without the country, formed people's thinking and actions in different ways.

6. Challenges come with the territory. If there was a common theme of how to face challenges, it would be attitude and perseverance. Kurt Gohde speaks of standing back to consider whether what he might first think of as an act of sabotage might simply be someone doing their job. Stacy Sauls speaks of looking at challenges as a game to figure out. Josh Nadzam and Everett McCorvey offer memorable images of times when it is necessary to try a different point of entry to accomplish your goal.

7. A small group of people who have passion for the work and commitment to it will accomplish more than a larger group that are not invested. Attrition is normal, and does not indicate failure. Part of other awareness is understanding that every person will have different interests and passions to which they will commit, and different skill sets, time and energy to devote. In awareness and understanding of these differences as facts rather than negativity toward your work lies the ability to connect people and participation.

8. Pioneering work requires new solutions rather than dependence on ideas which have been used successfully in the past. These leaders employed transformational thinking rather than transactional thinking.

9. Be aware that passion for the work of bringing societal change can become as exclusionary as the forces we are resisting. David

Wirtschafter reminds himself of the importance of creating safe spaces for all people to express themselves, rather than unintentionally marginalizing any part of a given constituency.

10. Trust your vision and do not give up on your dream. Everett McCorvey says that "you may see clearly what others do not see." Stacy Sauls of Love Must Act says that "plenty of people will say you cannot do what you are doing. Believe in yourself and your dream."

11. Systemic issues will exist, and although they may appear daunting, do not have to end the work of change agents. Jim Brown speaks of both the willingness to continue work through periods of time when elected leaders may not share his vision, and understanding the critical nature of both national and global situations which are the context for the work. Donald Lasserre emphasizes the importance of collaboration around shared values to accomplish larger goals.

A Project of Chapter Notes

Prologue: Beyond Dystopia and Utopia

Andreas, Brian. from Story People 2017 Calendar.
Used with permission. Brian Andreas is a contemporary poet and artist whose unique "Story People" with their sentences of wisdom that speak to universal concerns appear in a series of books, as well as on cards, calendars and wall art. I have requested permission to use Brian's quotes in two books now, and been impressed with the personal response which encourages passing these wise words widely. Permissions received from Annette Laitinen, Story People, by email, May 1, 2017.

1- Peck, M. Scott, MD.   A Different Drum. Reprinted with permission of Touchstone, a division of Simon and Schuster, Inc. Copyright 1987. All rights reserved. The renowned psychiatrist and author is referring to his response to his personal experience of diverse individuals coming together in small groups at National Training Laboratories in Bethel, Maine.

2- Definition of Civility from The Institute for Civility, P.O. Box 41804, Houston, TX 77241-1804. info@instituteforcivility.org. Cassandra Danke and Tomas Spath, Co-founders. Permission received August 10, 2017.

3- Friedman, Edwin H. A Failure of Nerve: Leadership in the Age of the Quick Fix. Seabird Books. New York. 2007. Used with permission. One of the books I keep close at hand as an ongoing reference and reminder of family systems theories and practices.

4- Newell, John Philip. A New Harmony: The Spirit, the Earth and the Human Soul. Josses-Bass: A Wiley Imprint. 2011.
Used with permission from Wiley Global Permissions, Sheik Safdar, Received May 15, 2017. Philip is one of many authors who has personally touched my life.

Chapter One: Discordance

5- "Eastern Standard" on WEKU Public Radio, June 2016. One of the multiple NPR programs which provides relevant content. Permission received by telephone from John Hungsbergen, August 18, 2017.

7- The Trump Effect, story in The Washington Post by Petula Dvorak. Permission received by telephone.

8- The Rivard Report, 13 September, 2016, used with permission.

Teaching Tolerance: A Project of the Southern Poverty Law Center. Founded in 1991 for the purpose of reducing prejudice, improving intergroup relations and supporting equitable school experiences for our nation's children. 400 Wabash Ave., Montgomery, AL 36104. Used with permission.

9- Keyes, Ken. The Hundredth Monkey.

The theory of the collective unconscious posits that when a new behavior or idea seems to spread rapidly from one individual or group to all related groups once a critical number of persons exhibit the behavior or acknowledge the new idea. The actual story about social change written by personal growth guru Ken Keyes was based on a report of a 30-year study of the behavior of monkeys on an island in Japan. Keyes presented the story as a legend or phenomenon, which added hopeful ideology to people seeking social or personal change in the 1950s-1960s. While some scientists have worked to disprove the theories, others point to its validity in pointing to ways simple innovation can lead to important change or paradigm shift. The research shows that the greatest change in monkey behavior happened for those who were between youth and adulthood in age, while a number of older monkeys never made the change. This information parallels experiences of the openness of younger generations to change, while older persons, in general, tend to cling to what they have known. In addition, the monkeys did extend their use of resources beyond what they had known previously. Keyes' book was not copyrighted and states that parts may be extrapolated without permission. The author states that he has done this deliberately to encourage the spreading of the concept as widely as possible.

Chapter Two: Shifting the Focus from Problem to Potential: Taking Back the Power

10- Treadwell, Margaret "Peggy", specialist in Family Systems presented training sessions for leadership groups at The Cathedral Domain Camp and Conference Center in Lee County, Ky., in 2009.

11- Oral conversation with David Sawyer; consultant and author on

Family Systems.

12- Peggy Treadwell lectures.

13- Elizabeth Workman Lecture on Appreciative Inquiry at Leadership Training Institute, Dubose Conference Center, Monteagle, Tenn., December 1993.

Chapter Three: The Why of It:
Behavior Makes or Breaks Relationships

Material in this chapter is largely experientially based, with narrative regarding work on the subjects of intention and intentionality beginning with Circles of Power Women's Leadership Initiative at the University of Kentucky, and intermingling with Edmond Friedman's work on intention and systems.

Chapter Four: Practice, Practice, Practice:
Foundations for Change

14- From a speech at The Carter Center to the annual Human Rights Defenders Forum in 2014.

15- McLaughlin, Kay Collier. The most recent adaptation of generic norms and standards by a working group led by Dr. Collier McLaughlin. While this exercise has been standard in the consulting repertoire for many years, in April of 2008, after completing the exercise, members of the Executive Council of the Diocese of Lexington decided to give their document a name. "With the behaviors we have named, we are trying to create a "culture of courtesy," said one member. "And we are covenantal people, said another. "So we need to call it the "Culture of Courtesy Covenant." The name has become ubiquitous, with variations from consulting group to consulting group. Some call it "A Covenant for the Creation of a Culture of Courtesy," while others calls it "A Culture of Curtesy Covenant." It is used to begin each Talking Together Seminar, setting a standard that any facilitator or member of a table group can bring to the attention of the gathering if the document is not being followed. It has proven extremely effective in setting the tone for any type of meeting.
16- McLaughlin, Kay Collier. Adapted from a document prepared in

1984 by Consultant Trainers Southwest, a now-defunct organization for consulting with faith-based entities. This document asks people to state the differences in dialogue and debate in order to recognize and name when the tone of the exchange moves away from dialogue, and to be aware of when it is appropriate to use each. The original document has been adapted over the ensuing years by working groups.

17- McLaughlin, Kay Collier. "The Public Conversation Project Modeled in Anaheim", THE ADVOCATE of the Episcopal Diocese of Lexington, September 1989. Marshall Ganz of the Harvard Kennedy School spoke to the Triennial Convention of the Episcopal Church in 1989, and conducted Public Conversations with a number of deputies to the convention, to model the process. I interviewed Ganz following his presentation in Anaheim, Calif., and wrote the article listed above.

18- The Maslow Hierarchy of Needs is now in the Public Domain. This current model was adapted for general use from a model entitled "Maslow Meets Jesus," created by The Rev. Hugh Major for the Department of Stewardship of the Episcopal Church in the United States of America.

Chapter Five: No Music Without Self and Other Awareness

19 and 20- McLaughlin, Kay Collier. Typology Continuum exercise designed by consultant Kay Collier McLaughlin. The use of the Typology Continuum is an efficient way to introduce people who are unfamiliar with the concept to the basics of typology theory, for individuals to self assess for self-awareness about their own styles of communication, energy gain or drain, giving and receiving of information, decision making and other aspects of typology. It is also a tool which encourages other awareness, and respect for individual differences. References to typology begin with the study of the work of Carl Jung on archetypes, Doctoral studies in psychometrics and include selected resources on the Myers Briggs Typology Indicator as well as a compilation of 30 years of experiences from workshops on typology, including a week-long intensive with Dr. Flavil Yeakeley at St. Louis University, Shadow workshops with Dr. Pearl Rutledge and the Rev. Dr. Paschal Baute in Lexington, Ky., workshops combining aspects of typology, emotional intelligence and human relations, workshops with the Mid-Atlantic Association for Training and Consulting. As an experiential consultant trained to adapt resources as current circumstances require, I may have long forgotten the names and dates of particular trainers or expe-

riences which led to the creation of exercises such as the continuum. I am forever indebted to Isabel Myers and Katherine Briggs for devoting years of their lives to creating a model that translated Jung's theories into a usable model that continues to serve human growth and development and to other typology theorists who have added to the conceptual resources with their work in Four Temperaments, Belbin Team Roles and other wellness instruments. There are many personality theories and models, all of which require for best usage, knowledge of supporting theories. The continuum exercise is intended to introduce or reinforce the concept of typology as important to self and other awareness, with emphasis on the fact that maximum understanding requires administration and explanation of a full instrument by a qualified practitioner of the model chosen.

See recommended reading for selected books on typology and emotional intelligence as tools for self and other awareness.

Additional resources for learning about typology are included in recommended reading.

22- McLaughlin, Kay Collier. Philosophical Quadrants exercise adapted as an experiential exercise. All too often groups trying to make a decision, whether the group be a business staff, a school faculty, a non-profit, etc. can sound as though they are talking about entirely different subjects, despite their stated goal. This exercise on the philosophical quadrants is ideologically inspired by an exercise experienced in a training session which was based loosely on the understanding of the four spiritual approaches identified by the Very. Rev. Urban T. "Terry" Holmes, Dean of the Seminary at St. Luke's School of Theology at Sewanee, Tenn. The philosophical quadrants share with the spiritual the head and heart approaches, but are more driven by philosophy than religion in the Quadrants into "philosophical" quadrants. The "heart" quadrant is driven by emotional; the intellectual by rational thinking, the connector by withdrawal from world for quiet reflection on internal resources to make foundational connections; the humanistic by social justice.

23- Lecture notes on Emotional Intelligence from Dr. Andrew Weiner, Application of Emotional Intelligence to Leadership, Circles of Power University of Kentucky Leadership Program, Wooded Glen Conference Center, Henryviille, Indiana, 2001. Dr. Weiner was a professor in the College of Education at the University of Kentucky.

and

Roy Oswald, Training session for The Center for Human Relations and Emotional Intelligence, Louisville Presbyterian Seminary, Louisville, Ky., 2008. Oswald was Executive Director and Senior Trainer for the Center for Human Relations and Emotional Intelligence.

Chapter Six: Every Behavior Has An Impact

24 - Training model. The leadership training model referenced here is an experiential process model in which participants of a leadership team experience exercises which illuminate a theory viscerally, and are then analyzed reflectively. The exercises are not content specific, but can be utilized and adapted for the content specified in the life of any system. Because a team (presenter and facilitators) have been trained in the same models and experiences, with awareness that circumstances of an event can call for an immediate adaptation of the design to meet a current crisis or need, team members can and will follow the lead of the presenter when a change is called for, as in the story demonstrated here.

24- McLaughlin, Kay Collier. Behavior/Impact exercise designed by consultant Kay Collier McLaughlin to provide the opportunity for experiential insight into the anxiety behaviors identified by family system theorists. The questions that drive the exercise are designed to trigger both self and other awareness in participants. This identification by participants helps them own the behaviors in their negative incidences, and invite the alternative positive behavior.

25- Anxiety behaviors from training session with Margaret "Peggy" Treadwell, LCSW, who has been active in fields of counseling and education for 35 years. She worked extensively with Dr. Edwin Friedman and edited his book Failure of Nerve Leadership training lecture 2009; The Cathedral Domain.

Chapter Seven: Bars, Measures and Boundaries

26- Cloud and Townsend handout at Crystal Cathedral Conference on Singles Ministry, 1990, adapted by numerous groups working experientially in the years since.

27- McLaughlin, Kay Collier. Circles of Core Values. 1987. Created to help participants in both group and private personal growth work to understand the relationship between personal boundaries and core values, and to be able to name and own their particular core values, and differentiate between those which they need to protect with a strong boundary, and those which are more open to porous boundaries.

28- Frost, Robert. A Mending Wall. 1914. This poem is in the public domain. http://copyright.cornell.edu/resources/publicdomain.cfm. Frost died in 1963; a few works were published prior to 1923, and are thus in public domain. It is not now copyrighted because of the date of publication. While "Mending Wall" can and is used without specific permission, unlike more obscure or lesser known works in the public domain, this information is provided as a courtesy to a well-known poet and one of his most popular and often quoted poems.

Chapter Eight: Finding Truth

29- Hirshfield, Jane. Post "On the Fifth Day" from the Collection The Beauty. Written for the 2017 March for Science in Washington, DC, by Hirsfield, the Chancellor of the Academy of American Poets. Email permission received from the poet May 2017

30- Phone interview with Jeffrey Sherwood, Senior Assistant Editor, Oxford English Dictionary, May 24, 2017.

31- Tutu, Archbishop Desmond. Notes from commencement address at Berea College, Berea, Ky., May 2005.

32- Notes from Institute for Servant Leadership session at Emory University with Bennett Sims, Marcus Borg and Margaret Wheatley, 2004. Sims' Hierarchy of Truth is detailed in his book *Servanthood: Leadership for the Third Millennium*. Cowley Publications, Cambridge, MA, 1997.

Chapter Nine: Good Grief, Charlie Brown

McLaughlin, Kay Collier - "Grief Emergency Kit." Self-published monograph. 1989. The author identifies and defines delayed grief, marginalized grief and collective grief as distinct from more generalized griefs, recognizing, however, that every loss is unique and special to some one.

Schneider, Dr. John - Grief model as taught at *Solo Flight Conference for Senior Adults*, Rosalind Conference Center, Richmond, Va.

33- McLaughlin, Kay Collier. Personal verbatim records of client interaction.

34- McLaughlin, Kay Collier. Suggestions developed and used in work 1985-2000.

Chapter Ten: Daunting Duet

Coontz, Stephanie. *The Way We Never Were* (1992) and The Way *We Really Are* (1997). These two books are references for people who wish to explore the topic of "mythical thinking" further, as part of a deeper understanding of how we can become so firmly attached to one aspect of a truth that we are unable to either see the totality of the picture or be open to new thinking. The reference to the titles hopefully opens up awareness that some ideas of the "way we were" is mythology, and in this time of resistance to facts, may help people understand that there is a difference in what we "remember" through the lens of our own experience and the facts of that time.

35- Commencement at Oklahoma City University, May 2017.

Chapter Eleven: Where Do We go From Here?

American War. As one who spends considerable time on the road, I am typically accompanied by NPR, and in this case, having heard Omar el Akid interviewed on Morning Edition, rushed to my independent book seller to purchase it, only to discover it had not yet hit the stores! Rather than a reference to a specific part of the book, it is mentioned to allow my personal response to the predictions of dystopian writing.

37- Friedman, Edmond. Family systems thinking and the work of Edwin Friedman, particularly in the book *Failure of Nerve* are foundational to my work. This particular statement from Friedman seems more true every day.

38- Walker, Frank X. Lines from poem entitled "Love Letter to the World," written for the Unlearn Fear and Hate campaign in Lexington, Ky. Used with permission, received July 26, 2017.

39- McLaughlin, Kay Collier. Notes from Bill Strickland's visit to Lexington, Ky. In 2015, Bill Strickland came to Lexington to speak to various groups who were interested in supporting the development of Manchester Bidwell job training and youth art centers in Lexington, based on the model Strickland developed in Pittsburgh and subsequently around the globe. Strickland spoke at a breakfast meeting at Mission House, the headquarters of the Episcopal Diocese of Lexington, with individuals who were interested in the project, and was interviewed by Kay Collier McLaughlin.

40- I first met Josh Nadzam when he was working with the effort to raise funds for a Manchester Bidwell Center in Lexington, Ky., and have followed his work in establishing On the Move Art Studio where I am proud to volunteer.

41- Telephone interview with Dr. Jennifer McCoy, Distinguished Professor of Political Science at Georgia State University on August 14, 2017. I became aware of Dr. McCoy's work when I heard part of an interview on the radio, and was led to seek a conversation with her, and learn more about her work.

Coda: The Beginning of a New Song

42 and 43- Andreas, Brian. *Bring Your Life Back to Life: A Guide to Effortless Joy*. *A Hundred Ways North*, Deborah, Iowa, 2016. Used with permission. Again, I am indebted to Brian Andreas and his team at STORY PEOPLE, and especially to Annette Lienen, whose swift responses, and enthusiastic and encouraging words, whether by phone or e-mail make an author rejoice in being able to share the words of this contemporary poet and artist.

READING ALONG THE WAY

Wherever I happen to be with people who are concerned about the state of our world, and hoping to be a part of the change they would like to see, invariably the question comes up of books I might suggest they might read to become better informed; books that have been important on my own journey. Considering both questions, I decided to try to offer some suggestions (certainly not a complete list in any category!) of books that have been important to me over the years. I am listing them in alphabetized categories, alphabetized by author within each category. Many may be out of print, as publication dates range from 1960 to books I purchased yesterday! May they enhance your journey.

Change

Bridges, William. *The Way of Transitions*. DeCapo Press. 2001.

Keyes Jr., Ken. *The Hundredth Monkey*. Vision Books. Coos Bay, OR. 1982.

Kotter, John. *Our Iceberg Is Melting: Changing and Succeeding Under Any Conditions.*

Senge, Peter. *The Dance of Change*. Currency Books, Random House. NY. 1999. See also Family Systems Theory.

Senge, Peter. *Presence*. See also Family Systems Theory and Living in Process.

Toffler, Alvin. *Future Shock*. Random House. 1970

Conflict and Violence

Buford, Bill. Among the Thugs: *The Experience and the Seduction of Crowd Violence*. Arrow Books. United Kingdom. 1991. See also Self and Other Awareness and Shadow Behavior.

Inazu, John D. *Confident Pluralism: Surviving and Thriving Through Deep Differences*. University of Chicago Press. 2016. See also Democracy and Politics and Understanding Multiculturalism.

Sawyer, David. *Hope in Conflict*. Pilgrim Press. 2007.

Yankelovich, Daniel. *The Magic of Dialogue: Transforming Conflict Into Cooperation*. Simon and Schuster. 1999.

Democracy and Politics

Bella, Robert. *Habits of the Heart*. Harper and Row. 1985.

Bella, Robert. *The Good Society*. Alfa Knopf. 1991

Inazu, John D. *Confident Pluralism: Surviving and Thriving Through Deep Differences*. University of Chicago Press. 2016. See also Conflict and Violence and Understanding Multiculturalism.

Lee, Harper. *To Kill a Mockingbird*. J.P. Lippincot. 1960. See also Understanding Multiculturalism.

Lee, Harper. *Go Set a Watchman*. Harper Collins. 2015. See also Understanding Multiculturalism.

Palmer, Parker. *Healing the Heart of Democracy: The Courage to Create a Politics Worthy of the Human Spirit*. Josses-Bass. 2011.

Warren, Robert Penn. *All the Kings Men. Harcourt, Brace and Company*. 1946.

Family Systems Theory

Friedman, Edwin. *Generation to Generation*. Guilford. 1985.

Friedman, Edwin. *Failure of Nerve: Leadership in the Age of the Quick Fix*. Church Publishing. 1997, 2007.

Friedman, Edwin. *Friedman's Fables*.

Friedman, Edwin. *What Are You Going to Do with Your Life? Unpublished Writings and Diaries*.

Gilbert, Roberta. *The Eight Concepts of Bowen Theory: A New Way of Thinking about the Individual and the Group*. Leading Systems Press, Falls Church, VA. 2004, 2006.

Gilbert, Roberta. *Extraordinary Leadership: Thinking Systems, Making a Difference*. 2006.

Senge, Peter. *The Dance of Change*. See also Change.

Senge, Peter. *Presence*. See also Living in Process and Change.

Forgiveness and Reconciliation

Smedes, Lewis. Forgive and Forget: Healing the Hurts We Don't Deserve. Harper and Row. San Francisco. 1984.

Stewart, Ann Kaiser. Triumphant Survivors. Doubleday. 1999.

Tutu, Desmond. No Freedom Without Forgiveness. 1999. See also Understanding Multiculturalism.

Grief and Loss

Angel, James. *O Susan!* Warner Press. Indiana. 1973.

Bozarth, Alla. *Life is Goodbye, Life is Hello*. CompCare Pub, MN. 1992.

Chethik, Neil. *FatherLoss*. Hyperion. 2001.

Marty, Martin E. *The Cry of Absence*. Eerdmans, Grand Rapids, MI. 1997.

Prend, Ashley Davis. *Transcending Loss: Understanding the Lifelong Impact of Grief*. Berkeley Books, NY. 1997.

Schneider, John. *Finding My Way*. Seasons Press, Traverse City, MI. 2011.

Stearns, Ann Kaiser. *Living Through Personal Loss*. Ballantine. 1984.

Harmony, Community, and Communication

Armstrong, Karen. *Twelve Steps to a Compassionate Life*. Anchor/Random House. 2010.

Breidenthal, Thomas. *Christian Households: The Sanctification of Nearness*.

Newell, John Philip. *A New Harmony*.

Peck, Scott. *A Different Drum: Community and Peace Making*. Simon and Schuster, NY. 1987.

Scott, Susan. *Fierce Conversations: Achieving Success at Work and in Life One Conversation at a Time*.

Schutz, William. *Here Comes Everybody*. Harper and Row. 1971.

Leadership

Collier McLaughlin, Kay. *Becoming the Transformative Church: Beyond Sacred Cows, Fantasies and Fears*. Church Publishing, NY. 2013.

Heifetz, Ronald A. and Linsky, Marty. *Leadership on the Line: Staying Alive through the Dangers of Leading*. Harvard Business Review Press, Boston. 2002.

Helgesen, Sally. *The Female Advantage: Women's Way of Leadership*. Currency. 1995.

Palmer, Parker. *The Courage to Teach*. Jossy-Bass. 1998.

Tjan, Anthony. *Good People: The Only Leadership Decision That Really Matters*. Portfolio. 2017.

Wheatley, Margaret. *Finding Our Way: Leadership for an Uncertain Time*. Barrett-Koehler, San Francisco. 2005.

Wheatley, Margaret. *Leadership and the New Science: Discovering Order in a Chaotic World*. 1999.

Memoirs, Novels, and Other Writings
Which Offer Perspective

Ali, Muhammad. *The Soul of a Butterfly*. Simon and Schuster. *2013*. See also Poetry and Other Inspiration and Understanding Multiculturalism.

Clinton, Hillary Rodham. *What Happened?* Simon and Schuster. 2017.

El Akkad, Omar. *American War*. Knopf. 2017.

Golding, William. *Lord of the Flies*. Penguin Classics. 1954.

Sweet, Leonard. Soul Tsunami: Sink or Swim in New Millennium Culture. Zondervan. 1999.

Tur, Katy. *Unbelievable: My Front Row Seat to the Craziest Campaign in American History*. Hey St. William Morrow. 2017.

Poetry and Other Inspiration

Ali, Muhammad. *The Soul of a Butterfly*. Simon and Schuster. *2013*. See also Understanding Multiculturalism and Memoirs.

Andreas, Brian. *Traveling Light*. StoryPeople Press, Deborah, IA. 2003.

Andreas, Brian. *Bring Your Life Back to Life: A Guide to Effortless Joy*. StoryPeople Press, Deborah, IA. 2017.

Berry, Wendell. *Collected Poems*. (especially "The Peace of Wild Things") North Point Press, San Francisco. 1985.

Dalai Lama and Tutu, Desmond. *The Book of Joy*. Avery/Random House. 2016.

Housden, Roger. *Ten Poems to Change Your Life*. (especially Mary Oliver's "The Only Life You Can Save") Harmony Press. 2001.

Housden, Roger. *Ten Poems to Change Your Life Again and Again.* (especially Jane Hirshfield's "Each Moment a White Bull Steps Shining Into the World") Harmony. 2007.

Instrata, Sam and Scriber, Megan. *Leading from Within: Poetry That Sustains the Courage to Lead.* Josses-Bass Wiley Imprint, San Francisco. 2007.

O'Donahue, John. *To Bless the Space Between Us.* Doubleday. 2008.

Walker, *Frank X. Love Letter to the World.* 2016.

Living in Process in a Product Oriented World / Gender / Counter-Cultural

Estes, Clara Pinkola. *Women Who Run With Wolves.* Ballantine. 1992, 1996.

Hays, Edward. *St. George and the Dragon and the Quest for the Holy Grail.* Forest of Peace Press, KS. 1986.

Rogers, Carl. *On Being a Person.* Houghton Mifflin. 1961.

Rogers, Carl. *A Way of Being.* Houghton Mifflin. 1980.

Senge, Peter. with C. Otto Scharmer, Joseph Jaworski and Betty Sue Flowers. *Presence: Exploring Profound Change in People, Organizations and Society.* Doubleday. See also Family Systems Theory and Change.

Schaef, Ann Wilson. *Living in Process.* Ballantine Wellspring. 1999.

Self and Other Awareness

Buford, Bill. *Among the Thugs: The Experience and the Seduction of Crowd Violence.* Arrow Books, United Kingdom. 1991. See also Conflict and Violence.

CPP (Consulting Psychologists Press) is the Myers Briggs Company and publisher/supplier of all official Myers Briggs instruments and related materials, including the following.

Gifts Differing: Understanding Personality Type. Isabel Briggs, and Myers; Peter C.

In the Grip: Understanding Type, Stress and Inferior Function. Naomi L. Quenk.

Introduction to Type. Isabel Briggs.

Introduction to Type and Careers. Naomi L. Quenk.

Introduction to Type in Organizations. Sandra Krebs Hirrsh and Jean M. Kummerow.

MBTI Manual: A Guide to the Development and Use of the Myers Briggs Type Indicator.

Goleman, Daniel. *Emotional Intelligence.* Bantam. 1995.

Goleman, Daniel. *Social Intelligence.* Bantam. 2006.

Goleman, Daniel. *Working with Emotional Intelligence.* Bantam. 2006.

Kearney, David and Bates, Marilyn. *Please Understand Me.* Prometheus Nemesis Books, Del Mar, CA. 1978.

Kroger, Otto and Theusen, Jane. *Type Talk.* Delacorte, NY. 1988.

Kroger, Otto and Theusen, Jane. *Type Talk at Work.* Delacorte, NY. 1992.

Laney, Marti Olsen. *The Introvert Advantage: How to Thrive in an Extrovert World.* Wordman. 2002.

Lawrence, Gordon. *People Types and Tiger Stripes.* CAPT, Gainesville, FL. 1979.

Pearson, Carol S. *Awakening the Heroes Within: Twelve Archetypes to Help Us Transform Our World.* Harper, San Francisco. 1991.

Tieger, Paul D. and Tieger, Barbara Barron. *Do What You Are.* Little Brown. 1992.

Weisinger, Hendrie, PhD. *Emotional Intelligence at Work.* Jossey-Bass. 1998.

Zweig, Conti and Wolf, Steve. *Romancing the Shadow: Illuminating the Dark Side of the Soul.* Ballantine. 1997.

Truth and Morality

Coontz, Stephanie. *The Way We Never Were: American Families and the Nostalgia Trap.* Basic Books, Harper Collins. 1992.

Coontz, Stephanie. *The Way We Really Are: Coming to Terms with America's Changing Families.* Basic Books, Harper Collins. 1997.

Hass, Aaron, PhD. *Doing the Right Thing: Cultivating Your Moral Intelligence.* Simon and Schuster/Pocket Books, NY. 1998.

Rohr, Richard. *The Naked Now: Learning to See as the Mystics Do.*

Sims, Bennett. *Servanthood: Leadership for the Third Millennium.* Cowley, Boston. 1997.

Understanding Multiculturalism and a Global Society

Al-Khataktbeh, Amani. *Muslim Girl*. Simon and Schuster. 2016.

Ali, Muhammad. *The Soul of a Butterfly*. Simon and Schuster. 2013. See also Memoirs and Poetry and Other Inspiration.

Citrin, Jack and Sears, David O. *American Identity and the Politics of Multiculturalism*. Cambridge University Books.

Geok-lin Lim, Shirley. *Among the White Moon Faces: An Asian-American Memoir of Homelands*.

Gish, Jen. *The Girl at the Baggage Claim: Explaining the East-West Culture Gap*. 2017.

Guerrero, Diane. *In the Country We Love: My Family Divided*. Holt and Company. 2016.

Hauser, Thomas with Muhammad Ali. *Muhammad Ali: His Life and Times*. Simon and Schuster. 1992.

House, Silas. *Clay's Quilt*. Ballantine Books, Random House. 2001. See also *The Coal Tattoo and A Parchment of Leaves*.

Inazu, John D. *Confident Pluralism: Surviving and Thriving Through Deep Differences*. University of Chicago Press. 2016. See also Conflict and Violence and Democracy and Politics.

Mandela, Nelson. *Long Walk to Freedom*. MacDonald Purnall. 1994.

Massive, Robert K. *Peter the Great: His Life and His World*. 1980.

Myers, Steven Lee. *The New Tsar: The Rise and Reign of Vladimir Putin*. 2014.

Paton, Alan. *Cry the Beloved Country*. Scribblers. 1948.

Pomerantsev, Peter. *Nothing Is True and Everything Is Possible: The Surreal Heart of the New Russia*. 2014.

Strickland, Bill. *Making the Impossible Possible*. Broadway Books. 2007.

Vance, JD. *Hillbilly Elegy: A Memoir of a Family and Culture in Crisis*. Harper Collins. 2016.

Wilkerson, Isabel. *The Warmth of Other Suns: The Epic Story of America's Great Migration*. Vantage. 2010.

BIBLIOGRAPHY

Andreas, Brian. *Story People.*

Cloud and Townsend. Boundary handouts. Crystal Cathedral Conference on Singles Ministry. California. 1990.

Collier McLaughlin, Kay. Leadership Manual of the Episcopal Diocese of Lexington (KY); Consultant resources (unpublished); Grief Emergency Kit; *The Advocate*, newspaper of the Episcopal Diocese of Lexington, 1985-2017.

Drakes, Cassandra and Spath, Thomas. The Institute for Civility. Houston, Texas.

Friedman, Edwin F. *A Failure of Nerve: Leadership in the Age of the Quick Fix.* Church Publishing. New York. 1997. 2007.

Frost, Robert. *A Mending Wall.* 1914. Public Domain.

Hirshfield, Jane. "On the Fifth Day." 2017 March for Science.

Keyes Jr., Ken. *The Hundredth Monkey.*

Maslow, Abraham. *Toward a Psychology of Being.* Van Nostrand Reinhold. 1968.

Newell, John Philip. *A New Harmony: The Spirit, The Earth and the Human Soul.* Jose Bass: A Wiley Imprint. 2011.

Oswald, Roy. Teaching on Human Relations and Emotional Intelligence. Training session for The Center for Human Relations and Emotional Intelligence. 2008.

Rivard Report. September 13, 2016.

Schneider, John M. *Finding My Way: Healing and Transformation Through Loss and Grief.* Seasons Press, Colfax, Wisconsin. 1994.

Sherwood, Jeffrey. Oxford Dictionary. Phone interview.

Teaching Tolerance. Southern Poverty Law Center. Montgomery, AL

Treadwell, Margaret "Peggy". Retreat with the Executive Council of the Episcopal Diocese of Lexington. 2009.

Tutu, Desmond. *No Future Without Forgiveness.* Doubleday. New York. 1999.

Walker, Frank X. Lines from "Love Letter to the World."

Weiner, Andrew. Application of Emotional Intelligence to Leadership. Circles of Power Leadership Initiative. 2001.

Workman, Elizabeth. Lecture on Appreciative Inquiry at Leadership Training Institute, Dubose Conference Center, Monteagle, Tennessee. 1993.

Meet

MICHAEL D. FITZPATRICK

Forward

Michael D. Fitzpatrick is the recipient of The Prince Charles Award for Musical Excellence, conferred by His Royal Highness The Prince of Wales.

He has performed for the leading world figures of our time including His Holiness, Pope Francis at The Vatican, His Holiness the XIVth Dalai Lama, the late Muhammad Ali, His Majesty King Abdullah II at the Jordanian Royal Palace, President Carter in Aspen, Nobel Peace Prize Laureate Shirin Ebadi of Iran, and as soloist at venues including the Hollywood Bowl, the United Nations, the John F. Kennedy Presidential Library and Museum, the Henry Crown Symphony Hall in Jerusalem, the United States Capitol West Lawn, and at the Rock & Roll Hall of Fame. Fitzpatrick has musically shared the stage with His Holiness the XIVth Dalai Lama for the past two decades, providing the Musical Keynote to set the tone for His Holiness' Public Talks around the globe, prompting His Holiness to state: "The emotion induced by Michael Fitzpatrick's music is so powerful it seems almost verbalized. His sound is Clear Light." Fitzpatrick is the architect of Tuning the Planet, the East-West musical recording inside of Mammoth Cave, the largest cave-system in the world. He is Music Director of the Muhammad Ali Humanitarian Awards, and is the Founder and Artistic Director of Earth's Call. Sir George Martin, Producer of The Beatles, stated: "He is beyond a marvelous talent and I could not agree with him more: "Music is the only thing that can change the world."

Meet

KAY COLLIER MCLAUGHLIN

Author

Kay Collier McLaughlin is a "blue" thought leader from the "red" state of Kentucky whose passion for creating harmony and civility was formed in the unlikely dual environments of classical music and NFL football, where she lived the experience of diverse individuals creating winning ensembles by blending their differences for a greater whole. She stepped briefly into the political arena at Girls' Nation during her high school years as a candidate for vice-president of the mythical country the rising seniors created in Washington, D.C., ultimately persuading her followers to join with her African American opponent, who in the late 1950s she believed "has the greater need for a voice." She holds

PHOTO BY CALLIE LINDSEY

a doctorate in Counseling Psychology from The Union Institute with sub-specialities in group dynamics, life transitions and bereavement, and has trained with the Association for Psychological Type, the MidAtlantic Association for Training and Consulting, National Training Laboratories, the Gestalt Institute of the Bluegrass and is a senior trainer for the Center for Human Relations and Emotional Intelligence. She is the author of six non-fiction books, four of which are responses to societal change, including, *They're Rarely Too Young and Never Too Old to 'Twinkle,': Teaching Insights Into the World of Suzuki Violin*; *Football's Gentle Giant: the Blanton Collier Story*; *Single in the Church: New Ways to Minister with 52% of God's People*; *Becoming the Transformative Church: Beyond Sacred Cows, Fantasies and Fears*; *Big Lessons from Little Places: Faith and the Future*, and has invited chapters in *What Shall We Become? (The Psychology of Change)* and *Re-Claiming the Gospel of Peace (Talking Together: Holy Conversations Get to the Root of Violence)*. She served as Deputy for Leadership Development, Transition Ministries and Communications for the Episcopal Diocese of Lexington under four bishops, two interim assisting bishops and three Presiding Bishops, covering 14 (national) Triennial Conventions dealing with such ground-breaking issues as the ordination of women, blessing of same sex relationships, the ordination of gay and lesbian individuals, issues with the world-wide Anglican Communion and more. As a keynote speaker, workshop leader and leadership development consultant, she travels widely, working in academic, religious, for-profit and non-profit systems. She is founder and President of Transformative Leadership Consulting and Talking Together Seminars. Her work has taken her to Japan, Australia, Canada, Germany, Russia and across the United States.

Her experiential trainings are based in theories which include family systems, Appreciative Inquiry, Emotional Intelligence, Typology, Human Potential Three Phase Training and Desmond Tutu's Truth and Reconciliation work.

An accomplished musician, she plays the French Horn, piano, violin, bowed psaltery and is teaching herself to play the folk harp. She is vice-chair of the Kentucky Pro Football Hall of Fame and a founding member of the Blanton Collier Sportsmanship Group for Excellence, Ethics and Education through athletics. She is a self-taught artist who enjoys creating pure paper wall collages and "Jane Bowls" — collages and decoupaged bowls named after her late sister under the name L' Art du Papier.

Kay and her master woodworker husband Raymond live on a small lake in Nicholas County, Ky.. She is the proud mother of two adult daughters, Diane Slone, a violinist who heads a Suzuki Music School in Hong Kong, and Laura Newsome, a realtor and event planner who lives in Lexington with her husband Brad, and passionate "Gamma" to Virginia Varden Newsome, a recent musical theater graduate of Oklahoma City University, now with the Florida Repertory Theater; Drew Newsome, a quarterback and baseball pitcher at Lexington Christian Academy, and MaryChun Slone, a swimmer and equine enthusiast in Hong Kong. Her "peace place and heart home" finds her in Door County, Wisc., where she will be in residence this spring at Write On Door County, and working with the Door County Civility Project.

Kay's work is guided and inspired by the following quotes:

"Vocation is where our deep gladness meets the world's deep need." Frederick Buechner.

" You can accomplish anything so long as you do not care who gets the credit" and "Teaching is the art of inspiring learning." Blanton Collier

" What is man's ultimate direction in life? It is to look for love, truth, virtue and beauty…" Dr. Shinichi Suzuki

" Perhaps it is music that will save the world." Pablo Casals after hearing the Suzuki children play.

Having known this author for 25 years as friend and trusted counselor I can attest to her big-hearted capacity to reach across personal division and to create unity where diversity might suggest otherwise. I find her writing in this latest book to be both practical and inspirational, speaking to her lifelong pursuit to find the humanity in every person and to seek the reconciliation brought on by honest dialogue. I cannot recommend "Talking Together" more highly!"

Bruce Neswick
Canon for Music
Trinity Episcopal Cathedral
Portland, Oregon

As an athlete and a businessman, I know the importance of bringing diverse people together around a common cause, regardless of differences. A coach or leader must create an environment where teamwork is possible, but it is the committment of individual players that builds a winning team. Talking Together Seminars, of which I was proud to be Honorary Chair for the pioneering event, and the book "Talking Together: Getting Beyond Polarization Through Civil Dialogue" teach the skills and provide the practice opportunities that can change the divided, losing negativity in our country into a winning, All-American team for the civility we must have for our country to survive and thrive. I heartily recommend it.

Frank Minnifield
Minnifield Enterprises
Six time All-Pro Corner Back for the Cleveland Browns

In her latest book, "Talking Together," Kay Colliere McLaughlin powerfully illuminates what it takes to move towards respectful and harmonious interactions with self and others. This important and timely labor of love is at once intimate, wise, and far-reaching.

Carrie Reuning-Hummel
Ithaca College, Ithaca, NY